Khorsabad

Nineveh

Mosul ● ● Balawat

Nimrud

ASSYRIA

Ashur ●

● Nuzu

MARI

Tigris

Euphrates

Baghdad ● ● Eshnunna

ACCAD

● Babylon

● Susa

BABYLONIA

ELAM

Lagash

Uruk

Ur of the Chaldees

Ancient coastline

—·—·—·— Route of the Patriarchs

················ King's highway

P E R S I A N

G U L F

IN ARDUIS AUDAX

HELEN & MICHAEL
OPPENHEIMER

The Bible as History IN PICTURES

WERNER KELLER

The Bible

with 329 illustrations and 8 colour plates

as History
IN PICTURES

HODDER AND STOUGHTON

For Helga *my indispensable assistant*

Pictures selected and arranged by
Dr Werner Keller

Typographic Design by George A. Adams

Originally published in Germany with the title
UND DIE BIBEL HAT DOCH RECHT IN BILDERN

Copyright © 1963 Econ-Verlag GmbH
Wien und Düsseldorf

English translation by Dr William Neil

Printed in Germany for Hodder and Stoughton Limited,
St. Paul's House, Warwick Lane, London E C 4
by DuMont Presse, Cologne
and bound by Klemme and Bleimund, Bielefeld

Contents

Defaulting taxpayers in court / Famine on the Nile / "Joseph opened all the storehouses" / "They bowed down with their faces to the earth" / Semitic prisoners / "They laded their asses with the corn" / At an Egyptian banquet / Cattle in the Nile delta / Measuring a field with a measuring line / Embalming a body / A nobleman's funeral.

BOOKS OF PICTURES about the Bible exist in plenty. What has so far been lacking is a pictorial history of biblical events in the light of archaeological finds. We have waited in vain for a picture book that would cover the whole field of biblical history—from the patriarchs right up to the apostles—relating it to the ancient documents and monuments of the Near East, some of which have come to light only in the very recent past.

This fact, coupled with the world-wide response to "The Bible as History", confirmed me in a long-cherished desire to compile just such a pictorial history.

A few decades ago such an undertaking would have been utopian. Not that there was a lack of illustrative material connected with the scriptures, for the great events of the Bible have always gripped men's imagination. Famous painters in the middle ages as in more modern times have chosen scenes from the Bible as their theme. But without concrete, genuine prototypes drawn from the past, without a knowledge of the ancient East, the content of the picture was bound to be largely the product of the artist's own imagination.

Thanks to archaeology, our knowledge of the background of the Bible has been immeasurably enhanced. Since the American scholar, Edward Robinson, laid the foundations of biblical archaeology with his work in Palestine 125 years ago, this branch of ancient studies has been crowned with extraordinary success. After thousands of years the forgotten world of the Near East has once again come within our ken. The empires, rulers and peoples of that wide semi-circle that stretches from Mesopotamia to the Nile—indeed the whole historical, cultural and religious background of those far off days with which the Bible is concerned—have suddenly become alive and real.

From Mesopotamia came evidence of the dynasties of Ur and of the empires of Assyria and Babylon. Cities referred to in the scriptures, like Nineveh, Ashur and Babylon, together with their palaces and royal homes, their sanctuaries and temple towers, their statues of gods and monarchs, have been discovered and excavated. On cuneiform tablets, found in their thousands, translators read in the annals of warlike Assyrian rulers descriptions of events which confirmed what had been handed down to us in the books of Kings and Chronicles. Archaeology has brought us closer to the Elamites, the "Horites" and the Hittites, or "sons of Heth" as the Bible calls them, while the Philistines have taken living shape on Egyptian temple walls.

Thanks to this wealth of documentation, the series of events, without parallel in human history, which is recorded in the Old and New Testaments, has suddenly in our own day once more become a visual experience. We have the good fortune to be the first generation to be able to look back into the world of the Bible more than four thousand years and see that world illuminated as if by a powerful searchlight.

What I have tried to do in this book is to select the pictures in such a way that following the illustrations step by step we get a panoramic view of that biblical history which is so deeply rooted in the eventful life of the ancient East. This new insight, this possibility of seeing backwards into the past, cannot but enrich our understanding of what the Bible has to say in its historical and cultural setting.

Of course there are many gaps in the panorama, many problems of biblical history which are still unsettled or obscure. Relatively little of note has come from Israel itself.

Where, however, actual finds have been lacking in Palestine, discoveries in neighbouring lands in the "Fertile Crescent" have often come to our aid—whether it be from Mesopotamia, or Asia Minor. An important role has also been played by Egypt. "Biblical scholars are coming more and more to value Egyptology as a means to a better understanding of the Bible", says Professor W. F. Albright. "Nowhere else have we anything remotely corresponding to the mass of material on the walls of temples and in tombs with which we can illustrate every aspect of life in Bible times."

In planning this book I have tried to associate with each picture an appropriate passage from the Bible, so as to show the connection between the historical document and the words of the Old or the New

Testament. With regard to the explanatory details attached to the pictures, what I have tried to do there is to bring out the typical or essential elements in a relief, a monument or a wall-painting in so far as they assist us in our understanding of a particular biblical passage. In the matter of dates I have followed Professor G. Ernest Wright's "The Westminster Historical Atlas to the Bible".

My warmest thanks are due to the great scholars, research workers, and excavators whose untiring efforts—indeed whose whole life's work has been devoted to gathering the fund of precious information about the world of the Bible and events in the ancient East upon which I have been able to draw for this picture book of mine. In this galaxy I want to name the great succession of pioneers no longer with us, each one associated with some unforgettable discovery: Paul Emile Botta who found Khorsabad, the royal city of King Sargon II, and Jean François Champollion, who deciphered Egyptian hiero-glyphics; A. Henry Layard, who discovered Nimrud, and H. C. Rawlinson who unearthed Nineveh; Sir Flinders Petrie who came upon the proto-Sinaitic inscriptions, James Lesley Starkey, who ex-cavated the Judaean fortress of Lachish, and Sir Leonard Woolley, who unearthed the famous "Ur of the Chaldees"; Richard Lepsius, too, who was the first to make an inventory of Egyptian monuments, as well as Hugo Gressmann with his collection of "Old oriental texts and pictures relating to the Old Testament", and Robert Koldewey, the excavator of Babylon. Special thanks are due to the foremost scholars and archaeologists of our own day, whose works have been indispensable for my project, and who have also generously put at my disposal their own valuable illustrations. Among them I would mention Professors William F. Albright, Nelson Glueck, André Parrot, James B. Pritchard, Claude F. A. Schaeffer, G. Ernest Wright.

I can only add the wish that this picture book may help to bring the world of the Bible closer to us.

Werner Keller

Ascona, Monte Verità 1963

I In the Land of Shinar

"For a thousand years in thy sight are but as yesterday when it is past, and as a watch in the night" (Psalm 90:4).

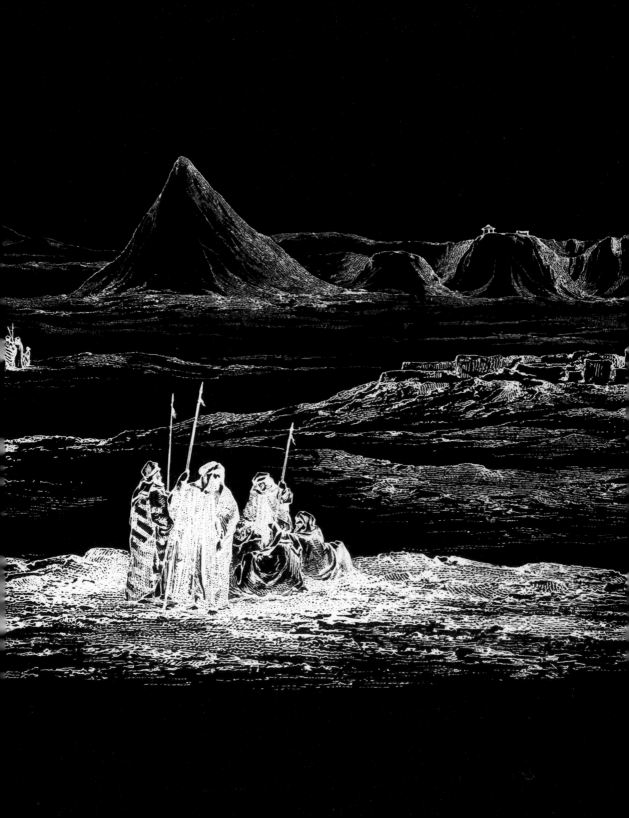

Beyond the River

(Genesis 1:1—11:9)

"Remember the days of old,
consider the years of many generations:
ask thy father, and he will show thee;
thy elders, and they will tell thee" (Deuteronomy 32:7).

IN RECENT YEARS our knowledge of the ancient East has been extended far beyond the times of the biblical patriarchs into the very beginnings of history. We have seen with astonishment civilisations come to life which flourished more than a thousand years before Abraham and whose existence was hardly suspected little more than a century ago. With all this new knowledge there has come at the same time the recognition that countless biblical narratives have their origins deeply rooted in Mesopotamian soil. The "Land of Shinar" so frequently mentioned in the Bible, is the name given to the Babylonian plain between the Tigris and the Euphrates. It is in that same part of Western Asia, where in very early times civilisation had reached such a high level, that the book of Genesis locates the first stories about the patriarchs. It is on the fringe of the "Fertile Crescent", the name given to the curved area extending from the Mediterranean across the Euphrates and Tigris to the Persian Gulf which contained these early civilisations, that the story of the patriarchs opens at Ur of the Chaldees, near the estuary of the two great rivers. From the south of Mesopotamia they journeyed through Syria to Canaan, and, for the first time, into Egypt itself.

Yet even before the family of Terah set out on its long journey to Haran and Canaan, names of countries, cities and mighty rivers crop up in the Old Testament like motifs which are destined to play a prominent part in the history of the people of Israel much later on. Similarly we find stories which preserve fragmentary and obscure recollections of events which, as we now know, took place in this part of the world in the dim and distant past.

Is it pure chance that the Garden of Eden is supposed to have been located here on Mesopotamian soil? Where today the desert has again assumed control, once upon a time artificial irrigation ensured fruitful pastures. "And a river went out of Eden to water the garden," says Genesis 2:10, "and from thence it was parted, and became into four heads." Two of these rivers of Paradise are known to us: the Tigris, which is the biblical "Hiddekel", and the Euphrates.

The discovery of the text of a heroic poem, the Epic of Gilgamesh, which goes back to the ancient Sumerians, brought to light an old Babylonian tale which at certain points comes very close to the biblical account of the judgment of God on sinful man in the story of the Flood. Excavations at the old Sumerian cities of Ur, Kish and other Mesopotamian sites revealed remarkable traces of extensive inundation.

According to Genesis 11 the Tower of Babel was erected in the "land of Shinar". Is it not like an illustration of the biblical story to find today in the heart of Mesopotamia so many ancient weather-beaten mounds which once upon a time were proud temple towers, ziggurats, reaching up towards the heavens?

Asleep and forgotten for thousands of years, the ruins of great cities have now once again been wrested from the desert, cities which Nimrod, the first of the despots, is said to have built: "And the beginning of his kingdom was Babel, and Erech, and Accad, and Calneh, in the land of Shinar", as is noted in Genesis 10:8-12. At Accad in northern Babylonia, possibly the modern Tell ed Der, a Semite by the name of Sargon founded the dynasty of Accad (about 2400–2200 B.C.) and became, according to the records, the first empire-builder in history. It was under this greatest of the kings of Mesopotamia in the third millennium B.C. that the Semites, who had for long enough been living side by side with the Sumerians, became the dominant power in the land. Under Sargon I and his successors, especially Naram-Sin, there came into being an empire that stretched as far as the Persian Gulf and from Elam to Asia Minor, indeed at times even to the Mediterranean. When, after the collapse of the empire of Accad, the third dynasty of Ur (about 2100–2000 B.C.) ushered in a last brilliant epoch of Sumerian culture, the hands of the cosmic clock were coming close to the point of time when the appearance of the family of Abraham marked the first stage in the story of the people of Israel.

"*And the Lord God planted a garden eastward in Eden . . . and a river went out of Eden to water the garden,
and from thence it was parted and became into four heads . . . and the name of the third river is Hiddekel:
that is it which goeth toward the east of Assyria*" (Genesis 2:8, 10, 14).
View of the upper reaches of the Tigris which the Bible calls Hiddekel and which it includes among
the four rivers of Paradise.

"*Now the serpent . . . said unto the woman, Yea, hath God said, Ye shall not eat of every tree of the
garden? . . . And the woman took of the fruit thereof, and did eat; and gave also unto her husband with her,
and he did eat . . . And the Lord God called unto Adam, and said unto him . . . Hast thou eaten of the tree,
whereof I commanded thee that thou shouldest not eat?*" (Genesis 3:1–11).
An old Babylonian cylinder-seal from the middle of the third millennium B. C.
almost looks like an illustration of the biblical story of the Fall of Man:
it shows a god, a tree of life, a woman and a snake.

"*And the flood was forty days upon the earth;
and the waters increased . . .*" (Genesis 7:17).
Archaeologists digging at Ur came upon a remarkable band
of clay about eight feet thick which pointed to some great
flood disaster in the area having taken place around
4000 B. C. Both above and below the clay deposit
were found traces of human settlement.

"And they said, Go to, let us build us a city, and
a tower whose top may reach unto heaven; and let us
make us a name . . ." (Genesis 11:4).
Not far from Baghdad, at Aqar-Quf, are these massive remains
almost 200 feet high, of what was once a mighty ziggurat.
Ruins of similar huge brick temple-towers, which call to mind
the famous Tower of Babel in the book of Genesis, are to be found
in plenty in the "Land of Shinar", ancient Mesopotamia.

Like the vision of the biblical Tower of Babel
this five-storied temple-tower appears
on an old Assyrian cylinder-seal.
In front of the edifice stands a priest.
The wavy lines underneath indicate
that the ziggurat is situated near a river,
as Babel lay on the banks of the Euphrates.
A desert fox (left) is apparently sniffing at a
dead fish.

"He was a mighty hunter before the Lord", says the
book of Genesis (10:9) about Nimrod.
This very early hunting scene was found at Uruk,
the biblical Erech. A priest-king with girdle,
fillet, top-knot and beard,
looses an arrow at a pouncing lion.

"Nimrod . . . began to be a mighty one in the earth"
(Genesis 10:8).
On the site of the biblical city of Calah (Genesis 10:11),
about twenty miles south-east of Nineveh near the Tigris,
Nimrud still bears the name of the "mighty hunter".
It was here that Layard began excavating in 1845:
one of the winged-oxen dug up from the rubble
is shown being sawn in pieces prior to removal.

"And the beginning of his kingdom was Babel, and Erech, and Accad, and Calneh, in the land of Shinar" (Genesis 10:10).
At Uruk, near the Lower Euphrates, archaeologists discovered the biblical Erech which Nimrod is said to have founded. Even in very early times it was a royal city. The "White Temple", approached by a long staircase, still witnesses to its ancient glory.

"And Abel was a keeper of sheep, but Cain was a tiller of the ground. And in process of time it came to pass, that Cain brought of the fruit of the ground an offering unto the Lord. And Abel, he also brought of the firstlings of his flock and of the fat thereof" (Genesis 4:2–4).

An alabaster vase found on the site of the biblical Erech and dating from the third millennium B. C. displays in relief the offering of the fruit of the ground and the firstlings of the flock at some religious rite.

"He began to be a mighty one in the earth" is what Genesis 10:8 says about Nimrod, the founder of Accad in northern Babylonia. Although every other great city of the ancient East has now been identified, the biblical Accad still remains undiscovered. At Nineveh, however, the bronze head of a mighty monarch came to light. This was Sargon I who, about 2400 B. C., founded both the Semitic dynasty of Accad and the first Semitic empire in history.

Naram-Sin, grandson of Sargon, was one of the greatest oriental rulers.
A stela of rose-coloured sandstone shows the king with a horned crown, carrying
in one hand his bow and battle-axe, in the other his javelin. He has fought his way
to the foot of a mountain and all that remain of the enemy forces are dead,
wounded or in flight. This column which was found in Susa
dates from the second half of the third millennium B. C.

Long after the collapse of the dynasty of Accad, the third and last dynasty of Ur begins
about 2100 B. C. with the Sumerian ruler Ur-Nammu. Here King Ur-Nammu is depicted
on a stela which is called after him, standing in front of a plant making an offering
to the god Nannar. Below we see the monarch walking behind the god and carrying
builder's tools on his shoulder as he makes his way to the site of a temple-tower.
When the third dynasty of Ur which was founded by Ur-Nammu succumbed
about 2000 B. C. before the onslaught of hordes of fighting bedouin from the Arabian desert,
we have reached the threshold of that period in the history of the ancient East
in which the patriarchs make their appearance.

25

II The Coming of the Patriarchs

"Thy servants' trade hath been about cattle from our youth even until now, both we, and also our fathers" (Genesis 46:34).

From Ur to Egypt

(Genesis 11:27–31:55)

*"The God of glory
appeared unto our father Abraham
when he was in Mesopotamia,
before he dwelt in Charran"* (Acts 7:2).

NO PEOPLE in the world have preserved in their tradition so clear a recollection of their origins as have the people of Israel. The early narratives in Genesis are nothing else but family history, featuring the venerable patriarchal figures of Abraham, Isaac and Jacob, who himself received the name Israel. Obviously biblical history is concerned to trace the threads by which Israel was tied up with so many peoples and countries in her immediate neighbourhood as well as with those who were more remote. So, like an overture, the biblical record takes us with the patriarchs on their journeys for thousands of miles in a great semi-circle which covers the whole of the ancient East: from the distant shores of the Persian Gulf through Mesopotamia, from the Euphrates and the Tigris to the Mediterranean lands of Syria and Palestine and on to the banks of the Nile.

Terah, the father of Abraham, lives with his large family, who still worship the ancient gods, in Ur of the Chaldees. It is from this corner of southern Mesopotamia, where around 2000 B.C. the third dynasty of Ur collapsed under the assault of nomadic Amorites from the desert, that the Bible launches the Israelites on their great world-wide journey. Their first major halt was at Haran. This town, lying on the Balikh, a tributary of the Euphrates, was an important trading centre at the intersection of the ancient caravan routes from Egypt, Canaan, Asia Minor and Mesopotamia. It belonged at that time to the kingdom of Mari.

After the death of his father, Abraham left Haran in response to the command of God, accompanied by his nephew Lot. With his family, his goods and his cattle he made his way to Canaan. Yet they did not strike roots in the new country that had been promised to their tribe and people. They remained sojourners among the Canaanite inhabitants.

We see Abraham as a typical nomad with his flocks and herds moving through the hill country and down into the Negeb, settling for a while at Shechem, Bethel and Ai. Famine drives him and his clan into Egypt, the country which is to play such a decisive role in the later history of the patriarchs and indeed of the whole Israelite nation.

After their return to Canaan comes the parting of the ways for the two families. Lot chooses for himself and his stock the lush pasture lands of Jordan and the Vale of Siddim, later to be overwhelmed by the disaster that came upon Sodom and Gomorrah. Abraham, however, from now on lives mostly in the south country. Beersheba, where ancient wells have been rediscovered, is mentioned in the Bible, as well as the oaks of Mamre near Hebron which became the last resting place of Abraham and his wife Sarah, a spot still held sacred to this day. All during their sojourn in Canaan the patriarchs remained in close contact with their kinsfolk in their homeland "beyond the River" Euphrates. Abraham sends his oldest servant to fetch a wife for his son Isaac from Haran, the city of Nahor. Likewise their son Jacob in his turn crosses the "River" to Haran to bring back Leah and Rachel, the daughters of Laban, as his wives.

"*Your fathers dwelt on the other side of the flood in old time, even Terah, the father of Abraham and the father of Nachor*" (Joshua 24:2).
The "flood" here refers to the Euphrates, the great river of Western Asia which the Bible includes among the four rivers of Paradise (Genesis 2:10-14). "Beyond the River" means Mesopotamia.

29

"Your fathers dwelt on the other side of the flood in old time . . . and they served other gods"
(Joshua 24:2).
The fear and horror of men face to face with incomprehensible heathen gods
and idols find expression in the fixed staring eyes of these twelve statues as with
clasped hands they gaze into the sky. They were found in a cache of sacred relics
in a temple at Tell Asmar, a mound of ruins north-east of Baghdad. Their date
is the first half of the third millennium B. C.

"And Terah took Abram his son, and Lot the son of Haran his son's son, and Sarai his daughter-in-law, his son Abram's wife; and they went forth with them from Ur of the Chaldees" (Genesis 11:31).

At Tell al Muqayyar, the "Mound of Bitumen", near the Lower Euphrates, it was possible to identify in this stumpy hillock of burnt bricks the remains of a three-storied temple tower many thousands of years old. Once upon a time it proudly raised its head above the surrounding buildings of a famous city of the ancient East, Ur of the Chaldees, as the Bible calls it. It was from here that the family of the patriarchs set out on their journey.

"And they came unto Haran and dwelt there" (Genesis 11:31).
It was on the river Balikh, an eastern tributary of the Euphrates, about 280 miles
N. N. E. of Damascus that the first stage of the patriarchal journey from Ur to Canaan
came to an end. Terah and his family stayed here for some time and it was here that he died.
Some of Abraham's relatives made their permanent home in the area (Genesis 24:4;
27:43; 28:2). Haran was an important centre of trade in the ancient East and the
junction of the caravan routes from Babylon to Asia Minor, Syria and Egypt.
Even today animals cluster round one of the ancient wells in front of the crumbling ruins
near the little village which still bears the name of Charran.

". . . and dwelt in Charran" (Acts 7:4).
The governor of Mari, the great kingdom to which Haran belonged, was, at
the time when the patriarchs lived there, Ishtup-Ilum. He is wearing a robe which
is draped over one shoulder and fringed at the edges.

"*These are the generations of Shem . . .
and Peleg lived thirty years,
and begat Reu . . . and Reu lived two
and thirty years, and begat Serug . . .
and Serug lived thirty years,
and begat Nahor . . . and Nahor lived
nine and twenty years, and begat
Terah . . . and Terah lived seventy
years, and begat Abram, Nahor,
and Haran*" (Genesis 11:10ff.).
This is the palace of Mari
on the Euphrates, containing
260 apartments and courtyards
and reckoned to be one of the
largest royal residences in the
ancient East. In a library
consisting of 25,000 clay tablets,
cuneiform texts were found which
contained important information
concerning the patriarchal period.
Reference is made in them to
places which bear the names of
patriarchs mentioned in the
Bible—Peleg, Serug, Nahor,
Terah, and Haran.

34

"*Now the Lord had said unto Abram, Get thee out of thy country, and from thy kindred, and from thy father's house, unto a land that I will shew thee . . . And Abram took Sarai his wife, and Lot his brother's son, and all their substance that they had gathered, and the souls that they had gotten in Haran; and they went forth to go into the land of Canaan*" (Genesis 12:1, 5).

Like the bedouin tribes of the present day, the family of Abraham with their herds of asses, goats and sheep made their way from water-hole to water-hole as they journeyed to Palestine.

"And into the land of Canaan they came" (Genesis 12:5).
Scene on the upper reaches of the Jordan, whose three sources spring from Mt Hermon –
"as the dew of Hermon . . . that descended upon the mountains of Zion"
(Psalm 133:3). When Abraham and his family crossed the river they had reached
their goal – the land of Canaan, in ancient times the country west of Jordan
(Numbers 33:51). Then for the first time members of the chosen race set foot
on the soil that was to have such a profound significance not only for the people of Israel
but for the whole of mankind.

"And Abram passed through the land unto the place of Sichem, unto the plain of Moreh" (Genesis 12:6).
Shechem, where Abraham made his first lengthy stay and where Joshua twice proclaimed the
terms of the Law before the people (Joshua 8:30–35; 24:1–28) was even in 2000 B.C.
a walled city with a city gate. Referring to Shechem the Bible says "(They) came unto the
gate of their city, and communed with the men of their city" (Genesis 34:20). The ancient
site has been excavated at Tell Balata.

"And the Canaanite was then in the land" (Genesis 12:6).
A painted potsherd found among the ruins of Beth-Shan, the city that was later to witness
the ignominious end of Saul (I Samuel 31:10), preserves a striking likeness of an unknown
Canaanite.

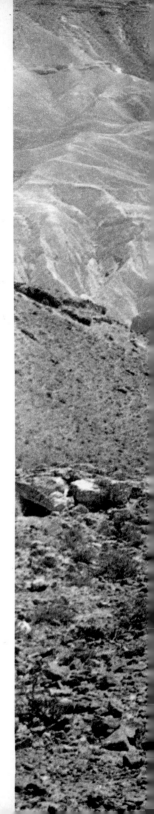

"*And Abram journeyed, going on still toward the south*" (Genesis 12:9).
The southern end of the country, which later became the outermost
area of the tribal territory of Judah (Joshua 15:1–4), is the Negeb—a
"dry, parched land" as the Bible says. "As whirlwinds in the south
(Negeb) pass through; so it cometh from the desert, from a terrible
land" (Isaiah 21:1). Shepherds in these parts can only keep their flocks
alive by moving from one water-hole to another.

"And there was a famine in the land" (Genesis 12:10).
When the rain and the dew no longer feed the crops hunger is not far behind.
"Therefore the heaven over you is stayed from dew, and the earth is stayed from her fruit.
And I called for a drought upon the land, and upon the mountains, and upon the corn,
and upon the new wine, and upon the oil, and upon that which the ground bringeth
forth, and upon men, and upon cattle, and upon all the labour of the hands"
(Haggai 1:10–11).
This Egyptian relief shows a starving bedouin, reduced almost to skin and bones,
supporting himself with a staff as he leads three oxen behind him.

"And Abram went down into Egypt" (Genesis 12:10).
When times were hard through drought or famine the pharaohs instructed their frontier
police to permit the entry of shepherds from Palestine into Egypt "so that they could
keep their flocks alive on the pharaoh's territory" as one of the hieroglyphic texts tells us.
Towards the delta of the Nile, in the region known to Bible readers as
the Land of Goshen (Genesis 45:10), grazing lands were reserved for such migrants.
Not far distant lay the proud city of Memphis, known to the Hebrews as Noph
(Isaiah 19:13).
Today palm fronds sway gently in the breeze, and on the horizon the "step-pyramid"
of Djoser, built in 2600 B.C., stands out against the sky, where once the pharaohs
of the old kingdom lived and died. Later on, after the destruction of Jerusalem at the
hands of the Babylonians, fugitives from Judah found refuge in the capital of lower
Egypt: "All the Jews which dwell in the land of Egypt . . . at Noph" (Jeremiah 44:1).

*"And Abram went down into Egypt to sojourn there;
for the famine was grievous in the land"* (Genesis 12: 10).
A wall-painting in a tomb at Beni Hasan in Egypt
gives us a lively impression of how we should think of the patriarch
and his family as they made their way into the land of the pharaohs.
This valuable record, dating from about 1900 B. C.,
shows us a caravan of desert bedouin led by a foreign prince.
The men have long hair which comes low over the brow and hangs down
at the back. They wear imperial beards (Leviticus 19:27; 21:5)
which are neatly trimmed (II Samuel 19:24). Their dress is varied:
some are clad in cloaks reaching just below the knee,
which could be given as surety only during the day and had
to be given back to the owner for his use at night (Exodus 22:26).
This cloak consisted of a square piece of cloth woven of coloured wool,
which was slung over one shoulder and reminds us of Joseph's coat
of many colours (Genesis 37:3).
Others are wearing simple leather aprons with a fringed border.
On their feet they have sandals reinforced at the heels.
The women's hair is held in place by a bandeau,
and hangs down over the shoulder with a little ringlet in front of the ear.
In addition to a three-quarter length dress they wear soft boots
covering the ankle, as does the small boy in front with the spear.
The third man from the left (above) carries a goatskin water-bottle
on his back: "Abraham . . . . took . . . . a bottle of water,
and gave it unto Hagar, putting it on her shoulder" (Genesis 21:14).
The men are armed with bows, spears and throw-sticks for protection
against robbers or wild animals (II Samuel 23:21).
One of the men is playing an eight-stringed lyre,
an instrument that is frequently mentioned in the psalms.

45

"*The princes also of Pharaoh saw her (i.e. Sarah), and commended her before Pharaoh; and the woman was taken into Pharaoh's house*" (Genesis 12:15).

At the time when the patriarchs had of necessity to interrupt their nomadic existence in the highlands of Palestine and in the Negeb to take refuge in Egypt because of famine, in the land of the pharaohs itself, the Middle Kingdom was drawing to its close. One of the best known and most important kings of the 12th Dynasty which was in power at that time (2000–1780 B. C.) was Sesostris III (1878–43).

"Then Lot chose him all the plain of Jordan; and Lot journeyed east . . . and pitched his tent toward Sodom" (Genesis 13:11, 12).

This happened after their return from Egypt. For "the land was not able to bear them, that they might dwell together: for their substance was great . . . and there was a strife between the herdmen of Abram's cattle, and the herdmen of Lot's cattle" (Genesis 13:6, 7). View from the west across the deep canyon of the Jordan valley just above the confluence of the river Jabbok. It is still as luxuriant and fertile today. The forest on the floor of the valley used to be the haunt of lions (Jeremiah 49:19).

"So Abraham returned unto his young men; and they rose up and went together to Beer-sheba: and Abraham dwelt at Beer-sheba" (Genesis 22:19).

A caravan has halted at Beersheba, literally "seven wells" or "the well of the oath", located in the deep south of Judah in the heart of the desert beside an ancient water-hole. It was here that Abraham and Abimelech made a covenant: they pledged themselves never to fight again over the well which Abraham had dug (Genesis 21:22 ff.) When Abraham left for Hebron the wells were stopped up by his enemies so that later his son Isaac had to dig them afresh. In the neighbourhood of present-day Beersheba there are still several wells that date back to patriarchal times.

"Abraham planted a tamarisk tree in Beer-sheba" (Genesis 21:33 – *R.S.V.*).
The tamarisk is a tree or bush whose small needle-shaped leaves
cling closely to the branches.
Several species grow in Palestine,
principally in the dry wadis of the desert and the steppes.
The largest of these, Tamarix Articulata,
reaches the height of an oak.
Here it is seen in springtime
in all the glory of its rose-coloured blossom.

"*And it came to pass in the days of . . . Chedorlaomer king of Elam . . . that these made war with Bera king of Sodom, and with Birsha king of Gomorrah . . . Twelve years they served Chedorlaomer, and in the thirteenth year they rebelled*" (Genesis 14: 1–4).
Suddenly out of the blue the father of the patriarchs enters the arena of the political struggles of the ancient East. When King Chedorlaomer of Elam with his royal allies from the smaller Babylonian kingdoms marched against Palestine he was routed by Abraham.
This fragment of a stela shows one of the kings of Elam, which lay E. N. E. of Babylon.

"*And in the fourteenth year came Chedorlaomer, and the kings that were with him . . . and smote . . . the Horites in their mount Seir, unto El-paran, which is by the wilderness*" (Genesis 14: 5–6).
The Horites, frequently mentioned in the Bible as living in Canaan (Genesis 36:20; Deuteronomy 2:12), probably belong to a people which came from an area south of the Caucasus and made its appearance in recorded history about 2400 B. C. This was the Hurrians, one of whose craftsmen produced this bronze lion.
The most important Hurrian source of information in the field of biblical studies is the collection of clay tablets from the city of Nuzu in Mesopotamia.

"All these were joined together in the vale of Siddim, which is the salt sea" (Genesis 14:3).
This was at the foot of the mountains of Moab, where now the peninsula of el-Lisan
thrusts a tongue of land into the Dead Sea. From this "shore of the salt sea,
from the bay (lit. tongue) that looketh southward" (Joshua 15:2),
it was possible in Roman times to wade across the sea to the Judaean shore.
The smooth surface of the lower part of the Dead Sea—in the foreground of the picture—
now covers what was once the fertile Vale of Siddim (Genesis 13:10) with the two cities
of Sodom and Gomorrah (Genesis 10:19). At the beginning of the second millennium B. C.
the ground subsided during a frightful natural disaster (Genesis 19), following which
the salt water from the north poured into the chasm and filled it up.

"But his wife looked back from behind him: and she became a pillar of salt" (Genesis 19:26).
Jebel Ustum is the name given by the Arabs to the ridge of hills which
stretches westward from the southern shore of the Dead Sea towards the Negeb.
Their slopes sparkle and glitter in the sunshine like diamonds. This is caused
by layers of pure rock salt. In the course of time the rains have worn away
many of these blocks of salt and have carved them into strange shapes.
Among the many remarkable salt formations,
some of them surprisingly human in appearance,
is one which still to this day recalls the punishment of Lot's wife—
a "standing pillar of salt . . . a monument of an unbelieving soul" (Wisdom 10:7)

"*Surely Moab shall be as Sodom,
and the children of Ammon as Gomorrah,
even the breeding of nettles, and saltpits,
and a perpetual desolation*" (Zephaniah 2:9).
As happened in ancient times, the
young state of Israel has begun to extract
salt from the Dead Sea near Sodom.
Water from the Dead Sea has eight times
as much salt content as water from
the Mediterranean.

"*So Abram moved his tent, and came and
dwelt by the oaks (or terebinths) of Mamre*"
(Genesis 13:18–R.S.V.).
Two miles north of Hebron, at what
is now Ramet el-Khalil, there was until
quite recently a huge and very old
terebinth which recalled the sacred place
where Abraham once had lived and
where he died (Genesis 25:8,9).
During a severe snowfall in the winter
of 1850 one of the lower branches broke
off and it required seven camels
to carry the wood to Jerusalem.

"... and built there an altar unto the Lord"
(Genesis 13:18).
King Herod the Great enclosed the
traditional site of the grove of terebinths
at Mamre with a massive stone wall.
Excavations in the south-west corner
of this area uncovered a well.
To the right of the picture a woman
is drawing water. Archaeologists also
came upon a levelled surface and, beside
the remains of very old roots of terebinths,
the site of an altar, easily identifiable
from the traces of ash.

"And Jacob went out from Beer-sheba,
and went toward Haran ... and, behold, a well
in the field ... and a great stone was upon
the well's mouth. And thither were all the
flocks gathered: and they rolled the stone
from the well's mouth, and watered the sheep,
and put the stone again upon the well's mouth
in his place (Genesis 28:10; 29:2, 3).
For thousands of years the custom of
covering the wells has been maintained
unchanged in Western Asia.
The purpose is to prevent wind or storm
from choking with sand the source
of the water that means life or death.

"*Then Jacob rose up . . . and . . . carried away all his cattle, and all his goods . . . for to go to . . . the land of Canaan. . . . and Rachel had stolen the images that were her father's*" (Genesis 31:17–19). Teraphim, the Hebrew word for household gods, seem to have been images or pictures with human shapes and features. Possession of them, as clay tablets discovered at Nuzu near Kirkuk have established, ensured that the owner would be head of the family and heir to the estate. That applied also to the son-in-law, so that Rachel's theft was a serious violation of her brothers' rights (Genesis 31:1). The Bible speaks elsewhere about household gods, such as those of Micah which were used in connection with oracles (Judges 17:5). Even David's wife Michal had her household god (I Samuel 19:13). As late as post-exilic times they are still being consulted: "For the teraphim have spoken vanity . . ." (Zechariah 10:2-R.V.).

"*So he fled with all that he had; and he rose up, and passed over the river . . .*" (Genesis 31:21). The "river" in this case—sometimes called the "great river" (Genesis 15:18; Deuteronomy 1:7) —is here also the Euphrates, which the patriarchs had to cross on the way between Haran and Canaan. In the foreground is a "quffa", a round boat which has been used from time immemorial on the Euphrates. Made of plaited reeds or osiers it is caulked with asphalt—called "slime" and "pitch" in the Bible—like Noah's Ark (Genesis 6:14). Since the quffa was specially used as a ferry for crossing the river, the patriarchs presumably used this type of boat in their day.

The prototype of the modern quffa, the Mesopotamian coracle. This relief
from Nineveh, dating from the time of Sennacherib, King of Assyria
(705–681 B. C.), shows a heavily laden boat being rowed across a river.
The boat is covered on the outside with animal hides and is manned
by four oarsmen.

III Joseph in Egypt

"He made him lord of his house, and ruler of all his substance"
(Psalm 105:21).

In the Land of the Pharaohs

(Genesis 39–50)

*"And the patriarchs, moved with envy, sold Joseph
into Egypt: but God was with him, and delivered him
out of all his afflictions, and gave him favour
and wisdom in the sight of Pharaoh king of Egypt;
and he made him governor over Egypt
and all his house"*
(Acts 7:9–10).

THE STORY of Joseph marks the transition from the simple day to day family life of the patriarchs to their involvement in the mainstream of world events. It was because of Joseph that Jacob and his household of seventy found themselves in Egypt, the land where this chosen family was to grow into the chosen people. For it was this group of Hebrew shepherds, settled on the grazing lands of the Nile delta, who formed the embryo of the people who later bore the name of Israel, and whose great assignment in history was to prepare the way for the coming of Christianity.

Joseph, the eleventh son of Jacob, was born while the family was still in Mesopotamia. His father loved him more than his other sons, since he had been the child of his old age by his favourite wife Rachel. The expensive "coat of many colours" which he gave to Joseph aroused the envy of his brothers, who sold him to a caravan of traders. They took Joseph with them to Egypt and sold him once again to Potiphar, an official in the royal household and captain of the pharaoh's bodyguard. After many mischances Joseph rose to fame and fortune in Egypt. Thrown into prison on account of a false accusation by Potiphar's wife, he suddenly found himself one day exalted to the rank of grand vizier in his adopted country.

If it seems surprising that this success story is given not even the barest mention in the otherwise meticulously accurate Egyptian records—at least so far as we possess them—we may put it down to the special circumstances of the period in which Joseph in all probability lived.

Shortly before 1700 B. C.—and this at least is certain—a new dark age overwhelmed Egypt which was to last for a century and a half. This came about through an invasion by Asian marauders whom the Egyptians called "Hyksos", meaning "rulers of foreign lands". In place of Thebes the Hyksos made their new capital at Avaris, in the eastern part of the Nile delta, not far from the grazings of the land of Goshen. In actual fact all the events described in the Bible as taking place at this time are located in the neighbourhood of the Nile delta.

Moreover, all that we learn from the book of Genesis about Joseph's stay in Egypt together with local customs and practices, corresponds exactly with what we know about ancient Egyptian life from excavations and other sources.

The Egyptians did in fact regard dreams and their interpretation as enormously important, and seven-year famines are confirmed in hieroglyphic texts. The titles of "chief of the butlers" and "chief of the bakers" can be identified in Egyptian inscriptions. So, also, the gifts which the pharaoh made to Joseph at his installation correspond with normal usage. When we are told that Joseph's brothers came down from Canaan in time of famine to buy food, and that eventually Jacob with his family and all his goods and chattels arrived in Egypt and received permission to settle in the land of Goshen, this too is nothing out of the ordinary. For we learn from Egyptian texts that it was customary for the pharaohs' frontier police to allow Palestinian bedouin to enter Goshen in times of hardship.

In effect, wherever we turn, the monuments and documents of Egypt's past—whether it be wall-paintings from the tombs, or mummified bodies, reliefs on temple buildings or sculptured figures—confirm the astonishing accuracy of the biblical record of the life and customs of the country.

"*Then there passed by . . . merchantmen; and they drew and lifted up Joseph out of the pit, and sold Joseph . . . for twenty pieces of silver: and they brought Joseph into Egypt*" (Genesis 37:28).
A group of Syrians has arrived in Egypt to offer gifts to the general of one of the pharaohs. As a token of their subjection and homage some of the princes shown in the picture are on their knees (II Kings 1:13).
One of them "bows himself toward the ground" (Genesis 18:2) which the Bible also rightly records as the normal ceremonial greeting. Among the costly gifts of jars and vases, stands a naked boy whom one of the servants holds by the hand.
"And the Midianites sold him into Egypt, unto Potiphar, an officer of Pharaoh's, and captain of the guard" (Genesis 37:36).

"And the patriarchs, moved with envy, sold Joseph into Egypt" (Acts 7:9).
After Abraham and Lot it was Joseph's turn to enter the land of Egypt.
Later on Jacob and his household joined him. The sojourn in Egypt,
during which Israel grew into the makings of a people in the four hundred years
before the Exodus under Moses, left an indelible impression on the minds
of the Israelite nation and is an established part of its history. Among the imposing
buildings which Joseph and many of his kinsmen must have seen are the massive
pyramids with the graves of the kings—Cheops, Khafre and Menkaure—at Giza.
The great Sphinx, in the centre of the picture, guardian of the pyramid on the right,
bears the head of Pharaoh Khafre. Near Giza, which lies north of Memphis, called
Noph in the Bible, is the beginning of the Nile delta, in the eastern part of which is the
area where Jacob and his family were allowed to settle, the "Land of Goshen".

61

"And the Midianites sold him into Egypt, unto Potiphar,
an officer of Pharaoh's, and captain of the guard"
(Genesis 37:36).
Like the pharaohs and the rulers of Assyria and
Babylon, the kings of Israel from Saul onwards had
their bodyguard or gentlemen-at-arms (I Samuel 22:7).
They furnished the heralds who proclaimed the
approach of the monarch and cleared the way for his
chariot (I Samuel 8:11) as well as providing the palace
guards. This is an Egyptian soldier of the bodyguard
from a relief in the temple-tomb of Ramesses II.

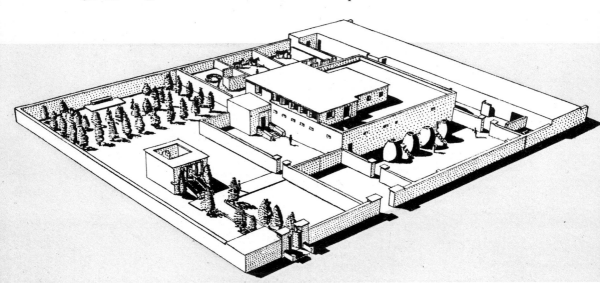

"And the Lord was with Joseph, and he was a prosperous man; and he was in the house
of his master the Egyptian . . . and he made him overseer over his house, and all that he had
he put into his hand" (Genesis 39:2, 4).
Model from a tomb of an Egyptian property: on the left, the garden with pool
and arbour; in the centre, the dwelling house; on the right and in the foreground,
offices; behind, on the right, stables. The roof-garden is of such a character that it
later became one of the laws of Israel that: "When thou buildest a new house,
then thou shalt make a battlement for thy roof, that thou bring not blood upon thine
house, if any man fall from thence" (Deuteronomy 22:8).

*"I made me gardens and orchards, and I planted trees in them of all
kind of fruits . . . I made me pools of water"* (Ecclesiastes 2: 5, 6).
Egyptian wall-painting of a luxury garden, such as would form part
of a nobleman's residence, with a pond in which fish and waterfowl are
disporting themselves. Among the trees and bushes can be seen date-palms,
greatly prized also in Palestine, and here well laden with bunches
of fruit. Their "branches" were used on festal occasions (Nehemiah 8: 15),
as a mark of homage to a sovereign (I Maccabees 13: 37–R.V.; John 12: 13)
or in celebration of a victory.

" *And it came to pass after these things,*
that the butler of the king of Egypt and his baker
had offended their lord the king of Egypt.
And Pharaoh was wroth against two of his
officers, against the chief of the butlers, and against
the chief of the bakers. And he put them . . . into
the prison, the place where Joseph was bound"
(Genesis 40: 1–3).
In view of the frequent attempts at murder
by poisoning in the ancient East
the position of cup-bearer was always one
of special trust. Here a cup-bearer serves
a drink to an Egyptian princess, while she is
having her hair done. Later, in the palace
of King Solomon there were cup-bearers
as in the court of the pharaohs
(I Kings 10: 5).

"And one night . . . dreamed . . . the baker of the king of Egypt" (Genesis 40:5–R.S.V.).
View of the bakehouse of one of the pharaohs: on the left, two slaves,
keeping their balance with long poles, are tramping out the dough
with their bare feet in a kneading trough (Deuteronomy 28:5–R.V.).
Two more are bringing liquid and dough to a third man who rolls it out
and makes it into different shapes. Recumbent cows and "snails" seem to have
been the most popular designs. One of the workers is seen bringing just such a
spiral-shaped coil of dough, spitted on two sticks, to a griddle which is placed
above a blazing fire—"all that is . . . on the baking pan shall be the priest's"
(Leviticus 7:9–R.V.). On the extreme right a man is taking the finished products
out of a cold oven and stacking them on a nearby table. The same oven
features again on the left of the lower series of pictures but this time the flames
are rising out of the opening at the top and an assistant is bringing the raw
material on a large board ready for baking.
This is what Hosea's "oven heated by the baker" looked like (Hosea 7:4).
It consisted of a clay cylinder which in Palestine was built into the ground,
as we can tell from excavations. The wood was tossed inside and then set alight.
As soon as the oven was hot the fire was removed and the bread was then
stuck to the warm inner surface of the oven and baked.

*"And Pharaoh said unto Joseph, See, I have
set thee over all the land of Egypt. And Pharaoh
took off his ring from his hand, and put it upon
Joseph's hand, and arrayed him in vestures of fine
linen, and put a gold chain about his neck"*
(Genesis 41:41–42).
A relief shows the solemn ceremony
at which a pharaoh installs a minister and
keeper of the seal, and invests him with the
symbols of his office. Part of the insignia
was a wand which was carried in the left
hand and a gold signet ring which was
worn on the right. On its surface it bore
an engraved circle with the name of the
particular pharaoh. Grooms-in-waiting
are seen in the act of hanging a heavy gold
chain round the neck of the new dignitary.

"*And he made him to ride in the second chariot which he had: and they cried before him, Bow the knee: and he made him ruler over all the land of Egypt*" (Genesis 41:43).

According to the biblical narrative Joseph's public appearances in his chariot must have been as impressive as a pharaoh's—the king shown in this relief is Akhnaten, Amenophis IV. Only very high-ranking officials were granted the royal privilege of riding through the streets in a state chariot. Pulled by a span of horses, the chariot was flanked and preceded by a couple of runners armed with sticks to clear the way. In the picture only two members of the public are represented (right), one of whom kneels in homage. Both of them greet the monarch with hand-clapping. Also in front of the chariot are detachments of the king's bodyguard marching at the double. Native troops as well as mercenaries can be recognised among them. In the top row are Libyans, Semites and negroes equipped with spears and bows; in the second row, warriors with battle-axes, spears and shields. Later this custom was adopted in court circles in Israel and Judah, and every notability had his escort when he undertook a journey: "Then Adonijah the son of Haggith exalted himself, saying, I will be king: and he prepared himself chariots and horsemen, and fifty men to run before him" (I Kings 1:5; II Samuel 15:1).

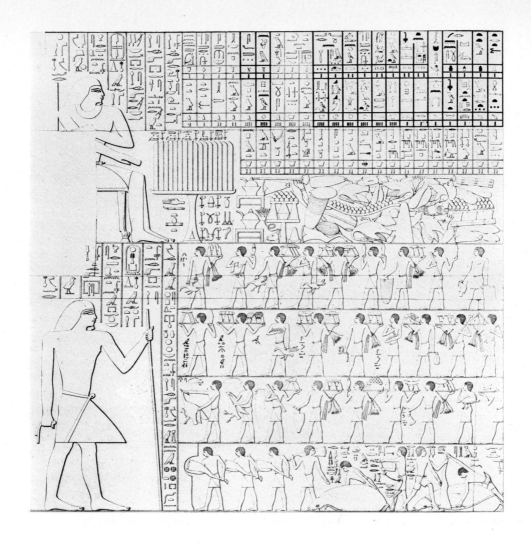

"*And in the seven plenteous years the earth brought forth by handfuls*"
(Genesis 41:47).
Above, rooms are chock-a-block and tables are piled high
with poultry, fruit and vegetables. A procession of servants
is laden with a variety of rich fare indicative of the affluent society
on the Nile—ducks and geese, trays of cakes and pastries,
local fruit and sheaves of ripe corn. Below are butchers with great
haunches of beef in their arms, while others are still engaged in
cutting up the carcasses.

"*And he gathered up all the food of the seven years, which were in the land of Egypt, and laid up the food in the cities: the food of the field which was round about every city laid he up in the same*" (Genesis 41:48).

Flocks of geese are rounded up by herds and packed into baskets for despatch to the cities.

In ancient Egypt food-storage was nothing out of the ordinary
as this wall-painting from a tomb at Thebes indicates. Top left, geese are hanging
on a frame ready for pickling in clay jars. They have already been cleaned
and stitched up. Two men are busy plucking the dead fowls and slitting
them up to remove the entrails. Others—right—have just caught a flock
of wildfowl in a seine-net.

"And Joseph gathered corn as the sand of the sea, very much, until he left numbering; for it was without number" (Genesis 41:49).

Corn is being cut in a field by hand, under the supervision of the land-owner and the overseer of the slaves. The harvesters—one of them is a child—grasp the stalks in their left hands (Psalm 129:7) and apply the sickle with the right. After it has been threshed the quantity of grain is recorded by scribes, while an overseer sitting on a heap of corn urges on the slaves to work faster as they pile up the grain (above). Below, the lord of the manor sits in the shade watching the operations. He holds a staff in his right hand and a sweat-rag in his left.

Top left, women are winnowing the grain. Their heads are covered with scarves to protect them from dust. The woman stooping down on the right is sweeping up the corn with a hand-brush, all the rest are wielding wooden winnowing-shovels. This throws the corn into the air so that the chaff is blown away. The grain is then piled up and measured against lines painted on the wall. Beside the overseer is the harvest-offering. Sheaves of corn can be seen above, together with quails, the birds which later were to provide sustenance for the people of Israel in the desert, and which they already had learned to relish during their stay in Egypt. "And he brought quails" (Psalm 105:40).

"*And let them gather all the food of those good years that come,
and lay up corn under the hand of Pharaoh, and let them keep food
in the cities*" (Genesis 41:35).

An interesting glimpse of the activity involved in filling one of
the state-owned granaries of ancient Egypt. This wooden model
which was found in a tomb illustrates the biblical narrative.
Above, left, is the door through which slaves bring tightly-packed
sacks of grain first of all into an office, where each sack is carefully
recorded by the scribes, who are seen squatting on the floor.
Then the corn is taken to the granary proper and emptied from an
upstairs gallery into one of the compartments.

"*Let Pharaoh . . . appoint officers over the land, and take up the fifth part of the land of Egypt in the seven plenteous years*" (Genesis 41:34).
Taxation in Egypt was strictly enforced. Three men are seen prostrated in an attitude of submission before scribes, who are seated in a covered bower, and who are noting down the amounts still to pay. Further defaulters are being marched in on the right and are being assisted by bailiffs to assume the proper posture.

"*And the seven years of dearth began to come, according as Joseph had said: and the dearth was in all lands; but in all the land of Egypt there was bread*" (Genesis 41:54).
Men, women and children reduced to skeletons, as they are seen on this Egyptian relief, show us only too clearly what a time of famine meant in those days for ordinary people.
This scene from Saqqara is almost like a contemporary illustration of the description in Genesis 41:55 where we are told: "And when all the land of Egypt was famished, the people cried to Pharaoh for bread."

71

"*And the famine was over all the face of the earth.*
And Joseph opened all the storehouses, and sold unto the Egyptians;
and the famine waxed sore in the land of Egypt. And all
countries came into Egypt to Joseph for to buy corn;
because that the famine was so sore in all lands" (Genesis 41:56–57).
This relief shows a whole row of state-granaries in Egypt.
They appear to have been round containers with vaulted
roofs. Underneath are clearly recognisable trapdoors
from which the corn was released for sale. Like the
Egyptian pharaohs (Exodus 1:11) King Solomon later
erected in his expanding monarchy "cities of store"
(I Kings 9:19) or "store cities" (II Chronicles 8:4, 6).

"*Now when Jacob saw that there was corn in Egypt, Jacob said unto his sons ...
get you down thither and buy for us from thence; that we may live, and not die ...
And the sons of Israel came to buy corn ... And Joseph was the governor over the land,
and he it was that sold to all the people of the land; and Joseph's brethren came,
and bowed down themselves before him with their faces to the earth*" (Genesis 42: 1–6).
Just such a scene as this may have taken place before Joseph. It is from a
bas-relief in a tomb near Memphis, and shows a group of foreigners in the
presence of high-ranking Egyptians. They are either prostrated or on their knees.
One lies flat on the ground and another lies flat on his back. Most of them are
Semites, easily recognisable by their features, their short beards and long tightly
bound hair. Ceremonial greetings of this kind are often referred to in the Bible:
"And so it was, when he came to David, that he fell to the earth, and did
obeisance" (II Samuel 1:2; 9:6).

"And Joseph said unto them, That is it that I spake unto you, saying,
Ye are spies ... ye shall be kept in prison ... And he put them
all together into ward three days" (Genesis 42: 14, 16, 17).
A column of Semitic prisoners. Each of the captives is
attached to an Egyptian by a rope round his neck and has
his hands tied across his chest.

"Then Joseph commanded to fill their sacks with corn,
and to restore every man's money into his sack,
and to give them provision for the way; and thus did he unto them.
And they laded their asses with the corn and departed thence"
(Genesis 42: 25–26).

"And Joseph . . . said, Set on bread . . . And they sat before him,
the firstborn according to his birthright, and the youngest according
to his youth . . . And he took and sent messes unto them from before him . . .
And they drank and were merry with him" (Genesis 43:30–34).
Picture of a banquet in Egypt such as Joseph may have arranged
for his brothers (wall-painting from a tomb).
Above, a naked slave-girl serves the distinguished men and
women guests. Below, musicians and dancing-girls.
Music and dancing were part of every banquet in the ancient
East: "As a signet of an emerald set in a work of gold,
so is the melody of musick with pleasant wine"
(Ecclesiasticus 32:6).

"And Pharaoh spake unto Joseph, saying, Thy father and thy brethren
are come unto thee: The land of Egypt is before thee: in the best of the land
make thy father and brethren to dwell; in the land of Goshen let them dwell:
and if thou knowest any men of activity among them, then make them
rulers over my cattle ... And Israel dwelt in the land of Egypt, in the
country of Goshen; and they had possessions therein, and grew, and multiplied
exceedingly" (Genesis 47: 5, 6, 27).

Not far from the Nile delta the location of the land of Goshen
has been established, an area with the most succulent grazings
that a pastoral people like the Israelites could possibly dream of.
This relief from Saqqara depicts a herd of cattle returning
from the lush pastures of the delta and being driven across
one of the arms of the river. The water is quite shallow.
First of all come the calves, a very small one having to be carried.
The second herdsman has a gourd-bottle slung over his stick
and a sleeping-mat hung over his shoulders.

76

PLATE I

"And they took their cattle, and their goods . . . and came into Egypt . . ."
(Genesis 46:6).
The "foreign prince"—for so he is described on the adjacent
hieroglyphic inscription—bows respectfully to a high Egyptian
official (not seen in the picture) and greets him with his right hand.
"Abishai"—his name recalls that of one of David's companions
(I Samuel 26:6)—has led a caravan of thirty-seven Semites
to Egypt in "the sixth year of his majesty king Sesostris II."
With his left hand the prince holds a tame ibex (Deuteronomy
14:5–R.S.V.) on a short cord. Between the animal's horns
he has placed a bent stick—the shepherd's crook—with separate
rings cut out of the bark. His black hair is worn long at the
back and over the forehead. He also wears sideburns, pointed beard
and no moustache—in the style of a "ruff". His cloak, which
is thrown over one shoulder, reaches to his knees and has a fringe
from top to bottom. The high quality worsted with its
variegated pattern gives us an idea of Joseph's famous coat
of many colours (Genesis 37:3).

"And when money failed in the land of Egypt, and in the land
of Canaan, all the Egyptians came unto Joseph, and said, Give us bread:
for why should we die in thy presence? for the money faileth.
And Joseph said, Give your cattle; and I will give you for your cattle,
if money fail. And they brought their cattle unto Joseph:
and Joseph gave them bread in exchange for horses, and for the flocks,
and for the cattle of the herds, and for the asses; and he fed them
with bread for all their cattle for that year" (Genesis 47:15–17).
Cattlemen bringing up their oxen. Below, left, a scribe stoops
over his task of checking the animals as they pass.

*"When that year was ended, they came unto him the second year, and said . . .
We will not hide it from my lord, how that . . . there is not ought left in the sight
of my lord, but our bodies and our lands . . . And Joseph bought all the land of Egypt
for Pharaoh; for the Egyptians sold every man his field, because the famine prevailed
over them"* (Genesis 47:18, 20).

A painting from a tomb at Thebes shows a field being measured.
This is what Joseph must have organised when he began to buy up land
in exchange for corn. Left and right of the picture are the men with the
measuring line. They are accompanied by three scribes, an old peasant
and some youths.

*"And . . . Jacob . . . yielded up the ghost, and was
gathered unto his people . . . And Joseph commanded
his servants the physicians to embalm his father:
and the physicians embalmed Israel"*
(Genesis 49:33; 50:2).

The Egyptian practice of embalming corpses
was intended to preserve the body after death.
It is only mentioned in the Bible in connection
with Jacob and Joseph (Genesis 50:26).
Here embalmers are processing a dead body.
Above, a priest wearing the jackal's mask
of Anubis, the god of embalming,
stands beside the corpse
which is laid out on the embalming-couch.
Below, the corpse is treated with natron which
draws the fluid out of the body.

"*And the Egyptians mourned for him threescore and ten days*" (Genesis 50: 3).
With uplifted hands a group of professional mourning-women and girls
are lamenting a death, as shown on this painting in an Egyptian tomb.
Some are naked to the waist, others wear full-length gowns.
Traces of tears can be seen on their faces. It later became the custom
in Israel to hire professional mourners, especially women, to express grief
at a bereavement: "Call for the mourning women . . . and let them make
haste, and take up a wailing for us, that our eyes may run down with tears,
and our eyelids gush out with waters" says Jeremiah 9: 17–18.

"And Joseph went up to bury his father: and with him went up all the servants
of Pharaoh, the elders of his house, and all the elders of the land of Egypt,
And all the house of Joseph, and his brethren and his father's house"
(Genesis 50:7–8).
A corpse, which has been ferried across the Nile, is being taken overland
to its last resting-place. The sarcophagus, in which can be seen the mummy
(underneath), sits in a boat which in its turn rests on a sledge drawn by
four oxen. Floral tributes are piled high round the coffin and two priests walk
in front. At the head of the cortège are the men, followed by the women.
As a mark of mourning they all have one hand placed on the head: "And
(Tamar) laid her hand on her head, and went on crying" (II Samuel 13:19).

IV Freed from Egypt's Bondage
"And I brought your fathers out of Egypt" (Joshua 24:6).

The Exodus and the Journey through the Wilderness

(Exodus—Deuteronomy)

"But when the time of the promise drew nigh,
which God had sworn to Abraham,
the people grew and multiplied in Egypt,
till another king arose which knew not Joseph . . .
In which time Moses was born . . .
He brought them out, after that he had showed wonders
and signs in the land of Egypt, and in the Red Sea,
and in the wilderness, forty years"
(Acts 7:17, 18, 20, 36).

THE BIBLE has nothing to say about the four centuries which the people of Israel spent in the land of Goshen. The record jumps from the death of Joseph immediately into the prelude (Exodus 1:8) to a new and significant development—the Exodus from Egypt.

Jacob's family, which once had migrated to Egypt to escape a famine, had in the meantime grown into a large people, whose increase in numbers was beginning to worry the Egyptians.

For a long time now Egypt had been free again from the oppressive foreign domination of the Hyksos, and in the New Kingdom, dating from about 1546 B.C., after a period of decline came the beginnings of a second golden age.

Towards the end of the fourteenth century B.C., when Seti I (1319–1301) acceded to the throne of the pharaohs, we have reached the time when the Bible takes up the narrative once more. A large number of scholars today are inclined to see in the second pharaoh of the Ramesside dynasty, Seti I, the "new king which knew not Joseph" referred to in Exodus 1:8. A hard time was now in store for the people of Israel. "They did set over them taskmasters to afflict them with their burdens" (Exodus 1:11). They were put to work to build the "treasure cities, Pithom and Raamses" which lay in the eastern part of the Nile delta.

Even when "in process of time the king of Egypt died" (Exodus 2:23) they were no better off. Under his successor Ramesses II

(1301–1234 B. C.) the oppression continued until at last their heaven-sent deliverer Moses prevailed on the pharaoh to let them go.

After the miraculous escape of the fugitives from their Egyptian pursuers at the Sea of Reeds, Moses led his people to Mt Sinai, where they received the Law. High up among the mountain peaks, where the name of Jebel Musa, the "mountain of Moses", still recalls the memory of this great man of God, the Lord revealed himself to his people, and Moses was given the injunctions which were to become the Law of the people of God, the Ten Commandments.

A year later they set out from Sinai. The forty years of wandering in the wilderness had begun. Among the many oases and places where they spent longer or shorter time, as listed in Numbers 33, Kadesh is perhaps the best-known. Lying about thirty-five miles south of Beersheba it forms the largest oasis in that desert area. It was from Kadesh that they finally set out for Canaan. When the Israelites had become masters of the territory east of Jordan, they reached the "plains of Moab" (Numbers 22:1) on the lower Jordan opposite Jericho. While they were encamped there, Moses climbed Mt Nebo, from where he was able to see the promised land and where he died.

"Now there arose up a new king over Egypt, which knew not Joseph. And he said unto his people, Behold, the people of the children of Israel are more and mightier than we"
(Exodus 1:8,9).
After the story of Joseph the Bible lapses into silence. When the narrative is resumed, four hundred years have passed, and the Ramesside dynasty, the nineteenth (about 1320–1200 B.C.), was in control on the Nile. Having reigned for barely two years the first Ramesses was succeeded by his son Seti I in 1319 B.C.
A limestone relief from the temple which he built to Osiris at Abydos shows us the warrior-king who restored Egyptian hegemony in Western Asia after a period of military ineffectiveness.

*"Come on, let us deal wisely with them; lest they multiply, and it come
to pass, that, when there falleth out any war, they join also unto our enemies,
and fight against us, and so get them up out of the land"* (Exodus 1:10).
In contrast to the bearded Semites, the Hittites—"sons of Heth"
as the Bible calls them (Genesis 10:15; 23:3)—were mostly clean-
shaven. They were the most dreaded of Egypt's enemies in the time of the
Ramessides. They wore their black hair long, hanging loosely down
their backs, and their sharp beak-like noses gave their people a
distinctive appearance. Short aprons fastened with a belt were worn
underneath long cloaks which were thrown over one shoulder,
leaving the other shoulder free. Egyptian artists found it difficult
to reproduce a hair-style and type of dress which were so unfamiliar.

This Egyptian relief takes us right into the confusion of a battle
between Egyptians (left) and Hittites (right). Under a hail of arrows
Hittite chariots are attacked by Egyptian forces. Dead and wounded
are already strewn over the battlefield. Pierced by arrows, Hittite
horses and charioteers plunge to the ground as their war-chariots
overturn.

▶

A king of Mitanni, the country on the upper reaches
of the Tigris and Euphrates which adjoined Hittite
territory and which had strong affinities with the
Hurrians. He wears the typical robe with padded edge
draped over one shoulder only.
The people of Mitanni were, however,
not always hostile to the Egyptians.
Many a time their kings sent their daughters
to Egypt as brides for the pharaohs.
The famous Queen Nofretete,
wife of Akhnaten the sun-king,
was probably one of these princesses of Mitanni.

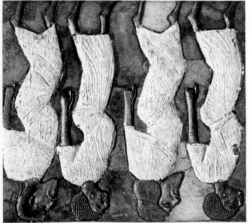

"... until I make thine enemies thy footstool"
(Psalm 110:1).
Inlaid with cedarwood, gold and ivory, this
magnificent footstool once stood before the throne of
Pharaoh Tutankhamen. As a symbol of his power
and of his mastery over his country's enemies,
the royal feet were placed upon this stool
when the pharaoh sat upon his throne in his capacity
as High Priest of Egypt.
Depicted on the stool are typical natives of countries
which were traditionally hostile to Egypt.
On the far left is a Libyan, with pointed beard,
hair cut evenly across the neck and a side pig-tail
at the temple. Second and fourth from the left are
negroes. Flat noses, full lips, clean-shaven faces,
woolly hair and earrings are their particular
characteristics. The figure in the centre with long hair,
fastened with a bandeau, and with full beard,
is a Syrian.

*"Therefore they did set over them taskmasters, to afflict them with
their burdens . . . And the Egyptians made the children of Israel to serve
with rigour . . . all manner of service in the field . . . wherein they
made them serve, was with rigour"* (Exodus 1 : 11–14).
Hounded on by an overseer, men in groups of five,
wearing loincloths, are trying to loosen the unyielding
sun-baked soil of Egypt.

*"And they made their lives bitter with hard bondage,
in mortar and in brick"* (Exodus 1:14).
Semites and dark-skinned slaves at work making bricks and building
a granary are shown on this wall-painting in a tomb at Thebes. Top left,
two slaves are fetching water from a tree-girt pool. One of them is in the water up
to his waist, the other is bending down. When the Nile clay has been moistened
it is lifted with mattocks and taken in baskets to the workmen in the background
who shape it into bricks using wooden moulds with handles attached. The rough
bricks, still moist, are then laid out in rows to dry in the sun (above left).
The finished products can be seen on the right being carried away by a slave,
who has them secured by straps and hanging from a pole laid across his shoulders.
An overseer with a stick urges the workers on. Underneath, workmen
are bringing bricks to build a ramp. At the same time Nile clay is being
brought to act as mortar. The overseer in this group also carries a rod.

"And it came to pass in those days, when Moses was grown, that he went out unto his brethren, and looked on their burdens: and he spied an Egyptian smiting an Hebrew, one of his brethren. And . . . he slew the Egyptian, and hid him in the sand" (Exodus 2:11–12).

Beating of slaves and impressed labourers was not uncommon in Egypt. Here a peasant is being beaten for not paying his taxes.

"But Moses fled from the face of Pharaoh, and dwelt in the land of Midian" (Exodus 2:15).
The country of the Midianites, who were supposed to have sprung from a son of Abraham and his wife Keturah (Genesis 25:2) lay to the east of the gulf of Aqabah.
Arabian geographers knew of a town in that area still bearing the name Midian.
The Midianites were nomads like the people who even today frequent the area, living in their black tents at the foot of the crags.

"*And it came to pass, in process of time, that the king of Egypt died;
and the children of Israel sighed by reason of the bondage, and they cried . . .*"
(Exodus 2:23).

After the death of Seti I in 1301 B.C., his son Ramesses II
succeeded him as king of Egypt. Many scholars today reckon that
this ruler was the pharaoh in whose reign the Exodus from
Egypt took place. Ramesses II whose ambition to build
for posterity became an obsession, left many memorials of his
enterprise, among them this massive rock temple of Abu Simbel
in Lower Nubia. Four stone statues of Pharaoh Ramesses II over
sixty feet high sit in front of the temple on the left bank of the Nile.

"*And Pharaoh commanded the same day the taskmasters of the people,*
and their officers, saying, Ye shall no more give the people (Israel)
straw to make brick, as heretofore: let them go and gather straw for themselves.
And the tale of the bricks, which they did make heretofore, ye shall lay upon them;
ye shall not diminish ought thereof..." (Exodus 5:6–8).

The accuracy of the biblical record, even in apparently unimportant
details, can be attested by this silent witness. It is a brick, made out of
clay from the Nile, into which pieces of straw have been kneaded—
exactly what the Israelites had to produce in their bond-service.
The stamp on the surface leaves us in no doubt as to the time when
this Egyptian brick was made nor as to who was responsible for its
creation—it bears the sovereign seal of Pharaoh Ramesses II.

*"But God led the people about, through the way of the wilderness
of the Red sea" (= sea of reeds)* (Exodus 13:18).
Between the shores of the Mediterranean and the gulf of Suez
on the Red Sea—now connected by the Suez Canal—there lies a
chain of inland lakes which in the time of the Ramessides were
artificially joined with the Red Sea: – the Bitter Lakes and Lake
Timsah or Lake of Crocodiles, lying further to the north.
Presumably the biblical "Sea of Reeds" lay in this region.
Lakes with tall reeds all along their banks suggest to us today
what a "Sea of Reeds" must have looked like.

"And it was told the king of Egypt that the people fled: and the heart of Pharaoh . . . was turned . . . And he made ready his chariot . . . and he pursued after the children of Israel" (Exodus 14: 5–8).

PLATE II

The majestic figure of Pharaoh Tutankhamen standing up in
his war-chariot pulled by two spanking steeds. Royal
vultures shield him overhead. The monarch wears his
war-helmet with heraldic viper and long ribbons, with a
broad collar round his neck. Driving at a furious speed the
pharaoh has far outpaced his own troops. They are attacking
their Asian enemies. His bow is fully stretched
(Psalm 18:34) and primed with an arrow. Dead and wounded
Asians, pierced by arrows, lie under the chariot wheels.
Such a scene as this picture portrays in the tomb of
Tutankhamen suggests the similar pursuit of the Israelites
by the "king of Egypt". "And he made ready his chariot . . .
and he pursued after the children of Israel" (Exodus 14:6–8).

"And he took six hundred chosen chariots, and all the chariots of Egypt, and captains over every one of them" (Exodus 14:7).

Egyptian war-chariots careering through meadows thick with flowers. Since ever the Hyksos introduced the horse into Egypt about 1700 B.C., the light two-wheeled chariot played an increasingly important role in Egyptian strategy. The chariot corps became a powerful striking force, operating in sections of twenty-five machines. Each car had a driver and a fighting-man, who was armed with bow, spear and shield. The quiver was fixed to the outside bodywork (as illustrated). Chariot units of the type seen in this Egyptian picture pursued the people of Israel, according to the biblical record.

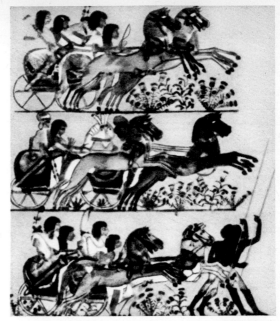

"But the Egyptians pursued after them, all the horses and chariots of Pharaoh, and his horsemen, and his army" (Exodus 14:9).

Forty soldiers on the march in four columns of ten (left). Each of them holds a six-foot lance in his right hand and a leather-covered shield in his left. Marching beside them, likewise in four columns of ten, is a company of Nubian archers (right). Each archer carries an unstrung bow in his left hand and a bundle of arrows in his right. This wooden model reproduces accurately what the Bible calls "Pharaoh's army".

"*And Miriam the prophetess, the sister of Aaron, took a timbrel in her hand;
and all the women went out after her with timbrels and with dances. And
Miriam answered them, Sing ye to the Lord, for he hath triumphed
gloriously; the horse and his rider hath he thrown into the sea*"
(Exodus 15:20–21).

The timbrel or tabret, here seen being played by Egyptian
dancing-girls, was a kind of tambourine, a wooden framework
covered with hide. It was used to provide a rhythmic
accompaniment for the choral dance which was led off by the
prophetess Miriam as an expression of joy and thanksgiving for the
miraculous escape of Israel from destruction at the hands of the
Egyptian army. Later on, King Saul is greeted joyfully in this manner
after the slaughter of the Philistines: "... the women came out of all
cities of Israel, singing and dancing, to meet king Saul, with
tabrets ..." (I Samuel 18:6).

"*So Moses brought Israel from the Red sea; and they went out into
the wilderness of Shur: and they went three days in the wilderness,
and found no water. And when they came to Marah,
they could not drink of the waters of Marah, for they were bitter:
therefore the name of it was called Marah*"
(Exodus 15:22–23).

Pilgrims and scholars alike have long sought to identify the
various stopping-places of the Israelites on their journey from
Egypt to Canaan. The first of these encampments—the
biblical Marah—is thought to have been found with
reasonable probability at Ain Hawara, almost fifty miles
south of Suez on the east side of the gulf and only a few
miles inland. Today a small clump of date-palms is all that
is left to indicate the miserable water-hole which desert winds
have now completely silted up.

99

*"And they came to Elim, where were twelve wells of water, and
threescore and ten palm trees: and they encamped there by the waters.
And they took their journey from Elim, and all the congregation
of the children of Israel came unto the wilderness of Sin . . ."*
(Exodus 15:27; 16:1).
View of the oasis in modern Wadi Garandel on the west coast
of the Sinai peninsula. It lies a day's march away from
Ain Hawara and its vegetation is rank. This is thought to
have been Elim, the second camping-ground of the Israelites.

"And the whole congregation of the children of Israel murmured against Moses and Aaron in the wilderness: And the children of Israel said unto them, Would to God we had died by the hand of the Lord in the land of Egypt, when we sat by the flesh pots, and when we did eat bread to the full! for ye have brought us forth into this wilderness, to kill this whole assembly with hunger" (Exodus 16:2–3).
View of an Egyptian slaughterhouse, well stocked with the meat the Israelites yearned for in the desert. This painted wooden model retained its life-like colouring for thousands of years in the tomb of a nobleman.

A wooden model of an Egyptian bakery. In the left background is the table on which the loaves were shaped. On the right two baking ovens with large loaves of baked bread, such as the Israelites knew from their stay in Egypt. Bread was an important element in the daily diet there and a price-list from the time of the New Kingdom specifies forty different kinds of bread and cakes.

"And the Lord spake unto Moses, saying, I have heard the murmurings of the children of Israel: speak unto them, saying, At even ye shall eat flesh ... And it came to pass, that at even the quails came up, and covered the camp" (Exodus 16:11–13).

Quails are found not only in Europe but also, as has been observed from ancient times, in Egypt and Arabia. Every spring, flocks of these migratory birds cross the Red Sea on their way to the Sinai peninsula, where they land exhausted near the coast and are easily caught. This is exactly how the Bible describes what happened during the Israelites' sojourn in the desert (Exodus 16:13 and Numbers 11:31). The birds were on their way northwards: "and there went forth a wind ... and brought quails from the sea". This wall-painting from a grave at Thebes shows that the trapping of quails was a normal occurrence on the Nile and indicates how it was done. Four men are walking through a cornfield holding a square fine-meshed net, extended in a horizontal position. When the birds fly up they are entangled in the net and can be readily caught.

"*In the third month, when the children of Israel were gone forth out of the land of Egypt, the same day came they into the wilderness of Sinai . . . and there Israel camped before the mount*" (Exodus 19:1–2).

If we follow the route taken by the Israelites through arid desert and sun-baked wadis, we come suddenly upon a vast plain overgrown with meagre shrubs. At the far end is the red granite massif which from earliest Christian times has been regarded as the mountain which the Bible calls Sinai or Horeb. The peak on the left beside the triple range is Jebel Musa—the "mountain of Moses"—7293 feet high.

"*And Moses went up . . . And God spake all these words, saying, I am the Lord thy God . . .*" (Exodus 19:20; 20:1–2).

View from the silent, lonely top of Jebel Musa on to the awe-inspiring
mountain-mass of Sinai.

"And when the people saw that Moses delayed to come down out of the mount . . . all the people brake off the golden earrings which were in their ears, and brought them unto Aaron. And he received them at their hand, and fashioned it with a graving tool, after he had made it a molten calf: and they said, These be thy gods, O Israel, which brought thee up out of the land of Egypt" (Exodus 32:1–4).

Bronze figure of Apis, the bull-god of Memphis. Between his horns he bears the sun-disk with heraldic viper; on his forehead is the distinctive white triangle of the sacred bull; round his neck he wears a ribbon, and a rug is spread over his back. It may be that the cult of this and other sacred bulls in Egypt influenced the Israelites in their decision to worship a golden calf. There is only one other example of this particular type of idolatry in the Bible, when King Jeroboam of Israel installed two golden calves in his new sanctuaries (I Kings 12:28–29).

"And the mixed multitude that was among them fell a lusting: and the children of Israel also wept again, and said, Who shall give us flesh to eat? We remember the fish, which we did eat in Egypt freely; the cucumbers, and the melons, and the leeks, and the onions and the garlick" (Numbers 11:4–5).

Fish was in plentiful supply in Egypt. One of the most popular subjects for wall-paintings in the tombs was fishing. On this painted relief from Saqqara two fishermen are seen on a skiff emptying the contents of an eel-basket into a receptacle. Two other eel-baskets are still in the water, lying beside a lotus flower. Farther to the right four men in two other boats are busy hauling out of the water quiver-shaped hand-nets, chock-a-block with fish.

Women returning from market. In the large wickerwork baskets which they carry on their heads they are taking home an ample supply of fruit and vegetables, including melons and cucumbers.

*"And Moses sent them to spy out the land
of Canaan, and said unto them:
Get you up this way southward, and go up
into the mountain: and see the land, what it is;
and the people that dwelleth therein . . .
And they returned from searching of the land . . .
and said, We came unto the land . . .
and surely it floweth with milk and honey . . .
Nevertheless the people be strong that
dwell in the land, and the cities are walled,
and very great"*
(Numbers 13:17, 18, 25, 27, 28).
The appearance of these strongly
fortified Canaanite towns as they
confronted the spies and struck terror into
their hearts, is strikingly conveyed
by contemporary Egyptian artists.
This relief from Medinet Habu
shows them to have resembled heavily
defended fortresses. The walls are
surmounted by ramparts on four
ascending levels, the topmost level being
crowned with three additional turrets.
The city colours emblazoned on a three-
cornered flag flutter gently in the breeze.
The turrets and ramparts are finished off
with semi-circular battlements, partly
for decoration and partly for the
protection of the defenders.
Every niche is packed with lancers ready
for action. Hostilities seem to have been
brought to a temporary standstill,
since on one of the turrets above the
gate (left) the governor of the city has
stepped forward holding a censer in
his right hand toward the invisible
enemy: ". . . and (he) had a censer in
his hand" (II Chronicles 26:19).

*"And when we departed from Horeb, we went through all that great and
terrible wilderness . . . and we came to Kadesh-barnea"*
(Deuteronomy 1:19).
It is thought that the Kadesh-barnea of the Bible can be
identified with the oases of Ain Qedeis, which still keeps the
old name, and Ain Qudeirat (seen here), five miles to the
north-west. This natural water supply in the heart of the
south Palestinian desert, where now as in ancient times
bubbling springs make a green island of shrubs and olive trees,
made the spot one of the main resting-places on Israel's
journey to the promised land. It was here that the
"wilderness generation" rebelled against Moses' orders and
refused to proceed to the conquest of Canaan. "So ye abode
in Kadesh many days" (Deuteronomy 1:46).

"And Moses sent messengers from Kadesh unto the king of Edom . . . Let us pass, I pray thee, through thy country: we will not pass through the fields, or through the vineyards, neither will we drink of the water of the wells; we will go by the king's high way, we will not turn to the right hand nor to the left, until we have passed thy borders. And Edom said unto him, Thou shalt not pass by me . . . wherefore Israel turned away from him . . . and pitched in the valley of Zared" (Numbers 20: 14, 17, 18, 21; 21: 12).

Soil research and aerial photography have combined in recent years to confirm the accuracy of the biblical narrative covering the Israelites' journey through the desert. The "high way" can be seen clearly from the air as a dark line stretching away to the north and eventually in the far background crossing the Zared, where the Israelites camped. This ancient road through Transjordan was known as the "king's high way" since it was used in Abraham's time by the four kings when they marched against Sodom (Genesis 14).

Soil research made it plain beyond any shadow of doubt that at the time of the Exodus it was flanked by cultivated land, as the Bible says.

"From thence (i. e. Zared) they removed and pitched on the other side of Arnon, which is in the wilderness that cometh out of the coasts of the Amorites: for Arnon is the border of Moab, between Moab and the Amorites" (Numbers 21:13). The waters of the Arnon have cut a deep canyon into the highlands to the east of the Dead Sea. The river bed lies over 1600 feet below the top of the cliffs. Above, the crumbling walls of a solitary Moabite frontier fortress in the neighbouring highlands—a silent witness that could recall the time when the Israelites in Transjordan on their way to the promised land were told: "Rise ye up, take your journey, and pass over the river Arnon" (Deuteronomy 2:24).

PLATE III

"And the whole congregation of the children of Israel murmured against Moses and Aaron in the wilderness: And the children of Israel said unto them, Would to God we had died by the hand of the Lord in the land of Egypt, when we sat by the flesh pots, and when we did eat bread to the full!" (Exodus 16:2–3).

After the Exodus, the poverty and misery of desert life stirred the memories of the Israelites and they yearned for the comforts of bygone days on the Nile. This colourful relief from a tomb in Saqqara with its harvest scenes, gives us a vivid picture of "Egypt's plenty". The first and fourth rows show donkeys being loaded with large baskets for carrying the sheaves. "Hup, hup! Slowcoach", says the inscription. In the second row, the mowers keep time to a tune played on a long flute. The corn, almost six feet high, is being cut with large sickles which the slaves hold in their right hands. A fat quail squats among their feet. The accompanying hieroglyphic text says "Hurry up, you people! This is very fine barley, my friend!" Threshing is shown in the third row. Goats, donkeys and oxen are driven over the corn on a threshing floor. The second row from the foot shows the harvesting of flax. Stalks are pulled out of the ground and bundled into sheaves. Bottom right shows slaves working with three-pronged forks, stacking the sheaves. On the left, the proprietor and his "sandal-bearer" watch the harvesting activities.

*"And we took at that time out of the hand of the two kings of the
Amorites the land that was on this side Jordan, from the river of
Arnon unto mount Hermon"* (Deuteronomy 3:8).

Statues of two kings found at Amman, the capital of
Jordan, which is called Rabbath-Ammon in the Bible. The
"kings of the Amorites" both wear broad sashes over
their long robes.

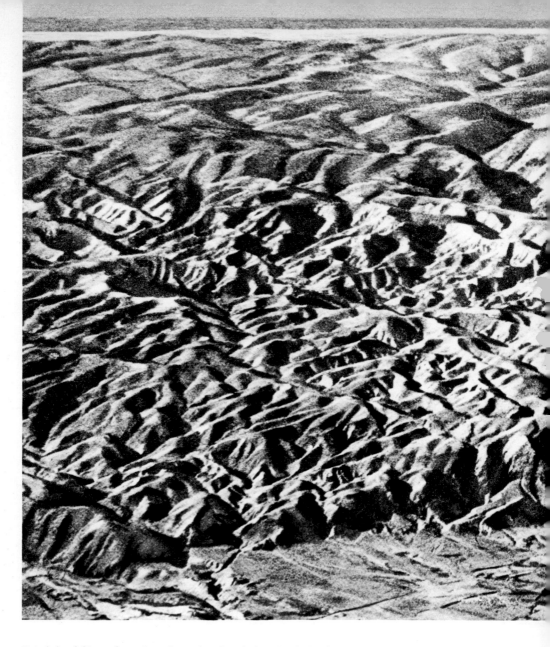

*"And the children of Israel set forward, and pitched in the plains of Moab, on this side
Jordan by Jericho"* (Numbers 22 : 1).
View of the hill country of Palestine from Transjordan. It was from here that the
Israelites were to advance and occupy the land. In the foreground lies the western
rim of the Jordan valley, with (centre) the maze of houses and alleys that make up

present-day Jericho. Behind the steep mountain face begins the "wilderness of Judah". In the far distance over the coastal plain lies the Mediterranean, a dark streak beyond the white sand-dunes. This is how Moses must have seen it from Mt Nebo before he died: "And the Lord showed him all the land . . . unto the utmost sea" (Deuteronomy 34 : 1–2).

117

V Into the Promised Land

"And thou subduedst before them the inhabitants of the land, the Canaanites, and gavest them into their hands" (Nehemiah 9:24).

The Struggle for Canaan

(Joshua, Judges—1 Samuel 7)

". . . and broughtest them into the land, concerning which
thou hadst promised to their fathers, that they should go in to possess it.
So the children (of Israel) went in and possessed the land . . .
and they took strong cities, and a fat land, and possessed houses
full of all goods . . ." (Nehemiah 9:23–25).

WHEN THE ISRAELITES under Joshua's leadership advanced across the Jordan, the political circumstances for such an enterprise could not have been more favourable. Egyptian suzerainty over Palestine had rarely been weaker. The native population was split up into a large number of city-states without any cohesion.

The conquest of western Palestine began about 1250–1225 B.C., using Jericho as the bridgehead. The most recent archaeological excavations substantially confirm the biblical account of Joshua's campaign. After a lapse of 3000 years the ruins of Bethel, Lachish, Debir and Hazor prove that the destruction of these cities undoubtedly took place at that time. Only the fall of Jericho remains a problem for the historians, since, according to the latest evidence, the city must have been destroyed a century before Joshua's time. The fact of the presence of Israelites in Canaan at this time is attested by a contemporary non-biblical authority. It comes from the thirteenth son who was also the successor of Ramesses II, who died at an advanced age after a reign of sixty-seven years. This pharaoh, whose name was Merenptah or Merneptah (1235–1227 B.C.), left behind a basalt stela at Thebes. The inscription dating from about 1230 B.C., mentions Israel as one of the races resident in Palestine.

After the Israelites had occupied the southern and northern areas of the country, the territory that had been taken over under Joshua's leadership was divided among the twelve tribes.

But when Joshua died, the Israelites were far from being in control of the whole country; a chain of fortified cities—Jerusalem and Megiddo among them—as well as the coastal strip and the plain of Jezreel were still in enemy hands. The Canaanites were not displaced; both peoples lived side by side. In their new role as townsmen, the Israelites, who had never previously lived in cities, now settled among the ruins of the places they had destroyed and proceeded to rebuild them. At the same time they became full-time farmers.

Lured by the fertility-cults of the Canaanite gods Baal and Astarte, the Israelites were unable to resist their attractions. When they were unfaithful to the one God, who had spoken to them through Moses, the people were punished. Their enemies oppressed them, made war upon them, and enslaved them. Then in their times of direst need they were delivered by the "judges", those resolute leaders of their people.

Their most brilliant achievement was the victory won by Barak, roused to action by the prophetess Deborah, in the Plain of Jezreel. Under their leadership the northern tribes routed the Canaanites, despite their dreaded "chariots of iron". The Midianites, too, wild bedouin tribes from the desert who year by year had crossed the Jordan on their swift camels and plundered the terrified villages of Canaan were soundly thrashed by Gideon, a "judge" from the tribe of Manasseh. But the most powerful enemy the Israelites had to face was in the end the Philistines. As part of the "Peoples of the Sea" these warriors had attacked Egypt in the reign of Ramesses III at the beginning of the twelfth century B.C. and had been decisively beaten in two battles. After their defeat the Philistines had settled on the coastal plain of Palestine and had established a federation of five cities—Gaza, Askelon, Ashdod, Ekron and Gath.

"*And Joshua rose early in the morning; and they removed from Shittim, and came to Jordan, he and all the children of Israel, and lodged there before they passed over*" (Joshua 3:1).

From their last camping ground on the "plains of Moab" the route taken by the Israelites lay across the Arabah (Deuteronomy 1:7; 4:49—R.S.V.) the name given in the Bible to this area north of the Dead Sea on either side of Jordan. It is a desolate expanse of limestone through which the Jordan has cut a gorge half a mile wide.

In the background, to the west of the depression, the hills of Judah rise above Jericho.

It was here "in the plains of Jericho" that the Babylonians later captured King Zedekiah of Judah when he fled from Jerusalem (Jeremiah 39:5).

"*And the people passed over right against Jericho . . . and all the Israelites passed over on dry ground, until all the people were passed clean over Jordan*" (Joshua 3:16–17).

Near Jericho the river is almost twenty feet deep and is fringed by a narrow, sub-tropical thicket, the "jungle of the Jordan", which at one time harboured lions (Zechariah 11:3–*R.S.V.*). It is on record that several times when the river has been in spate masses of marl have crashed down the banks and temporarily stopped up the channel. According to the Arab historian, al-Nuwairí, the river was completely dammed for ten hours on 8th December 1266 near the confluence of the Jabbok, a striking reminder of the biblical story. Similar occurrences have been reported in more recent times, as in October 1914, when the Jordan was blocked for twenty-four hours at the Jericho bridge.

"So Joshua made flint knives, and circumcised the people of Israel at
Gibeath-haaraloth . . . Though all the people who came out had been
circumcised, yet all the people that were born on the way in the
wilderness after they had come out of Egypt had not been circumcised"
(Joshua 5:3, 5–R.S.V.).
This relief from a tomb at Saqqara shows young Egyptians being
circumcised with a type of flint knife.

"And the Lord said unto Joshua, See, I have given into thine hand
Jericho . . . and they took the city" (Joshua 6:2, 20).
Archaeologists have cut this deep shaft through Tell es-Sultan,
the mound of rubble that lies to the north of modern Jericho. On
top of layers that go back to the Stone Age and to the earliest
human settlements, are the remains of the biblical stronghold
dating from the Israelites' invasion of the promised land when
Jericho was the first city they conquered. In the background
rises the "Mountain of the Temptation" (Matthew 4:8).

"The plain of the valley of Jericho, the city of palm trees", as
Deuteronomy 34:3 describes it, still preserves some semblance
of its appearance in ancient times. On the edge of the
treeless basin of the Jordan with its tropical climate,
date palms flourish even today beside the spring
Ain es-Sultan, whose waters have never ceased to flow
throughout the centuries.

"Come near, put your feet upon the necks of these kings. And they came near, and put their feet upon the necks of them . . . And Joshua said unto them, Fear not, nor be dismayed, be strong and of good courage; for thus shall the Lord do to all your enemies . . ." (Joshua 10:24–25).
Joshua's treatment of the five captive Amorite kings after his famous victory—"Sun stand thou still upon Gibeon; and thou Moon in the valley of Ajalon"—was a common practice in the ancient East. As confirmation of a victory the conqueror placed his feet upon the necks or—as shown in the relief on the left—upon the backs of the vanquished. The same gesture was used as a symbol of power and ascendancy. The future Pharaoh Amenophis II, shown sitting on his nurse's lap, is already at this tender age credited with royal authority—his footstool consists of the heads of conquered foes.

"*And Joshua did unto them as the Lord bade him: he houghed their horses, and burnt their chariots with fire. And Joshua at that time turned back, and took Hazor, and smote the king thereof with the sword; for Hazor before time was the head of all those kingdoms . . . utterly destroying them: there was not any left to breathe: and he burnt Hazor with fire*" (Joshua 11:9–11).

At Hazor, not far from the Sea of Galilee, recent excavations on the site of this important biblical city have revealed not only evidence of Joshua's destruction of the town but the remains of a Canaanite temple dating from the same period. These stelae (above) were still standing in a small shrine, one of them showing two outstretched hands reaching up to the crescent of the Canaanite moon-god. Beside them was this seated stone figure. Libations were poured into the hollow between its open arms.

*"And the border was drawn from the top of the hill unto the
fountain of the water of Nephtoah"*
(Joshua 15:9).
These words come from the definition of the area allotted
to the tribe of Judah. Just under two miles north-west
of Jerusalem there is still to be found on the site thus described
a spring and a large enclosed well. The name Nephtoah
(in modern Hebrew: Mei Neftoah) is probably derived
from the name of the pharaoh to whom we owe the first
documentary evidence outside the Bible of Israel's existence
in Canaan at the time of the conquest.
This statue of Merneptah, who reigned from 1235–1227 B.C.,
shows the Egyptian monarch wearing the famous royal head-dress.
His name is inscribed in the cartouche on his right shoulder.

This monument of Pharaoh Merneptah has often been called the "Israel-stela" since it is so far the only contemporary Egyptian document containing the name of the Israelite people. The relief above the inscription is divided into two almost identical scenes. On each side, in the centre, the god Amon stands under the winged sun-disk. He is giving Merneptah the sickle-sword with his right hand and holding the sceptre of the gods in his left. The pharaoh wears the decorative war-helmet, and above him hovers the sun-disk with pendant heraldic vipers. With one hand he grasps the sword offered to him by the god Amon, with the other he holds his crook. Behind Merneptah, to the right of the picture, stands the falcon-headed god Horus, while on the far left is Mut, wife of Amon and goddess of Thebes. Horus and Mut both have one hand raised in greeting, in the other hand they hold a notched stick.
The inscription on the stela is dated the third day of the third month of summer in the fifth year of the pharaoh's reign—
i. e., about 1230 B. C.

From Pharaoh Merneptah's hymn of victory:
"In Egypt there is great rejoicing,
Her cities shout for joy . . .
All men speak of Merneptah's conquests . . .
The princes are prostrate and cry: Peace!
The vanquished are laid low . . .
Libya is devastated, the Hittites are pacified.
Canaan is conquered and all her wickedness.
Askelon is captive, Gezer is fallen,
Yenoam is no more.
Israel is ravaged and has no offspring.
Palestine is widowed"

The name "Israel" in hieroglyphs. Extract from the second line from the foot of the inscription, on the left.

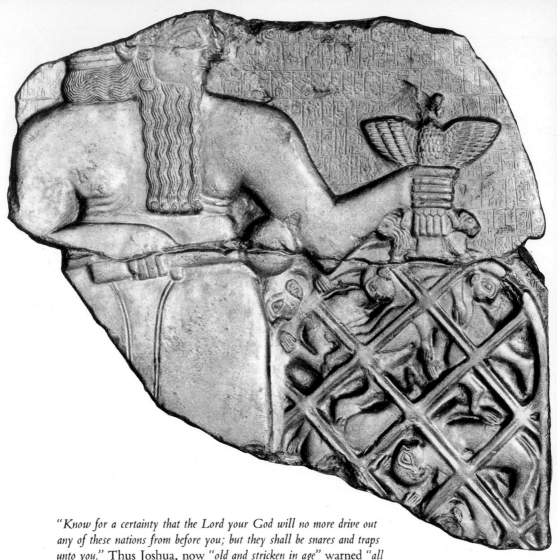

"Know for a certainty that the Lord your God will no more drive out any of these nations from before you; but they shall be snares and traps unto you." Thus Joshua, now *"old and stricken in age"* warned *"all Israel"* when he had summoned the people before him (Joshua 23:13, 1, 2).

A net—whether the fishing or hunting type, or as a symbol of judgment, misfortune or waylaying enemies—is a poetic image repeatedly used in the Bible, above all in the psalms (9:15; 10:9 etc). On the famous "Stela of the Vultures", a Sumerian victory monument of the third millennium B. C., the god Ningirsu has imprisoned the enemy captives in a wide-meshed net held in his left hand. With his right hand he is getting ready to smash them to pieces with a stone club.

"And Joshua . . . died . . . and also all that generation were gathered unto their fathers: and there arose another generation after them, which knew not the Lord, nor yet the works which he had done for Israel. And the children of Israel did evil in the sight of the Lord . . . and served Baal and Ashtaroth" (Judges 2:8–13).

Clay figures such as these, depicting naked goddesses of fertility, among whom was the Ashtaroth (Astarte) so frequently referred to in the Bible, have been found by archaeologists all over Palestine. The fact that they occur in such numbers in the layers dating from Israelite times confirms all that the Bible has to say about the danger of idolatry spreading through the whole people. The noticeable accentuation of sexual characteristics not only makes it clear what was the nature of these Canaanite cults, but also explains why the prophets thundered against them with all the power at their command and denounced them as a menace to society.

The discovery of such statuettes also helps us to see the point of many frequently misunderstood passages in the Old Testament.

Right: Figure of Baal, one of the gods whose worship was forbidden.

"Now after the death of Joshua . . . Judah took . . . Askelon with the coast thereof" (Judges 1:1,18).

It was only for a short time that the tribe of Judah was able to hold Askelon. A little later, by the time of Samson, the Philistines captured this Mediterranean port and made it one of their five city-states. The last moments before the surrender of Askelon, after a fierce struggle, have been caught on this relief, which dramatically portrays the taking of the city by Pharaoh Ramesses II in 1280 B. C., a few decades before the event referred to in the Bible. It can hardly have been much different when Judah "took Askelon". The fortress is shown perched on a hill, as was indeed the case, and the battle rages on the slopes. In the right foreground, the battlefield is covered with dead or wounded Canaanites. The city is surrounded by a double wall. Scaling ladders have been propped against the outer fortifications and warriors are in the act of climbing them, protected by shields covering their backs. A soldier with a battleaxe is proceeding to smash open one of the two gates, above which are three open windows. In the inner wall, with its battlements and turrets rising behind the outer wall, can be seen two more windows. The one on the right is barred, the one on the left is open. The ramparts are packed with Canaanites. Some of the men are wearing shirts with short sleeves (on the upper battlements), others (in the row below) are wearing capes. Their features, especially the long noses, are typically Semitic. They wear their beards in what can best be described as a "ruff" consisting of sideburns, pointed beards but no moustaches; the hair is worn shoulder-length and fixed with a bandeau. With uplifted hands they beg mercy from their conquerors. The Canaanite standing on the far right on top of the battlements is holding out a burning censer over the ramparts as a token of submission. The man in front of him is lowering his child over the wall, another (top left) is doing the same with his wife. Women can be seen above crouching between the men. Their hair, cut evenly across the forehead, hangs in long tresses down their backs. Such, then, was the appearance of the people with whom the Israelites likewise had to contend.

"And the house of Joseph, they also went up against Beth-el: and the Lord was with them . . . And the spies saw a man come forth out of the city . . . And when he shewed them the entrance into the city, they smote the city with the edge of the sword . . ." (Judges 1:22–25).

The name of this town, which lay among the mountains of Ephraim ten miles north of Jerusalem, crops up for the first time in the Bible during the period of the patriarchs. After Jacob on his way to Haran had his dream of the ladder that reached to heaven, he set up a votive pillar and "called the name of that place Beth-el" (Genesis 28:19). Excavations at modern Beitin have in fact uncovered the layer which confirms the destruction of the town when the Israelites conquered it, as described in the Book of Judges. Among the ruins were found the remains of a large house which could have been built in the time of the judges.

"And the children of Israel again did evil in the sight of the Lord . . .
And the Lord sold them into the hand of Jabin, king of Canaan,
that reigned in Hazor; the captain of whose host was Sisera . . .
And the children of Israel cried unto the Lord; for he had nine hundred
chariots of iron" (Judges 4: 1–3).
These iron-clad war-chariots gave the Canaanites superiority
in battle and terrified the Israelites. The charioteers,
as we learn from Ugaritic texts found at Ras Shamra in Syria,
formed the hard core of the Canaanite army.
Chariots, mostly drawn by a pair of horses,
were also used for hunting. This hunting scene on a gold salver
from Ugarit gives us a clear picture of what a chariot
looked like.

"And Deborah a prophetess . . . judged Israel at that time . . . and she sent and called Barak . . . and said unto him . . . Go, and draw toward mount Tabor, and take with thee ten thousand men . . . And I will draw unto thee . . . Sisera, the captain of Jabin's army, with his chariots and his multitude; and I will deliver him into thine hand" (Judges 4:4–7).

Just over five miles from Nazareth, in the north-east corner of the Plain of Jezreel, is the round hump of Mt Tabor, 1300 feet high. It was here that the men of Naphtali and Zebulun gathered before they came down with Deborah and Barak to attack the Canaanites under Sisera.

". . . then fought the kings of Canaan in Taanach by the waters of Megiddo; they took no gain of money. They fought from heaven; the stars in their courses fought against Sisera" (Judges 5:19-20).

After more than three thousand years this ivory plaque was found at Megiddo, where the battle was fought between the ill-equipped Israelites and the Canaanites with their "chariots of iron".
It provides a unique pictorial record of these times,
with its scenes from the victory celebrations of a Canaanite king.
The ruler is seated on his sphinx-sided throne, drinking from a bowl.
His embroidered robe reaches to his feet, which rest upon a stool.
A close fitting cap or helmet covers his head. His beard is trimmed into
a "ruff". A royal lady offers the king a lotus blossom
and the fringe of her shawl.
Beside them a musician plays upon a nine-stringed lyre.
Next comes a warrior equipped with shield and spear leading two
naked, circumcised prisoners, roped together and manacled.
The king himself appears again on the right seated in his chariot
and pair. The "armoured car" with its quiver, arrows and spear
shows what it was that gave rise to so much panic among
the Israelites: . . .
"all the Canaanites . . . have chariots of iron" (Joshua 17:16,18;
Judges 1:19;4:3,13).

*"And the children of Israel did evil in the sight of the Lord; and the Lord
delivered them into the hands of Midian seven years . . . For they came up with
their cattle, and their tents, and they came as grasshoppers for multitude; for
both they and their camels were without number: and they entered into the land
to destroy it"*
(Judges 6:1,5).

For years bedouin raiders mounted on camels had been a scourge
in the land until one day Gideon was able to tell the Israelite army:
"Arise, for the Lord hath delivered into your hand the host of Midian"
(Judges 7:15).

Assyrian artists have conveyed on this relief the various
phases of a turbulent battle with Arabian camel troops so realistically
and excitingly that we can almost see it happening.
The desert folk are in full flight. Many of them already lie dead on the field.
Pursued by the Assyrian footsoldiers armed with bows and spears,
as well as by horsemen and charioteers, the saddled camels gallop away
with prodigious strides. On the left of the lower panel,
one of the two on camel-back turns round to shoot an arrow,
while, on the right of the same panel, a camel has just collapsed
throwing his rider to the ground.
Similar scenes—though without cavalry and chariots—must have been
witnessed between the Israelite army and the predatory Midianites.

"Behold I will put a fleece of wool in the floor; and if the dew be on the fleece only, and it be dry on all the earth beside, then shall I know that thou wilt save Israel by mine hand, as thou hast said. And it was so; for he rose up early on the morrow, and thrust the fleece together, and wringed the dew out of the fleece, a bowl full of water"
(Judges 6:37–38).

What happened to Gideon, the judge of Israel, scientists in the new state of Israel have learned at first hand for themselves. While they were investigating problems of precipitation and humidity they recalled the biblical story and decided to put it to the test. They spread out a fleece overnight in harvest-time on a village threshing-floor. Next morning so much dew had collected on the fleece that they could squeeze a bowl full of water out of it. Knowledge of the life-giving properties of dew is reflected in the Blessing of Isaac when he says:
"God give thee of the dew of heaven and the fatness of the earth and plenty of corn and wine"
(Genesis 27:28).

*"And the children of Israel did evil again in the sight of the Lord; and the Lord
delivered them into the hand of the Philistines forty years"*
(Judges 13:1).
"The Philistines from Caphtor"—this is what they looked like: clean-shaven,
"Greek" profile, with hardly any break between forehead and nose.
They wore a plumed head-dress held in place by a bandeau decorated
with a string of pearls or with zig-zag ribbons.

Their necks were protected by an attachment to the head-dress—they also
had chinstraps. Only occasionally are they depicted with breast-plates.
The manacled Philistine prisoners in this picture are wearing braided kilts
fastened with a belt, as they are carried off by an Egyptian soldier.
They were known in hieroglyphic language as "peles et" from which
the whole country later derived its name "Palestine". "O Canaan, the land
of the Philistines" (Zephaniah 2 : 5).

*"Now . . . he thought to reign over Egypt, that he might have the dominion of two realms.
Wherefore he entered into Egypt with . . . chariots . . . horsemen and a great navy."*
What Antiochus Epiphanes later succeeded in doing, as I Maccabees 1 : 17–18
tells us, the Philistines, banded together with their allies in a great coalition of the
"Peoples of the Sea", had also in mind to do about 1200 B. C. Their bold plan,
however, misfired. Under Ramesses III, a fierce naval engagement took place in
the Nile delta between the Egyptians and the invading forces, including the
Philistines, which has been immortalised on this relief in the temple at Medinet Habu.
The pharaoh himself with supporting archers joins in the battle from land, already
treading underfoot the heads of his stricken foes. "I have wounded them that they
were not able to rise: they are fallen under my feet" (Psalm 18 : 38; Joshua 10 : 24).
Nekbet, the hawk-goddess, queen of the gods of Upper Egypt, hovers above his
head with a whisk in her talons, pledging him the victory. Three lines of ships are
locked in fierce combat. The fleets are for the time being becalmed, all sails are
reefed—an advantage for the Egyptians since they also have oarsmen. The prow of

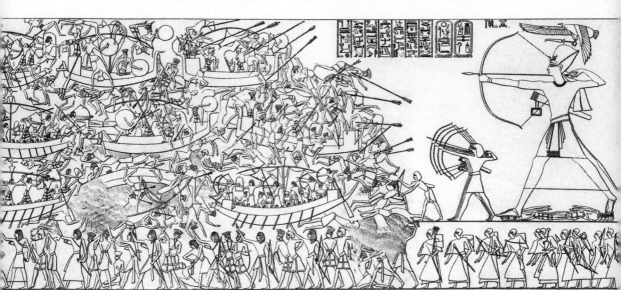

the Egyptian ships has a lion's head, the helm tapers off into a spike. The rowers sit
level with the bulwarks, fighting-men stand beside them. Most of these are archers,
only an occasional warrior is armed with lance or dagger.

The ships of the Sea-Peoples have high prows and sterns. They are built for sail alone.
One of their boats has already capsized. The Philistines and their allies fight with
daggers and lances; bows and arrows are lacking. They are thus equipped for
close fighting only. They wear horned helmets or plumed head-dresses and carry
round shields for protection. The crow's-nests in both fleets are manned with officers
directing the battle. Those on the side of the Sea-Peoples are all represented as mortally
wounded. The hail of Egyptian arrows coming from the right suggests that it was
this weapon that brought about the downfall of the enemy.

Already, at the foot of the picture, Philistine prisoners are being led away.

Below: Part of the relief, which is reproduced as a drawing
on the previous page, in the original.

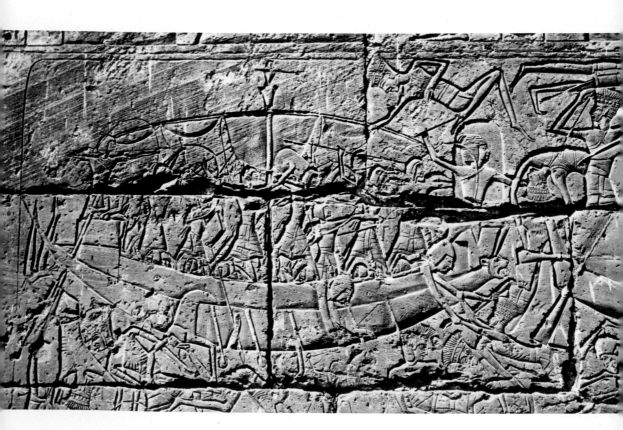

*"And the Philistines called for the priests ...
Then said they, ... Now therefore make a new
cart, and take two milch kine, on which there
hath come no yoke, and tie the kine to the cart ...
and take the ark of the Lord, and lay it upon
the cart ... and send it away that it may go ...
And the men did so ... And the kine took the
straight way to the way of Beth-shemesh,
and went along the highway, lowing as they
went, and turned not aside to the right hand
or to the left ..."* (I Samuel 6: 2, 4, 7–12).
Egyptian representations of their struggle
with the Sea-Peoples on land show us
this characteristic Philistine cart with its
two great solid wheels. We may conjure
up a similar picture of the cart on which
the Philistines, on the advice of their
priests, sent the ark of the covenant back
to Israel. We are told that it was after
"a very great slaughter" that "the ark of
God was taken" (I Samuel 4: 10–11).

*"Then took I the cup ... and made to drink ...
all the kings of the land of the Philistines,
and Ashkelon, and Azzah, and Ekron, and the
remnant of Ashdod."*
These words are used of the cup of the
wrath of God against all the nations in
Jeremiah 25: 17, 20.
Beautifully painted clay jars have been
found among piles of rubble on the sites
of the five Philistine cities by the sea
which the Bible refers to—still another
proof that these mortal enemies of the
Israelites actually once lived on this coastal
plain. These stylised swans are typical
designs on Philistine pottery.

VI The Palmy Days of the Monarchy

"... we will have a king over us ..." (I Samuel 8:19).

The Golden Age

(I Samuel 8–I Kings 11)
(I Chronicles 10–II Chronicles 9)

"And afterward they desired a king: and God gave unto them Saul the son of Cis"
(Acts 13:21).

IT WAS in the years around 1000 B. C. that Israel's material fortunes reached their zenith. These were the days of Saul, David and Solomon, striking, controversial personalities, who within a few decades made Israel into a strong nation of considerable influence and importance in the ancient world. Within two generations the confederation of twelve tribes, which had been in the first instance based on a common religious allegiance, blossomed into a full-grown monarchy with undreamt of economic prosperity. It was the danger of Philistine expansion from the coastal plain into the hill country that compelled the tribes to unite under one king. The example of their neighbours, Edom, Moab and Ammon, who had already become kingdoms, was also not without its own influence.

The greatest achievement of the first king, Saul (about 1020–1004 B. C.), was the expulsion of the Philistines from the hills. David (*c.* 1004–965 B. C.) made it his aim so to circumscribe both their power and their territory that they would never again become serious rivals. With the subjugation of the Philistines, and later of the Edomites, Moabites, Ammonites and Syrians, Israel vastly extended her frontiers and became a small-scale empire embracing subject nations. The creation of a new capital at Jerusalem, on the site of a captured Jebusite fortress, destroyed the individual identity of the tribes and imposed heavy burdens on the whole people (I Samuel 8:10ff.).

In Solomon (965–926 B. C.) the nation found a brilliant and peace-loving monarch to succeed the warlike David. He inherited his father's skill and was able to carry out the plans David had been unable to bring to fruition. The country was divided into twelve districts and government officials imposed heavy taxes to pay for the King's ambitious building projects.

With its new temple—which Solomon built in accordance with his father's intentions—its royal palace and its government buildings, Jerusalem became a sight worth seeing. Solomon enlisted the help of Hiram, King of Tyre, whose Phoenician craftsmen and artists hewed the stones and carved costly Lebanon timber for these building operations. Splendid cities arose as garrisons for the king's new chariot corps. The money for all this extravagance came, apart from taxation, from brisk foreign trade with Egypt and Asia Minor and with Ophir on the other side of the Red Sea. By exploiting his copper resources in the south Solomon also built up a centre of heavy industry at Ezion-Geber on the Red Sea.

"And when Samuel had caused all the tribes of Israel to come near . . . Saul the son of Kish was taken . . . And all the people shouted, and said, God save the king . . . And Saul . . . went home to Gibeah" (I Samuel 10:20–26).

At Tell el-Ful, the "hill of beans", three miles north of Jerusalem, excavations confirmed the biblical statement: "Gibeah belongeth to Benjamin" (Judges 20:4). The remains of Saul's citadel were discovered there, a fortress of rough-hewn stone, no more than a hundred and thirty by eighty feet square. Such was Israel's first royal castle. Once more in ruins, its walls crumble on the lone hill-top where once, as the Bible tells us: "the king sat upon his seat, as at other times, even upon a seat by the wall" (I Samuel 20:25).

*"And the Philistines gathered themselves together to fight with
Israel . . . as the sand which is on the sea shore in multitude:
and they came up and pitched in Michmash . . . and the garrison
of the Philistines went out to the passage of Michmash"*
(I Samuel 13 : 5, 23).
View of the site of Michmash about eight miles north of
Jerusalem. On the rocky hillside beyond the gorge the
Philistines had pitched their camp. There is still a pathway
up the cliff-face leading to the spot where on "an half acre of
land" Jonathan and his armour-bearer carried out their
surprise attack by night on the Philistine sentries.
An incident during the first world war showed the extreme
accuracy of the biblical record of Israel's struggle against the
Philistines. A British detachment basing its tactics on those
of Saul and Jonathan, as recounted in the first book of
Samuel, successfully routed Turkish forces encamped at
Michmash.

"And they smote the Philistines that day from Michmash to Aijalon" (I Samuel 14:31).
A group of Philistine prisoners being led off in chains. This Egyptian wall-carving from Medinet Habu suggests what must have happened after the surprise attack at Michmash, for "there was sore war against the Philistines all the days of Saul" (I Samuel 14:52).

"And Saul said unto his servants: Provide me now a man that can play well, and bring him to me ... And David came to Saul ... and became his armourbearer ... And it came to pass, when ... David took an harp, and played with his hand: so Saul was refreshed, and was well, and the evil spirit departed from him" (I Samuel 16: 17, 21, 23).

A musician of ancient Babylon playing a harp. David used the same kind of instrument. "A psalm of David, on stringed instruments" or "set to the eighth" occurs frequently in the psalter (Psalm 4; 6; 12 etc—R. V.).

These stringed instruments were made of cypress or sandalwood (I Kings 10: 12). The strings were mostly of cat-gut.

"And David said unto Saul, Thy servant kept his father's sheep, and there came a lion ... and took a lamb out of the flock. And I went out after him, and smote him, and delivered it out of his mouth: and when he arose against me, I caught him by his beard, and smote him and slew him" (I Samuel 17: 34–35).

This formidable beast of prey was to be found all over Palestine in biblical times, not only in the "pride of Jordan" (Jeremiah 49: 19), but also in Samaria (II Kings 17: 25), in Moab (Isaiah 15: 9), and, as in David's case, in the mountains of Judah. The kings of the ancient east appear to have had a passion for the hair-raising sport of lion-hunting, especially the Assyrians. Among many reliefs is one from Nineveh which is quite astounding. It shows Ashurbanipal, the Assyrian king, in a situation which is as unusual as it is dangerous. With extraordinary courage the monarch stands face to face with the lion, which has already been pierced by an arrow and wounded in the bowels. While Ashurbanipal grasps the lion's mane in one hand—just as the Bible describes young David's daring feat—he delivers the death-blow with a sword held in the other hand.

"And Saul and the men of Israel were gathered together, and pitched by the valley of Elah,
and set the battle in array against the Philistines. And the Philistines stood on a mountain on the
one side, and Israel stood on a mountain on the other side: and there was a valley between them"
(I Samuel 17:2-3).

The vale of Elah, or "valley of the terebinth" is the present-day Wadi es-Sant,
a broad well-wooded and fertile valley. As the only dale on the western frontier
of Judah which opened on to the coastal plain it was an obvious route for a
Philistine attack. This was the scene of the single combat between David and Goliath.
On the hill (centre) where the Israelites had mustered, Solomon's son Rehoboam
later made Azekah into a fortified city (II Chronicles 11:9)—a place which was
also one of the last cities of Judah to be besieged and conquered by Nebuchadnezzar
of Babylon in his campaign of 589-7 B. C. (Jeremiah 34:7).

"And he (David) took his staff in his hand, and chose him five smooth stones out of the brook, and put them in a shepherd's bag which he had, even in a scrip; and his sling was in his hand: and he drew near to the Philistine" (I Samuel 17:40).
The sling stones which David selected must have looked like this. With their surfaces rounded and smoothed by river-action, stones of this kind (pictured here) have been unearthed in excavations of the Israelite period and can still be found in the dry wadi of the Vale of Elah, where David fought Goliath. Shepherds used them in slings to ward off wild animals (Job 41:28) and they were also used in battle (Judges 20:16; II Kings 3:25).

"And it came to pass, when the Philistine arose, and came and drew nigh . . . that David hasted, and ran . . . to meet the Philistine. And David put his hand in his bag, and took thence a stone, and slang it . . ." (I Samuel 17:48–49).
What happened as he did so has been handed down in such drawings from real life as this relief of a slinger from Tell Halaf. The sling was generally made of textiles, woven in such a way that there was a broader section in the middle to hold the stone.

"*And there went out a champion out of the camp of the Philistines,
named Goliath ... And he had a helmet of brass upon his head, and he
was armed with a coat of mail ... And David ... smote the Philistine
in his forehead, that ... he fell upon his face to the earth. So David
prevailed over the Philistine with a sling and with a stone, and smote the
Philistine, and slew him*"
(I Samuel 17:4–5, 49–50).

With sightless eyes and outstretched arms, this Philistine in full
armour lies dead on the battlefield, like Goliath after David's
fatal slingshot.

His cuirass is cut well away at the shoulders and covered
from the chest downwards with a series of bands
which stretch across both sides of the body like ribs.

His plumed helmet is kept in position by a head-band
decorated with zig-zag braid.

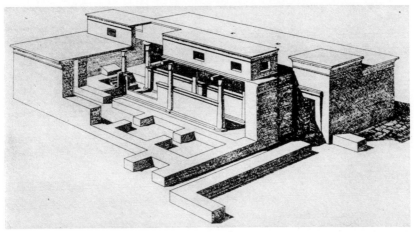

"Therefore Saul took a sword, and fell upon it . . . And it came to pass on the morrow, when the Philistines came . . . that they found Saul . . . and they put his armour in the house of Ashtaroth; and they fastened his body to the wall of Beth-shan . . . and fastened his head in the temple of Dagon" (I Samuel 31:4–10; I Chronicles 10:10).

This is what remains of the city whose walls must once have seen what the Philistines did to the body of King Saul after their victory. On the edge of the Plain of Jezreel, towards the Jordan valley, archaeologists found among the masses of rubble at Tell el-Husn—the site of biblical Beth-Shan—the remains of four temple buildings (above). Religious objects discovered among the ruins of one of the temples, chiefly a stela with the inscription ". . . queen of heaven and leader of all the gods" indicate that this building was dedicated to the worship of Astarte, the Canaanite fertility goddess.

Another temple (see reconstruction) is thought to be the "House of Dagon", one of the Philistine gods.

157

"*And the Lord said unto David, Go up; for I will doubtless deliver the Philistines into thine hand . . . And David did so, as the Lord had commanded him; and smote the Philistines from Geba until thou come to Gezer . . . and subdued them*" (II Samuel 5:19,25;8:1).

This dramatic relief from the temple of Ramesses III at Medinet Habu enables us to see for ourselves the bloody hand-to-hand fighting and general mêlée in the great land battle about 1200 B. C. between the Egyptians and the "Sea Peoples". It ended in disaster for the Philistines, as did the encounters of these oppressors of Israel with King David later on. The picture gives us some idea of the type of experienced and powerful warriors the Israelites had to contend with.

The Philistines, readily recognisable by their plumed helmets, are markedly taller than the Egyptians.

They are still fighting in little groups at various points on the
battlefield with swords, lances, daggers and circular shields. Some are
already manacled, others lie dead and stripped on the field (upper rows).
In the midst of the confusion can be seen occasionally Philistine
transport—ox-drawn carts filled with crouching women and children.
The square bodywork is either of timber or of wattle. The wheels are
solid wooden disks fixed with a peg to the axles. The Philistine women
hold out their children to the enemy, begging for mercy (above right).

*"And the king (David) and his men went to Jerusalem . . . So David
dwelt in the fort, and called it the city of David. And David built round
about, from Millo and inwards"* (II Samuel 5:6,9).
After almost three thousand years of oblivion, and in the course
of excavations which have often presented the archaeologists
with considerable difficulties, these meagre and insignificant-looking
fragments of walls are all that have so far come to light from the
time when David captured Jerusalem and his son Solomon built its
temple. On the east side of the "city of David" lie side by side
the remains of the Jebusite fortress and a square tower dating
from Solomon's day—venerable mementoes of Jerusalem in the
time of the monarchy.

"And David reigned over all Israel; and David executed judgment and justice unto all his people . . .
Seraiah was the scribe" (II Samuel 8:15, 17).

From the time of David onwards, one of the high ranking officials attached to the
Israelite court, in addition to the chamberlain and the chancellor, was the scribe.
He occupied an extremely important position, the modern equivalent being that of a
secretary of state. His name, which as the Bible tells us was Seraiah, suggests that this
dignitary was an Egyptian, as indeed David's whole administration seems to have
largely followed the Egyptian pattern. The office of these "scribal-cabinet-ministers"
was no sinecure. They were in charge of the king's economic policies, they were
responsible for communications with foreign powers and compiled the official records
of state. Later on, scribes are also mentioned in connection with the administration
of the temple, the civil service and the armed forces. The scribes of ancient Palestine had
their own "guilds of scribes", like the "families of the scribes which dwelt at Jabez"
(I Chronicles 2:55).

"*The wisdom of the scribe cometh by opportunity of leisure; and he that hath little business shall become wise*"
(Ecclesiasticus 38:24 *R.V.*).
View of an Egyptian office: three scribes are hard at work.
They use pointed reeds as pens and each of them has a reserve supply
behind his ears. Two of the men have little mussel-shaped palettes
for ink fastened with a strap to their left hands. The third man's palette is
rectangular and like the others has two ink-wells.
Above their heads the hieroglyph for "scribe" is repeated thrice—
a reed with its fibres clipped at the base, and next to it, tied with a string,
a receptacle for water and an ink-pot.
Black ink—mostly made of soot
mixed with water or vinegar—was used for writing on leather, papyrus
—as here—or on potsherds.

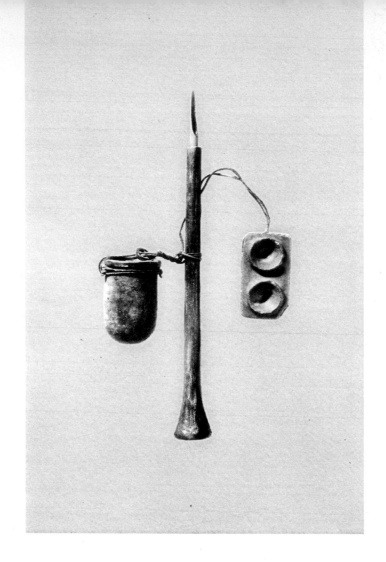

"... one man among them , .. with a writer's inkhorn by his side ..."
(Ezekiel 9:2).
From Egyptian sources it is possible to get a fairly clear picture of
a scribe's equipment in Old Testament times.
The tools of his trade were three in number—a reed pen, a gadget
holding two kinds of ink (right) and a water-pot (left).
These three articles seemed to the Egyptians so typical that they
made them the hieroglyph for "writer" or "writing"
(see relief on previous page).

*"And Solomon made affinity with Pharaoh, king of Egypt,
and took Pharaoh's daughter, and brought her into the city of David"*
(I Kings 3:1).
Likeness of an Egyptian princess, such as the one King Solomon
brought to Jerusalem. Having regard to her royal
upbringing, he provided for her special apartments
of "costly stones" with "cedar beams".
"Solomon made also an house for Pharaoh's daughter,
whom he had taken to wife" (I Kings 7:8).

"But king Solomon loved many strange women" (I Kings 11:1).
When a princess in the ancient East married out of her own country it was
customary to send her off accompanied by a group of her friends. When the pharaoh's
daughter left Egypt to wed King Solomon we may therefore take it that her
ladies-in-waiting accompanied her. This painting from a tomb at Thebes introduces
us to the ladies at a banquet. Dressed and coiffured for the occasion,
dangling with jewelled necklaces and earrings, these Egyptian society ladies
are being waited on by a naked slave-girl.

"And he had seven hundred wives, princesses, and three hundred concubines . . ."
(I Kings 11:3).

A glimpse of life in a harem in a palace at Tell el-Amarna on the Nile,
which like Jerusalem was the seat of government—in this case of Pharaoh
Akhnaten, husband of the famous Nofretete—is provided by this copy of a
relief. The entrances are well guarded. The warder in the lower panel
carries a broom for sweeping the courtyard, but at the moment he is
having a rest. The man on duty in the upper panel is leaning against the
wall, propped on one leg, gossiping with a visitor. Each of the doors
behind the two sentries leads into a pillared hall. In a corner of the upper
room an inmate is having a meal (right), two women opposite are engaged
in hairdressing operations (left). In the foreground others are dancing to the
strains of a harp. The girls' hair styles are Syrian, not Egyptian.

As in Solomon's establishment, it was not only native women who were
installed. Foreign singers were very popular (Song of Songs 2:14).

The lower hall is given over to music and dancing. The girl at the top is
playing a lyre, the one on the left, underneath, a harp, and the one in the
centre, a lute. In the four closets on the left beside the sitting-rooms can be
seen, apart from bedsteads, a variety of musical instruments: harps, lyres
and lutes. The women of the harem were expected to entertain the pharaoh
with music as well.

"Only the people sacrificed in high places, because there was no house built unto the name of the Lord, until those days"
(I Kings 3:2).
The "high places", whose attractions proved too much
for the Israelites, despite the admonitions of the prophets,
were part of the pagan cults of Canaan. This bronze plaque
was found in Elam, which is referred to in the Bible.
It is by an unknown artist of the twelfth century B.C.,
and represents a pagan cult of the ancient East.
Action and setting recall many biblical passages.
Presumably the ceremony took place at sunrise.
Two naked men are squatting on a hill, engaged in ritual
ablutions (II Chronicles 4:6). Around them are the various
objects pertaining to the cult. Two ziggurats can be seen,
at one time great temple-towers dedicated to the deities of
Mesopotamia, where their massive ruins still dominate the plains.
The trees recall the words of II Kings 16:4—
"And he sacrificed ... on the hills and under every green tree".
The great jar behind one of the men reminds us of the "brazen sea"
in the Old Testament, which later stood in the court of Solomon's
temple: "Also he made a molten sea ..." (II Chronicles 4:2).
As well as an altar and basins there are two upright pillars: "And
he brake in pieces the pillars, and cut down the Asherim and
filled their places with the bones of men" (II Kings 23:14—*R.V.*).

166

"And this is the reason of the levy which king Solomon raised; for to build . . . the wall of Jerusalem, and Hazor, and Megiddo"
(I Kings 9:15).

No other spot in Palestine affords such clear evidence of Solomon's building activities as Megiddo, the city which has been excavated in the north of the Plain of Jezreel. Right round the hill a new wall was erected. On the northern side, as this reconstruction based on the excavated layers demonstrates, was the unusually strongly fortified entrance to the city. Anyone approaching the town from outside (reconst., left) had first to pass through a double gateway, covered over for defensive purposes. Thereafter the road turned sharp left through the outer courtyard to the main gateway itself, which was likewise covered over and fitted with double doors. Behind the main gate were three further entrances, each of them with the additional protection of a guardroom. The remarkable thing is that the construction of this gateway into Megiddo, as revealed by excavations, corresponds exactly with the description given by the Prophet Ezekiel of the east gate of the temple at Jerusalem (Ezekiel 40:5–16).

167

"And Solomon built . . . all the cities of store . . . and cities for his chariots, and cities for his horsemen, and that which Solomon desired to build . . . And Solomon had forty thousand stalls of horses for his chariots, and twelve thousand horsemen" (I Kings 9:17,19;4:26).

Today anyone can visit the imposing and up-to-date stables of King Solomon, despite the fact that their existence has often been questioned. Only a few steps from the main gate of Megiddo one comes upon a paved road to the south-east, where the great stables were situated. The horses stood in double rows, with their heads towards the centre passage. They were tied to posts—the stumps in the picture—which also served to support the roof. Between them were the stone troughs for food and water. The stalls were cobbled but the passage down the middle was treated to prevent the horses from slipping.

"And Solomon gathered together chariots and horsemen:
and he had a thousand and four hundred chariots and twelve thousand horsemen,
whom he bestowed in the cities for chariots" (I Kings 10: 26).
One of the great stables. By following the outline of the walls,
buildings and paved roads it was possible to reconstruct the lay-out
fairly accurately. This is therefore in all probability what the south end
of King Solomon's stables at Megiddo looked like . . . Can one imagine
a better illustration of the vast scale on which this monarch carried out
his building operations, both as a display of his power in the best
oriental tradition and also for the safety of his realm?
This section of the stable alone had room for 450 horses.
Ruins of royal stables have been found on other sites—
in Taanach, near Megiddo, and at Eglon on the borders of Judah.

"*And Solomon had twelve officers over all Israel, which provided victuals
for the king and his household . . . And these are their names: . . . Baana,
the son of Ahilud; to him pertained Taanach and Megiddo*"
(I Kings, 4:7,8,12).
Behind the loose-boxes, a flagged road led to the courtyard
of the official residence of the governor of the district. This office was
occupied in King Solomon's day by Baana. His house, shown
in this reconstruction, was solidly built, probably of two storeys.
From the top he could see over the city walls. Nearby were more
stables with a large cobbled courtyard. "And those officers"
says I Kings 4:27–28, referring to their official duties, "provided
victual for king Solomon . . . Barley also and straw for the horses . . ."

" *And the horses which Solomon had were brought out of Egypt;
and the king's merchants received them in droves, each drove at a
price . . . and an horse (went out of Egypt) for an hundred
and fifty (shekels)*" (I Kings 10:28–29–*R.V.*).
This lovely fragment of an Egyptian horse's head
gives us some idea of the splendid breeds that were
at stud in Old Testament times.

"And a chariot came up and went out of Egypt for six hundred shekels of silver" (I Kings 10:29).

This original Egyptian wooden chariot, covered with gilded leather, has survived for thousands of years in a tomb in the Valley of the Kings. The same type of chariot must have been imported from Egypt by Solomon, either for his own use or for re-sale to Syria and the Hittite kings.

". . . and so for all the kings of the Hittites, and for the kings of Syria, did they bring them out by their means" (I Kings 10:29).

This is how we must picture Solomon's commercial associates to the north of his kingdom. Here is a Hittite from Zinjirli, with his beard curled in the Assyrian style. The long sharp nose is characteristic. His hair is neatly coiled at the back of his neck. He wears a peaked cap with a large pom-pom, trimmed with braid. The main garments are a tight-fitting coat with half-length sleeves, and a braided kilt fastened with a broad belt. The pointed shoes are typically Hittite. He is armed with a sword fixed at his waist, a tall spear and an indented shield.

Hittite chariot with rectangular bodywork.
Behind the driver, who whips on the horses,
stands the archer in the act of loosing an arrow.
A dead man between the horses' feet shows that the
scene is a battlefield.

"*And king Solomon made a navy of ships in Ezion-geber, which is beside Eloth,
on the shore of the Red sea, in the land of Edom*" (I Kings 9:26).

Instead of these Egyptian carpenters, seen here building a ship, Solomon engaged
Phoenicians for work in his shipyards. This scene shows the assembling of a ship's hull.
Many of the craftsmen are busy cutting out the bung-holes. For this purpose they use
mallets and chisels, clearly seen on the right, below. The Prophet Ezekiel lists the various
expensive items that go to make up a Phoenician merchantman: "Thy builders have
perfected thy beauty. They have made all thy ship boards of fir trees . . . they have taken
cedars from Lebanon to make masts for thee. Of the oaks of Bashan have they made
thine oars . . . thy benches of ivory . . . Fine linen, with broidered work from Egypt,
was that which thou spreadest forth to be thy sail" (Ezekiel 27:4–7).

"*And Hiram sent in the navy his servants, shipmen that had knowledge of the sea,
with the servants of Solomon*" (I Kings 9:27).

Phoenician merchantmen being unloaded at an Egyptian river port. In building up an
Israelite merchant navy—the first and only one, which was for a time successful—
Solomon had the benefit through his alliance with Tyre of the knowledge and experience
of the most skilful mariners and shipbuilders in the ancient world. "Thy wise men,
O Tyrus, that were in thee, were thy pilots", says Ezekiel 27:8. King Jehoshaphat
of Judah later on fitted out ships at Ezion-Geber to try to revive the trade with Ophir but
without success. "And the ships were wrecked, and were not able to go . . ."
(II Chronicles 20:37–R.S.V.).

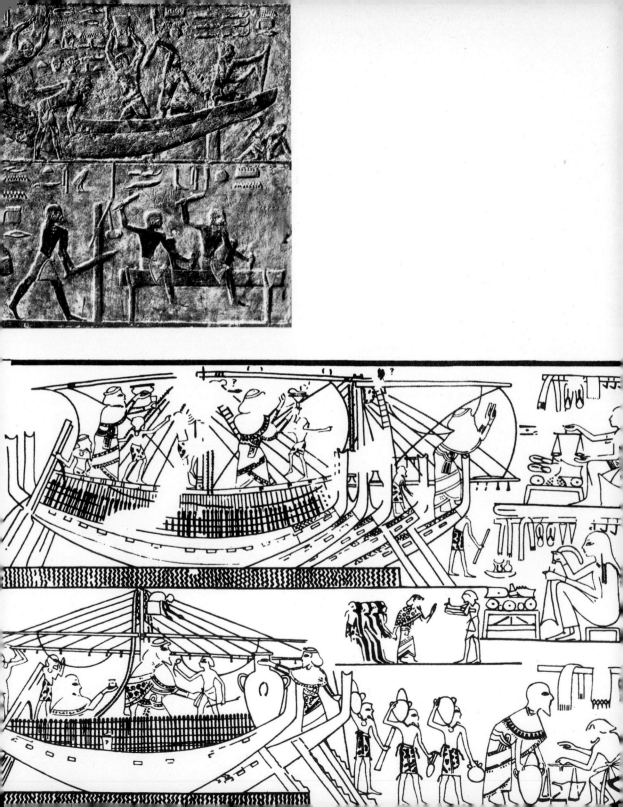

"In Ezion-geber, which is beside Eloth, on the shore of the Red sea,
in the land of Edom" lay King Solomon's harbour (I Kings 9:26).
On the shores of the Gulf of Aqabah, where ships once sailed from
the Port of Elath to Ophir, there is now the harbour of Aqabah
(above) belonging to the state of Jordan. To the north-west
of it a surprising discovery was made. At Tell el-Kheleifeh (below)
were found the remains of the port of Ezion-Geber, which Solomon
himself used to frequent (II Chronicles 8:17). Among the ruins large
copper-smelting installations came to light. Ezion-Geber was at the same time
a trading post and an important centre of industry. It was here that
they processed the ore from the copper mines in the Arabah (see p. 191).

"And they came to Ophir, and fetched from thence gold, four hundred and twenty talents, and brought it to king Solomon" (I Kings 9:28). "Gold from Ophir for Beth-Horon" is the translation of this inscription found at Tell Qasile. The potsherd establishes both the existence and the wealth of Ophir, which the Bible refers to. Its location, however, is still a mystery. Ophir, which means "light soil" or "dust", may have been in the Yemen, in the south of Arabia, well known for its gold resources, or else on the African coast on the opposite side of the Red Sea. Ophir was still famous for its gold in Palestine long after the time of Solomon, as can be seen from the frequent references in the Bible. The Prophet Isaiah speaks of it almost two hundred years later as he foretells the destruction of Babylon by the Medes: "I will cause the arrogancy of the proud to cease, and will lay low the haughtiness of the terrible. I will make a man more precious . . . than the golden wedge of Ophir" (Isaiah 13:11-12).

For the king's ships went . . . with the servants of Huram: every three years once came the ships . . . bringing gold, and silver, ivory, and apes, and peacocks" (II Chronicles 9:21). Had King Solomon learned an old secret about Egyptian foreign trade? It could be so, if, as is sometimes suggested, Ophir is the "Punt" referred to in Egyptian texts. A relief shows us one of the ships of the famous expeditionary fleet which Queen Hatshepsut of Egypt (1504–1483 B.C.) sent out to this mysterious "Punt" on the west coast of the Red Sea. The hieroglyphic inscription tells us that the fleet "arrived safely in Punt" and that they were able to exchange their own Egyptian produce for precious items like sandalwood, ivory, and gold. In the picture one of the ships is being loaded in "Punt". Porters are carrying up the gangway containers with myrrh trees in them. Other myrrh trees are already on board. Several apes can also be seen clambering about the ship.

"And there was peace between Hiram and Solomon; and they two made a league together" (I Kings 5: 12).

This portrait of a Phoenician king with almost the same name as Hiram of Tyre is that of King Ahiram of Byblos—the Gebal of the Bible (Ezekiel 27:9). Since the inscription on this relief from his sarcophagus is dated to the tenth century B. C. we cannot go far wrong if we think of Solomon's ally and trading partner as similar to this monarch in appearance and attire. King Ahiram is clearly an Amorite type. His features are Semitic; he wears side-burns but no moustache; his hair falls in thick locks to shoulder-length. The king of the "land of the Giblites" (Joshua 13: 5) sits on a throne decorated with two sphinxes; his feet rest upon a stool. In his right hand he holds a jar of ointment, in his left a lotus-flower. A table with offerings upon it stands in front of him. A procession is approaching the king from the right and we can see the first figure in it, a man bringing gifts

PLATE IV

"Horses (were) brought out of Egypt" by King Solomon,
also chariots (I Kings 10: 28–29).
An Egyptian stable-boy curbs a pair of horses,
a black and a chestnut bay (above). The horses are yoked to a
war-chariot. The bodywork of this light two-wheeled vehicle
is of wood with metal fittings. It rests directly on the axle
and has a handrail in front and at the sides. In contrast
to the two fiery, temperamental colts rearing to go, a couple
of quiet mules are pictured underneath.

"*. . . Tyrus, O thou that art situate at the entry of the sea*" (Ezekiel 27:3).
This aerial photograph of present-day Sur, twenty-five miles north of Acco,
shows all that remains of the once powerful city of Tyre, renowned
throughout the Mediterranean shores. Here, on the coast of Palestine,
lay the fortified island-city of the Phoenicians. Its sea-girt security came to
an end when Alexander the Great built an artificial mole from the mainland
to the island during siege operations in 332 B.C.
The siege lasted for seven months and ended with the Greeks destroying
the city and deporting the people. It was the end of Tyre's predominance.
Gradually the action of the sea added silt to the mole until there was
a broad tongue of land joining the island-fortress to the mainland.
Robbed of its strongest defence it met the fate which the prophets
had foretold: "Howl, ye ships of Tarshish; for it is laid waste . . .
Be still, ye inhabitants of the isle . . . Who hath taken this counsel
against Tyre, the crowning city?" (Isaiah 23:1,2,8)

"O Tyrus, . . . thy borders are in the midst of the seas" (Ezekiel 27: 3–4).
Embattled amid the ocean waves is how Shalmaneser III, King of Assyria,
pictures Tyre when he had this bronze tablet made to commemorate his
receipt of tribute from Solomon's ally. The Prophet Ezekiel has also
left us this expressive description of the power and glory of this great
centre of international trade: "O Tyrus, thou hast said, I am of perfect
beauty. Thy borders are in the midst of the seas, thy builders have
perfected thy beauty . . . All the ships of the sea with their mariners were in
thee to occupy thy merchandise. They of Persia, and of Lud, and of
Phut, were in thine army, thy men of war: they hanged the shield and
helmet in thee: they set forth thy comeliness . . . Tarshish was thy merchant
by reason of the multitude of all kinds of riches: with silver, iron, tin,
and lead, they traded in thy fairs. Javan, Tubal, and Meshech, they were
thy merchants: they traded the persons of men and vessels of brass in thy
market. They of the house of Togarmah traded in thy fairs with horses,
and horsemen, and mules. The men of Dedan . . . brought thee for a
present horns of ivory and ebony. Syria was thy merchant by reason of
the multitude of the wares of thy making: they occupied in thy fairs with
emeralds, purple, and broidered work, and fine linen, and coral, and
agate . . . Arabia, and all the princes of Kedar . . . were . . . thy
merchants . . . The merchants of Sheba and Raamah . . . occupied in thy
fairs with chief of all spices, and with all precious stones, and gold . . .
The ships of Tarshish did sing of thee in thy market; and thou wast
replenished, and made very glorious in the midst of the seas"
(Ezekiel 27: 3, 4, 9–16, 21, 22, 25).

"And Solomon sent to Hiram (king of Tyre), saying . . . behold, I purpo⟩
to build an house unto the name of the Lord my God . . . Now therefore
command thou that they hew me cedar trees out of Lebanon"
(I Kings 5: 2, 5, 6).

Growing to a height of a hundred and fifty feet, cedars of Lebanon
—cedrus libani—were among the most famous and most sought-
after trees in the ancient world. The Bible has much to say about
them. They were regarded as the stateliest of trees (I Kings 4: 33),
symbols of strength and power (Psalm 92: 12), but also of pride and
haughtiness (Isaiah 2: 13). Ancestors of these splendid trees pictured
here provided the timber which the Phoenicians supplied
to David for the building of his palace (II Samuel 5: 11)
and to Solomon for both his temple and his own palace
(I Kings 7: 1–12). One of the palace buildings was in fact called
the "House of the Forest of Lebanon" on account of the large
proportion of cedar wood used in its construction.

Today little remains on the heights of Lebanon to remind us
of the vast tracts of cedars that once grew here in what
Isaiah 37: 24 *(R.S.V.)* calls "densest forest".

"Then Huram the king of Tyre answered in writing, which he sent to Solomon . . .
We will cut wood out of Lebanon, as much as thou shalt need" (II Chronicles 2:11, 16).
This Egyptian relief shows how cedars were felled in Lebanon—as at King
Solomon's behest. The lofty trunks of the conifers were chopped close to the
ground with axes and then lowered with ropes. According to the hieroglyphic
inscription (top right) the tree-fellers are "great princes of Lebanon", i.e.,
Phoenician potentates like Hiram. Presumably therefore the King of Tyre looked
like them. They wear long wrappers with capes. The men on the right have their
long hair tied with headbands, those on the left are wearing close-fitting caps.

"And Hiram sent to Solomon, saying, . . . My servants shall bring them (i.e. the cedars)
down from Lebanon unto the sea; and I will convey them by sea in floats . . . and will cause
them to be discharged . . . and we will bring it to thee in floats by sea to Joppa, and thou
shalt carry it up to Jerusalem" (I Kings 5:8–9; II Chronicles 2:16). ▶
This expensive timber was always ferried across the Mediterranean.
The picture shows logs of cedarwood, which King Sargon II of Assyria had
ordered for his palace at Khorsabad, lashed together into rafts.

"*And the king commanded, and they brought great stones,*
costly stones, and hewed stones, to lay the foundation of the house.
And Solomon's builders and Hiram's builders did hew them,
and the stonesquarers: so they prepared timber and stones
to build the house"
(I Kings 5: 17–18).
"Solomon's quarries" is the name still given to part of the rock
on which Jerusalem stands. Traces of quarrying are plainly visible.

"*Then Solomon began to build the house of the Lord at Jerusalem
in mount Moriah, where the Lord appeared unto David his father . . .
In the fourth year of Solomon's reign over Israel . . . he began to build
the house of the Lord*" (II Chronicles 3:1; I Kings 6:1).
In all probability Solomon's temple looked like this.
The building stood on a platform about ten feet high
(Ezekiel 41:8). Ten steps led up to the entrance which was
flanked by two pillars: "*And he set up the right pillar,
and called the name thereof Jachin; and he set up the
left pillar, and called the name thereof Boaz.
And upon the top of the pillars was lily work*" (I Kings
7:21–22). The vestibule ended in double doors with folding
leaves, decorated with carved palm trees, flowers and cherubim.
The carved figures glittered with fitted gold-plating
(I Kings 6:35). The double doors gave access to the
"Holy Place" which had various windows (I Kings 6:4).
A gallery with three floors surrounded the temple on three
sides. On each floor were about thirty small rooms
(Ezekiel 41:6) used as treasure chambers, dressing rooms and
dining rooms for the priests. The "Holy of Holies"
lay beyond the "Holy Place". It had no windows and was
in complete darkness.

"... a worker in brass ... filled with wisdom and understanding and cunning to work all works in brass. And he came to king Solomon, and wrought all his work" (I Kings 7:14).

In contrast to other crafts it is not often that the skill of the metallist is portrayed in the fine arts. These tomb-paintings from Egypt show us metal-workers smelting and casting. In the top picture two men with tongs are gripping a crucible containing molten metal. Under it is a little clay oven. To keep the charcoal glowing properly two of their mates are taking turns with foot-bellows. When they have pressed the air out they refill the bellows by pulling up the strings. How they overcame the difficulty of casting large objects can be seen from the wall-painting on the left, showing the casting of a bronze door. At the top are two of the finished articles, doors complete with pivots, while, underneath, a further casting of a large mould is taking place through the inlet funnels. The "worker in brass" whom King Hiram sent must have been a master of this craft to make the "brazen sea" and the shafts of the temple pillars. "In the plain of Jordan did the king cast them, in the clay ground between Succoth and Zarthan" (I Kings 7:46).

"And he made a molten sea, ten cubits from the one brim to the other:
it was round all about, and his height was five cubits . . .
It stood upon twelve oxen" (I Kings 7:23, 25).
The "brazen sea", a huge bronze basin—this is a reconstruction—
stood beside the altar of burnt offerings in the inner court of the temple.
It rested on the backs of twelve oxen, which, in groups of three, faced
the four points of the compass, as we are told in I Kings 7:25.
Its rim "was wrought like the brim of a cup, with flowers of lilies"
(I Kings 7:26). With a diameter of about seventeen feet and about
half as deep this massive tank must have weighed about thirty tons.
Such an enormous quantity of costly bronze sealed its own fate. In
734 B. C. King Ahaz removed the oxen from under the "sea" to pay
his tribute to the king of Assyria. "And (he) took down the sea from off
the brazen oxen that were under it, and put it upon a pavement of
stones" (II Kings 16:17). The "brazen sea" itself "did the Chaldees
break in pieces, and carried the brass of them to Babylon"
(II Kings 25:13)—that happened in 587 B. C., after the capture
of Jerusalem by Nebuchadnezzar.

"*Then made he ten lavers of brass*" (I Kings 7:38).

A mobile laver, found in a tomb in Cyprus, gives us some idea of what the "bases" in Solomon's temple may have looked like. It has four wheels, each with six spokes, and connected by two axles—"and the work of the wheels was like the work of a chariot wheel" (I Kings 7:33). Above them is a square frame with long legs and side supports, its panels ornamented with winged sphinxes—it was "cherubims, lions, and palm trees" according to verse 36. Fitting into the frame is a round bowl. These mobile lavers of the Bible stood in the inner court and were used for purifying sacrificial offerings— "such things as they offered for the burnt offering they washed in them" (II Chronicles 4:6).

The idea of making the lavers mobile must have arisen because of the difficulty of moving the heavy bronze vessels.

"For the Lord thy God bringeth thee into a good land . . . a land whose stones are iron, and out of whose hills thou mayest dig brass" (Deuteronomy 8:7–9).

These were King Solomon's copper mines. It was at the southern end of Palestine, between the Dead Sea and the Red Sea, that archaeologists in our own day came upon traces of an extensive metal industry which Solomon had brought into existence. In a bleak gorge, bearing the name of Wadi Timna, it was this oddly shaped rock-face that produced the surprising discovery that the holes on the surface are entrances to three tiers of galleries in the biggest of Solomon's copper mines. It was here that the ore was quarried according to proper mining procedure as Job describes it: "He breaketh open a shaft . . . as for the earth . . . underneath it is turned up . . . he bindeth the streams that they trickle not; and the thing that is hid bringeth he forth to light" (Job 28:4–11—*R.V.*).

VII Under the Yoke of Assyria

"Wherefore the Lord brought upon them the captains of the host of the king of Assyria" (II Chronicles 33:11).

The Division and Decline of the Kingdom

(I Kings 12–II Kings 17)
(II Chronicles 10–28)

*"So Israel rebelled against the house
of David unto this day . . . there was none
that followed the house of David, but the tribe of
Judah only"* (I Kings 12:19–20).

HARDLY HAD KING Solomon closed his eyes for ever (926 B.C.) when trouble broke out. Rehoboam, his son and legal heir to the throne, was unable to command the loyalty of the whole kingdom. Discussion arose at once over his accession. The ten northern tribes broke away and elected as their king, Jeroboam, a man of the people who had been banished to Egypt. From now on the country is divided. The Kingdom of Israel in the north has its capital at Samaria, the Kingdom of Judah in the south has its capital at Jerusalem. A time of bitter trials and heavy reverses set in which slowly but surely was to lead to ultimate collapse. About two hundred years after the disruption the northern kingdom was no more.

War between north and south, to which the recently excavated frontier fortress of Mizpah still bears witness, was the first consequence of the split. To make the national calamity complete, Pharaoh Sheshonk I, called Shishak in the Bible, invaded the country in 922 B.C. Judah and Jerusalem were his chief targets but the northern kingdom did not escape without scathe. In the general disorder of the time four kings who followed Jeroboam I in the north died violent deaths. Then about 882 B.C. an army commander, Omri by name, founded a new dynasty. His reign was occupied with an unending struggle against his warlike neighbours to the north, the Syrian kings of Damascus. It was in the reign of Omri's son Ahab that there came the first clash with the imperial power of Assyria which ultimately sealed the fate of Israel. In 853 B.C. at Karkar on the Orontes, Israel and her allies had to face the might of Shalmaneser III. The importance of the Omri dynasty is evidenced not only by frequent references in Assyrian inscriptions but also by excavations at Samaria, the

194

northern capital. At home, however, Ahab's marriage with the daughter of the King of Sidon brought about a religious crisis. Queen Jezebel reintroduced the fertility cult of Baal. Under the influence of the prophets Elijah and Elisha, Jehu, an officer in the army, not only demolished all traces of this idolatrous worship including its priests but also exterminated the whole family of Ahab.

In the first half of the eighth century B. C. both kingdoms enjoyed a period of economic prosperity—in the north under Jeroboam II (787–747 B. C.) and in the south under the leprous King Uzziah (785–747 B. C.). Material advance was, however, matched by moral decay. In vain the prophets Amos and Hosea thundered against the luxury and social injustice of the times. Amos was convinced that the people of the north must pay the price of their moral and religious depravity. Events proved him right. More than a century earlier than Judah, the kingdom of Israel met her fate. Under Tiglath-Pileser III (745–727 B. C.), the King of Assyria who is called Pul in the Bible, Palestine was invaded in 733 B. C. and both Galilee and Transjordan were torn from the kingdom of Israel. There followed the first deportation of exiles to captivity in Assyria. Ten years later Israel's last king, Hoshea, stopped his payments of tribute and the Assyrians attacked Samaria. When the city fell in 721 B. C., the conqueror Sargon II carried off large numbers of the remaining inhabitants of the northern kingdom, principally the upper classes, and scattered them throughout the various parts of his empire. In return, foreigners were settled as colonists in Israel. The ten tribes of the north were no more.

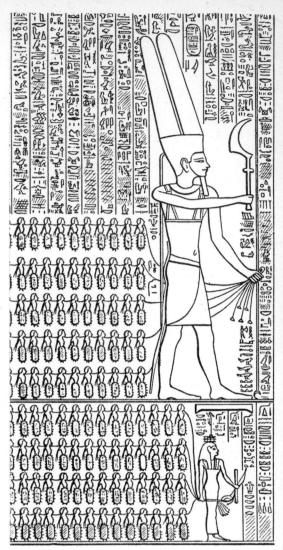

"And it came to pass, in the fifth year of king Rehoboam, that Shishak king of Egypt came up against Jerusalem" (I Kings 14:25).

In a victory relief on the south wall of the great temple at Karnak, Pharaoh Sheshonk I, whom the Bible calls Shishak, has immortalised in stone his raid on Canaan referred to in I Kings. The god Amon, with his sickle-sword in his hand, and below him his wife, the goddess of Thebes, are shown leading the conquered cities on cords to present them to the pharaoh.

PLATE V

"The Lord shall bring a nation against thee from far, from the
end of the earth . . . A nation of fierce countenance . . . And he
shall eat the fruit of thy cattle, and the fruit of thy land,
until thou be destroyed" (Deuteronomy 28:49–51).
This is what the conquerors from the Tigris looked like.
Their rise to power was fateful for Israel, bringing bitter
defeat and deportation. These court officials,
whose heads are pictured here, have the grim expression
and the large, hard piercing eyes which were characteristic
of this cruel race of warriors from Assyria.
Their black curly hair is caught up in a headband.
The twisted moustache and the long spade beard
done up in artistic ringlets were fashionable among
the Assyrian nobility.

"And he (Shishak) took the fenced cities which pertained to Judah" (II Chronicles 12:4).
Each one of the 138 towns and cities which he conquered has been represented
by Shishak as a prisoner roped to his neighbours. The captives shown in this section
of the relief symbolise, according to the hieroglyphic inscriptions on the ovals,
four Israelite towns: Rehob, Beth-Shan, Shunem and Taanach.

*"And there was war between Asa and Baasha, king of Israel, all their days . . . Then king Asa made
a proclamation throughout all Judah . . . and built . . . Mizpah"* (I Kings 15:16, 22).
Reconstruction of the powerful fortress of Mizpah on the frontier between the northern
and southern kingdoms. Remains of this stronghold have now been excavated,
symbolising the inexorable conflict between Judah and Israel, despite their common heritage.

199

"And Omri reigned . . . over Israel . . . And he bought the hill Samaria of Shemer for two talents of silver, and built on the hill, and called the name of the city . . . Samaria" (I Kings 16:22, 23, 24). It was on this hill, brilliantly chosen for strategic purposes, that the new capital of the northern kingdom was established. Lying about eight miles north of Shechem on two important main routes and almost six hundred feet above a "fat valley" (Isaiah 28:4), Samaria very quickly developed into a powerful stronghold. About 880 B. C. King Omri built an enclosing wall, to be followed by a strong casemated wall which his son Ahab erected round the whole hill top. Yet despite all these defences the city did not escape the fate foretold by the prophets. In 721 B. C. Samaria fell into the hands of the Assyrians and was destroyed. Its people were sent captive into exile. "Woe to them that . . . trust in the mountain of Samaria . . . therefore will I deliver up the city, with all that is therein . . . and Israel shall surely be led away captive out of their own land" (Amos 6:1, 8; 7:11).

These excavated walls, which must have been constructed with the assistance of Phoenician builders, indicate the efficiency with which the massive fortifications were carried out by Omri. This was the reason why, almost 160 years later, it took a three years' siege on the part of the Assyrians to conquer the city.

"*But, behold, I will raise up against you a nation, O house of Israel . . . and they shall afflict you*" (Amos 6:14). With the Assyrian campaigns into the west under their king, Shalmaneser III (859–824 B. C.)— whose commanding figure we see here—disaster loomed ahead for Israel and Judah. "I set out from Nineveh and crossed the Tigris" is how this monarch begins his account of his first campaign against Damascus. In the fighting which led up to the Battle of Karkar in 853 B. C. King Ahab of Israel, who took part in the Syrian coalition against Assyria, had his first encounter with Assyrian troops.

This relief, which once adorned
the bronze doors of the palace of
Shalmaneser III, takes us into the
midst of a bloody conflict such as
Israel was shortly afterwards to
experience. Assyrian archers are
attacking a Syrian town, which is
protected by a double wall and
towers. Under cover of a hail of
arrows they are beginning to storm
the battlements with scaling-ladders
(right). To strike terror into the
hearts of the beleaguered garrison
the Assyrians have staged an
exhibition outside of a row of
impaled captives (below).

"... the acts of Ahab ... and all the
cities that he built ..." (I Kings 22:39).
Among the imposing structures
for which King Ahab was responsible
was this strong citadel with its great
pillared hall. It was excavated at
Hazor in Upper Galilee.

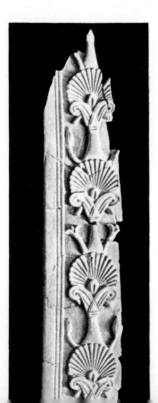

". . . and the ivory house which he made . . ."
(I Kings 22:39).
Beside the ruins of a palace of the time of King Ahab—
above—excavators at Samaria made a surprising
discovery. They came upon fragments of exquisite
ivory carving, such as had been inlaid in furniture
or used for interior decoration generally.
Some of these pieces, like this attractive beading
with palm-motif (left), undoubtedly come from
the period of the Omri dynasty. Experts believe that
they are evidence of Ahab's "ivory house"
which the Bible expressly refers to.

We are told in I Kings 16:31 that King Ahab
"took to wife Jezebel the daughter of Ethbaal king of the Zidonians".
This painted carving preserves the likeness of a Phoenician woman
of the time. She used red lipstick. Jezebel too "painted her face"
(II Kings 9:30).

"And he reared up an altar for Baal in the house of Baal,
which he had built in Samaria" (I Kings 16:32).
This stela of a Baal was found in Phoenicia, the home
of Queen Jezebel. He holds a spear which flashes lightning
in his left hand and wears a pointed hat with horns.

"*And when Jehu was come to Jezreel, Jezebel heard of it; and she painted her face, and tired her head, and looked out at a window . . . And he lifted up his face to the window, and said . . . Throw her down*"
(II Kings 9: 30–33).
Both scenes are uniquely illustrated by archaeological finds. A little Egyptian drawing shows how women used cosmetics in those days. The lips are being reddened with a fine paint-brush. The prophets have nothing good to say of women who have a passion for dress and cosmetics like Jezebel: "Though thou deckest thee with ornaments of gold, though thou enlargest thine eyes with paint, in vain dost thou make thyself fair"
(Jeremiah 4: 30—*R.V.*).
An ivory plaque was discovered at Nimrud which shows a low window, looking out over a pillared balcony. It frames a lady's head. The hair-style is Egyptian, suggesting Phoenician work with Egyptian influence. It was probably carried off by the Assyrians to Nimrud as loot.

"And Mesha king of Moab, was a sheepmaster, and rendered unto the king of Israel an hundred thousand lambs, and an hundred thousand rams" (II Kings 3:4).

"I am Mesha . . . king of Moab". Thus the king mentioned in II Kings 3:4 introduces himself on this basalt stela. The Bible goes on to say: "But it came to pass, when Ahab was dead, that the king of Moab rebelled against the king of Israel" (v. 5). This black monument, discovered by chance in Transjordan in 1868, contains the account of King Mesha's campaign against Israel and Judah after he refused to pay tribute as described above. After the stone had been laboriously hoisted out of the sand, enterprising nomads shattered it to get more money by selling it in small pieces (note cracks).

208

*"How say ye, we are mighty and strong men for the war? Moab is spoiled, and gone up
out of her cities, and his chosen young men are gone down to the slaughter."*
So runs Jeremiah's prophecy against Moab for her arrogance (48:14–15).
This is a relief of one of the warriors of Moab, with which Israel was often at war.

"Then they hasted, . . . saying, Jehu is king" (II Kings 9:13).
This unique portrait of Jehu, the army commander who was elected king in 845 B. C., has been preserved on an Assyrian relief. It is an enlargement from the famous Black Obelisk of Shalmaneser III from Nimrud (see p. 213).

"Take ye the heads of the men, your masters' sons, and come to me" (II Kings 10:6–8).
This was the command of the newly elected King Jehu, to exterminate the house of Ahab which had gone over to the worship of Baal. So "they took the king's (Ahab's) sons, and slew seventy persons, and put their heads in baskets, and sent him them to Jezreel".
The counting of heads of enemy dead on this Assyrian relief illustrates vividly the gruesome biblical narrative.

"And the anger of the Lord was kindled against Israel;
and he delivered them into the hand of Hazael king of Syria, and into the
hand of Ben-hadad the son of Hazael, all their days" (II Kings 13:3).
Clad in a costly fringed mantle, with folded hands and bearded
face, King Hazael of Damascus is caught in contemplative mood.
This wonderful ivory carving of the great contemporary and
relentless opponent of King Jehu was found at Arslan Tash in Syria.

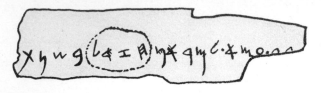

"Our lord Hazael in the year of . . ." is written
on this ivory tablet. The inscription dates
from the time described in II Kings 10:32:
"In those days the Lord began to cut Israel short:
and Hazael smote them in all the coasts . . ."

*"So Hazael went to meet him, and took a present
with him, even of every good thing of Damascus,
forty camels' burden"* (II Kings 8:9).
"In the wall of Damascus" (Jeremiah 49:27)
stood the palace of King Hazael, once adorned
with these elegant ivory carvings.

It was in 1845 that Henry Layard, an Englishman who was one of the first and one of the greatest Assyriologists of the nineteenth century, dug up this now world-famous black basalt obelisk.

It is a victory monument over six feet high, commemorating the campaigns of Shalmaneser III of Assyria, who reigned from 859–824 B. C. Both the reliefs in the second top row and the cuneiform text are of great interest for biblical studies of the period. They tell us that King Jehu of Israel paid tribute to this Assyrian king.

How King Jehu paid tribute to
Shalmaneser III is shown in the
series of reliefs in the second row
of the black obelisk. The king
of Israel grovels in the dust
before the Assyrian king, who
is making a libation. Behind
Shalmaneser III stand two officers, one
holding a parasol and the other a
club. Opposite the monarch two
grooms-in-waiting have taken
up their stance, one waves a fan
and a censer, the other, carrying
a sceptre under his arm,
has his hands respectfully clasped
in front of him. Then comes
a bearded officer with an attendant,
leading a procession of thirteen
Israelites laden with precious
gifts for the Assyrian king. All
the Israelites are bearded, and
wear peaked caps and
bandeaux. A long robe with
fringes round the hem and a
girdle, a long cloak with fringed
end thrown over the shoulder,
and pointed shoes complete
their outfit.

PLATE VI

"And they transgressed against the God of their fathers, and went a whoring
after the gods of the people of the land, whom God destroyed before them.
And the God of Israel stirred up the spirit of Pul king of Assyria, and the spirit
of Tiglath-Pileser king of Assyria . . ."
(I Chronicles 5:25–26).

This portrait of "Pul", as the Bible calls him, was discovered among
the ruins of a palace at Til Barsip on the banks of the upper Euphrates.
He was one of the greatest militarists of the ancient East and his rise to power
was to bring about the subjection of the whole of Palestine.
Here he sits upon his throne, granting an audience, with two officers
of the royal household standing behind him. The monarch, with his
handsome beard and flowing locks, wears the typical Assyrian crown—a
conical fez-type hat with a peaked top, and a headband tied with two long
ends hanging down at the back. Outstanding among his various
adornments are his long earrings and rosette-bracelets. In his right hand
the king is holding a long sceptre. Pul, who was the real founder of the great
Assyrian Empire, was the first to undertake on a large scale the systematic
transfer of people from conquered countries. When he came to the throne
as Tiglath Pileser III in 745 B. C. it was not long before subjugation
loomed ahead for both Judah and Israel and the beginning of the
deportations. In his annals this monarch, who came into contact with the
northern kingdom of Israel after his first battles in Syria against King
Rezin of Damascus, gives a list of payments of tribute by King Menahem of
Israel (II Kings 15:19–20). In 734 B. C. Tiglath-Pileser's campaign
was directed against Philistia. At that time King Ahaz of Judah
was hard pressed by King Pekah of Israel and King Rezin of Damascus,
since he had refused to join with them against Assyria.
In II Kings 16:7–9 we are told how King Ahaz in this situation bought
the help of the Assyrian king with treasure from the temple and from
his own palace. This tribute too is recorded in Assyrian annals.
Tiglath Pileser's chronicles go on to describe his campaign against Gaza
and Damascus in 733–732 B. C. At the time he confirmed the accession of
Hoshea, who had killed King Pekah, as King of Israel (II Kings 15:30).
After the conquest of northern Israel and Transjordan Pul carried into
exile the people of Naphtali, Gad, Reuben and half of Manasseh
(II Kings 15:29; I Chronicles 5:26).
King Ahaz had to appear at Damascus before Tiglath Pileser
as a vassal and a tributary (II Kings 16:10). The whole of Palestine
was now Assyrian.

*"And Jehoash, the son of Jehoahaz, took again out of the hand
of Ben-hadad, the son of Hazael, the cities which he had taken . . ."*
(II Kings 13:25).

Only a cow and her calf, carved in ivory, remain now to
remind us of Benhadad III of Damascus, referred to in II Kings,
in whose regency decline set in in Syria, which for so many
years had pressed Israel hard. The ivory plaque was part of
tribute that the King of Damascus had to pay to Assyria.

217

"That lie upon beds of ivory, and stretch themselves upon their couches . . ." (Amos 6:4).
Ivory plaques, often inlaid with gold and precious stones, decorated with cherubs and
religious motifs of foreign origin, have been found by the hundred at Megiddo and
Samaria. They testify to the luxury and extravagance of the upper classes in Israel
in the first half of the eighth century B. C., against which the Prophet Amos
thundered in vain.

"Jeroboam the son of Joash king of Israel began to reign in Samaria, and reigned forty and one years" (II Kings 14:23).
This fine seal, found at Megiddo in 1904, belongs to the time of Jeroboam II, who reigned from 787–747 B. C.
Above the roaring lion it reads:—"Shema", and, underneath, "Servant of Jeroboam".

"And the Lord smote the king",
says II Kings 15:5 of Uzziah of Judah, "so that he was
a leper unto the day of his death, and dwelt in a several house".
Two and a half miles from Jerusalem at Ramat Rahel,
the remains of the residence of Uzziah, the leprous king
in the Bible, were quite recently discovered.
Part of the walls can be seen above.

"*So Azariah slept with his fathers; and they buried him with his fathers*
in the city of David: and Jotham his son reigned in his stead"
(II Kings 15:7).
This modest stone tablet marks the grave of King Uzziah,
who is called Azariah in II Kings, and who died in 747 B. C.
The weather-beaten seal is that of his son Jotham.

"In the days of Pekah king of Israel, came Tiglath-Pileser king of Assyria ..." (II Kings 15:29).

An Assyrian artist has given us on a relief this portrait of the fierce and inexorable Tiglath-Pileser III. It comes from his ancient capital at Nimrud. When this terrifying monarch, the real founder of the Assyrian Empire, ascended the throne in 745 B. C. it was the beginning of the end for the northern kingdom of Israel.

"The days of visitation are come, the days of recompense are come: Israel shall know it" (Hosea 9:7).
Among the armed units of Tiglath-Pileser III which forced their way into Syria, there was, besides infantry and charioteers, an element which was used for the first time in history on a large scale by the Assyrians, namely cavalry. This relief shows mounted Assyrians engaged in battle with Syrian rebels. Behind the horsemen flies a vulture which has snatched up a dead man's entrails.

"Ushna, servant of Ahaz" is written on this cornelian seal which is shaped like a scarab. It belonged to an official of Ahaz of Judah, the king who invited the Assyrians to come to his aid, for "Rezin king of Syria, and Pekah . . . king of Israel, came up to Jerusalem to war: and they besieged Ahaz . . ." (II Kings 16: 5, 7).

"And he shall set engines of war against thy walls, and with his axes he shall break down thy towers" (Ezekiel 26:9).

These ancient sculptures with their wealth of detail enable us to share in the excitement and sense the cruelty of the tumultuous times when the Assyrians fell upon the northern kingdom, destroying and plundering. An officer in a long coat and a soldier are fighting behind a shield higher than themselves. In front of them a powerful mobile battering ram is being driven up a ramp specially built for an attack on the walls, which it has already breached. In the background three men have been impaled. On the left, soldiers are storming the fortress with scaling ladders.

225

"... came *Tiglath-Pileser king of Assyria, and took ... Hazor ...*" (II Kings 15:29).
The extent of the damage caused by Tiglath-Pileser's forces when they captured
Hazor in 732 B. C. can still be seen from this photograph of the excavated ruins.
In the foreground are the remains of the city walls and gateway dating from the
time of Solomon. Beyond them, in the middle of the eighth century buildings,
is all that was left of King Ahab's pillared hall.

"... *and carried them captive to Assyria*" (II Kings 15:29).
While two scribes outside a town which has just been conquered by Tiglath-
Pileser III are busy recording the plunder, the cattle are already being driven off.
Underneath, the waggon train is setting out, with women and children packed into
the bullock-carts. The long sad journey has begun to a far-off land and an unknown
future. Tiglath-Pileser's own words in his annals of "The Campaigns against the
west, and against Gaza and Damascus" (733–732 B. C.) confirm the biblical
description:— "All their people and their goods I carried off to Assyria".

*"In the ninth year of Hoshea
the king of Assyria took Samaria"*
(II Kings 17:6).
This was Sargon II, conqueror
of the capital of the northern
kingdom of Israel. His portrait
has been preserved on this
limestone relief for over two
thousand five hundred years.

Dur-Sharrukin—"Sargon's citadel"—was inscribed on cuneiform
tablets which Emile Botta, the great French archaeologist,
discovered at Khorsabad north of Nineveh in 1842. They were
found among the ruined walls of what had been a gigantic royal
establishment. Its builder was "Sargon, the king of Assyria",
referred to in Isaiah 20:1. The frontage of the city wall itself
with its twenty towers—not counting the entrance gateway—
was over 2000 feet long. The palace, which can be seen farther back,
with its temple-tower, was built on an artificial platform 45 feet high
(reconstruction).

"Then the king of Assyria came up throughout all the land, and went up to Samaria, and besieged it three years. In the ninth year of Hoshea the king of Assyria took Samaria, and carried Israel away into Assyria . . ."
(II Kings 17:5–6).
"I besieged and captured Samaria, and carried off 27,290 of its inhabitants as booty." The Assyrian text of this victory inscription of Sargon II dealing with his campaign in Israel, which is preserved in the original, reads like a confirmation of the biblical statement.

"So was Israel carried away out of their own land to Assyria unto this day"
(II Kings 17:23).
Accompanied by their sheep, and with their belongings
slung over their shoulders, captives are being driven out
of Ashtaroth, a town to the east of the lake of Galilee,
by Assyrian warriors.

*"Woe to them that ... trust in the mountain
of Samaria ..."* (Amos 6:1).
The Assyrians "besieged it three years"
(II Kings 17:5) before its resistance was finally
broken. Samaria fell in 721 B. C. This relief
from Nineveh, depicting the Assyrians taking
a city, shows the inhabitants being driven off
into exile while the battle for the city is still
in its last stages. A similar fate befell
the people of Samaria.

VIII The Road to Babylon

"Behold, the days come, that all that is in thine house . . . shall be carried into Babylon" (II Kings 20:17).

The Last Days of Judah

(II Kings 18–25)
(II Chronicles 29–36)

"I will remove Judah also out of my sight,
as I have removed Israel,
and will cast off this city Jerusalem which I have chosen,
and the house of which I said,
My name shall be there" (II Kings 23:27).

AFTER THE FALL of the northern kingdom, Judah too became a tributary of the all-powerful Assyrians. Despite the fact that the fate of Israel twenty years before was still fresh in men's minds, King Hezekiah of Judah determined to shake off the intolerable burden of tribute imposed by the Assyrian kings. After he had made secret treaties with Babylon—whose king, Merodach-Baladan, sent emissaries to Jerusalem—and with Egypt, the King of Judah rebelled against the oppressor. Probably envisaging a siege of Jerusalem he instructed his engineers to build the Siloam tunnel to ensure an adequate water-supply for the city. In 701 B.C. the Assyrian army under King Sennacherib (705–681 B.C.) marched into Palestine. Forty-six towns were taken by storm, among them Lachish, one of the largest cities in Palestine at that time. Jerusalem escaped the same fate and got off with payment of tribute.

Now completely a vassal state of Assyria, Judah was ruled for the first half of the seventh century B.C. by Hezekiah's son and successor Manasseh (696–642 B.C.). His submission to Assyria certainly saved the country in a political sense, but almost destroyed its religion. For Manasseh adopted the astral cults of his Assyrian overlords and went as far as to erect altars to pagan gods in the courts of the temple. During his reign the Assyrians pulled off the greatest triumph of their whole history. In 663 B.C. King Ashurbanipal (669–626 B.C.) took Thebes, the capital of Upper Egypt, called No-Amon in the Bible. But within fifty years of reaching this pinnacle of success as a world-power, Assyria herself was finished. Attacked by Medes and Babylonians, her metropolitan cities fell one after the other—Ashur in 614 B.C. and Nineveh two years later.

Nevertheless Judah's hope that with the fall of Assyria her own freedom would be assured was bitterly disappointed. In place of Assyrian oppression came the no less severe suzerainty of Babylon, under whose yoke Judah's last hour was soon to come.

Despite the Prophet Jeremiah's insistent demand that Judah should submit to Babylon, her ineffective King Jehoiakim preferred to take advice from his nationalistic ministers and rebelled. He died before the Babylonian nemesis could overtake him. In 598 B. C. Nebuchadnezzar's army reached Jerusalem and compelled it to surrender. Jehoiakim's son, who had succeeded him, the eighteen-year old Jehoiachin was carried off into exile in Babylon. With him went a large number of the most important people in Judah including the Prophet Ezekiel. This was the year of the first deportation. Eleven years later the fate of the country was finally settled.

In 589 B. C. Zedekiah, an uncle of the young king in exile, made an alliance with Egypt and refused to recognise the claims of Babylon any longer. The arrival of Nebuchadnezzar's army heralded the end. City after city in southern Judah was stormed and razed to the ground. After a hopeless resistance of eighteen months Jerusalem itself was over-run and destroyed in 587 B. C. For the second time thousands of captives left Judah for exile in Babylon. The southern kingdom now too had ceased to exist.

*"In the year that Tartan came unto Ashdod, (when Sargon the king of Assyria sent him,)
and fought against Ashdod and took it ..."*
(Isaiah 20:1).
Here, standing face to face, are Sargon, conqueror of Samaria and Israel,
and the Tartan, his commander-in-chief, who is making his report in the audience
chamber. With staff in one hand and sword in the other, the king embodies
a power that brooks neither opposition nor contradiction.
Submission alone is permitted. None dared counter his inexorable will.

"*This same Hezekiah also stopped the upper watercourse of Gihon, and brought it straight
down to the west side of the city of David. And Hezekiah prospered in all his works . . . and
. . . he made a pool, and a conduit, and brought water into the city . . .*"
(II Chronicles 32 : 30; II Kings 20 : 20).
View of the tunnel, accidentally discovered in 1880, which King Hezekiah built
in 701 B. C. in anticipation of a long siege of Jerusalem by Sennacherib, King
of Assyria. The tunnel runs for about 1700 feet through the rock on which the city
is built and carries the water of the Gihon spring into the pool of Siloam,
inside the old city walls.

237

"The boring through is completed."
So begins the inscription, written in ancient Hebrew characters, which was found
in the famous tunnel which King Hezekiah built.
"And this was the story of the boring through. While the workmen were
hacking their way from opposite ends, and while there were still three cubits
to be bored through, they heard voices calling from each side, for there was a
crevice in the rock. And on the day when the boring was completed the
stone-cutters hacked their way towards each other until they met. Then the water
flowed from the spring to the pool twelve hundred cubits, and the height of
the rock above the heads of the stone-cutters was a hundred cubits."

"... ye gathered together the waters of
the lower pool ... ye made
also a ditch between the two walls for the
water of the old pool" (Isaiah 22:9, 11).
The diagrams show the route of
Hezekiah's great Jerusalem tunnel. It
begins at the Gihon spring in the
Kidron valley east of Jerusalem, and
makes something like an 'S' bend
through the rock to reach the pool of
Siloam about thirty feet lower down.
Work began at both ends at the same
time, as the inscription says.
The remarkable curved course of
the tunnel gave rise to the belief that it
could not have been cut in a direct line
without disturbing royal graves.

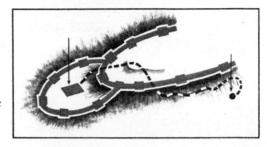

"Go, wash in the pool of Siloam"
(John 9:7).
The pool of Siloam, which King
Hezekiah made inside the walls of
Jerusalem to ensure that the vital
water-supply from the Gihon spring
should be available for the
townsfolk even during a siege,
is still today, as it was then,
a hive of activity. Arab women
and girls use the ancient reservoir
as a public wash-tub.

"*At that time Merodach-baladan, the son of Baladan king of Babylon, sent letters and a
present unto Hezekiah: for he had heard that Hezekiah had been sick*"
(II Kings 20:12).

"And Hezekiah was glad of them, and shewed them the house of his precious
things . . . and all the house of his armour" (Isaiah 39:2), for the visit was of
considerable political significance. This Chaldean Merodach-Baladan
(Marduk-apaliddin)—who made himself king of Babylon for a time and was
an inveterate enemy of the Assyrians all his days—was a rather mysterious figure
to all readers of the Bible until the discovery of this basalt relief brought him to life.
Here we see him as a paunchy figure, in a long belted coat, pleated at the back,
wearing a pointed helmet with streamers. This secretive ally of King Hezekiah
of Judah is participating in a solemn ceremony, the bestowal of estates
upon one of his nobles.

"And Elam bare the quiver with chariots of men and horsemen ..."
(Isaiah 22:6).
The Elamites formed part of the mounted auxiliaries whom
Sennacherib, the successor of Sargon II of Assyria,
brought with his army to Judah. In those days they roamed
all over the tiny land:
"thy choicest valleys shall be full of chariots, and the horsemen
shall set themselves in array at the gate" (Isaiah 22:7).

"Sennacherib king of Assyria came, and entered into Judah,
and encamped against the fenced cities, and thought to win them
for himself"
(II Chronicles 32: 1).
King Sennacherib, Hezekiah's most relentless foe,
seated on his throne in front of Lachish, the Judaean city.
He has a stool at his feet and a rug hangs over his high-backed
seat. In addition to a cone-shaped hat, encircled by double
rosetted braid, the Assyrian monarch wears the long military
cloak with a cape, decorated with wide fringes and trimmings.
The odd position of the two arrows—both pointing upwards—
means: Peace—Mercy.
(Section of the relief drawing on p. 249 in the original).

When *"Sennacherib king of Assyria did come up against all the fenced cities of Judah"* with
his army, *"Hezekiah king of Judah sent to the king of Assyria to Lachish, saying, I have
offended, return from me . . ."* (II Kings 18:13,14).
The full force of the Assyrian attack fell upon Lachish. This ancient and
powerful Canaanite royal city, once conquered by Joshua (Joshua 10:31–33)
and refortified by Rehoboam, Solomon's son and successor (II Chronicles 11:9),
lay on the edge of the mountains of Judah about twenty-five miles south-west of
Jerusalem. A double wall, strengthened with towers, and a triple entrance
gateway made the fortress well-nigh impregnable, as this reconstruction based on
the excavated foundations clearly shows.
Nevertheless the judgment pronounced on it by the Prophet Micah was fulfilled:
"Harness the steeds to the chariots, inhabitants of Lachish; you were
the beginning of sin to the daughter of Zion, for in you were found the
transgressions of Israel" Micah 1:13–R.S.V.).

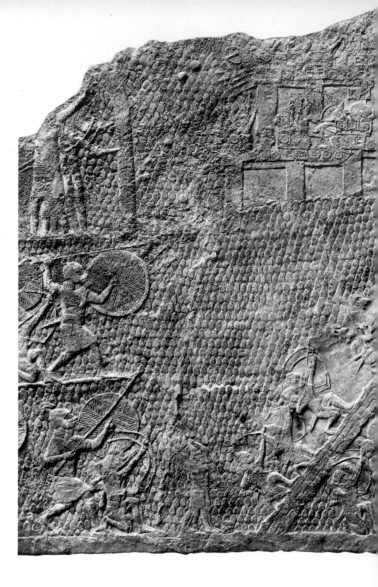

"Now in the fourteenth year of king Hezekiah, did Sennacherib king of Assyria come up against all the fenced cities of Judah, and took them" (II Kings 18:13).

After more than two thousand five hundred years this relief from Nineveh reproduces for us the attack of Sennacherib's army upon the biblical city of Lachish, with overwhelming force and with all the techniques of war. The defenders fight desperately from the towers, protected by shields between the battlements—"like the tower of David, builded for an armoury, whereon there hang a thousand bucklers, all shields of mighty men" (Song of Solomon 4:4). They are shooting arrows, slinging stones or throwing them with their bare hands and hurling firebrands down upon the enemy.

They wear pointed helmets like the Assyrians or close-fitting caps with chin-straps. Assyrian sappers have built a series of sloping brick ramps on which the siege-engines are pushed up the hillside against the fortress walls. The battering-rams are fitted with a long shaft in front, the purpose of which was to gouge stones out of the masonry. A soldier was posted in the front of the machine to keep throwing ladlefuls of water on the flying firebrands, thus preventing the flames from spreading. The archers advance under cover of the battering-rams. Behind them come the spearmen with large round shields. Captives, both men and women, are already leaving the city, passing three impaled victims.

"*The Lord shall bring a nation against thee from far . . .*
And he shall besiege thee in all thy gates, until thy high and fenced walls
come down, wherein thou trustedst, throughout all thy land . . ."
(Deuteronomy 28:49, 52).

Shattered stonework in the fortifications of the old city of Lachish,
which archaeologists came upon unexpectedly in the course
of excavations. It still bears traces of the siege-technique
of Sennacherib's assault troops, since the holes in the wall
were made by Assyrian battering-rams (Ezekiel 26:9).

Right: Picture of a mobile battering-ram
(from the relief on p. 225). The machine was manned by sappers
inside, was completely armour-plated, and equipped with
prongs in front with metal tips.

"And when he (Sennacherib) heard say of Tirhakah king of Ethiopia, Behold,
he is come out to fight against thee; he sent messengers again unto Hezekiah,
saying . . . Let not thy God in whom thou trustest deceive thee . . ."
(II Kings 19:9, 10).
"And they brought archers, chariots and horses of the king of Ethiopia,
soldiers without number . . ."
With these words taken from the annals of his campaign,
Sennacherib corroborated the statement in the Bible.
This is a bronze statuette of Pharaoh Taharka, called Tirhakah in the
Bible. The short curly hair, high cheek bones, thick lips, round chin
and short neck mark him out clearly as an Ethiopian. On the top of his
close-fitting cap sat the double crown of Egypt with two heraldic vipers.
When Taharka set out in 701 B. C. to assist Hezekiah he was in fact only
commander-in-chief of the Egyptian army.
His intervention was unsuccessful as his army was defeated by
Sennacherib's forces and he had to return to Egypt. In 689 B. C. Taharka
became King of Egypt.

"Sennacherib, King of the world, King of Assyria, took his seat upon the throne and caused the spoil of Lachish to pass before him". So runs the inscription to the left of the monarch's head (on the right of the picture). The background is the hilly, fertile country around Lachish, with its vines, its palms and other trees. On the far right, as the notice above it indicates, "the tent of Sennacherib, King of Assyria" has been pitched. Not far away stands the royal chariot. Behind the throne two attendants cool the air with fans, while facing Sennacherib and surrounded by officers, stands the grand vizier, bare-headed, making his report to the king. At the same time helmeted warriors armed with swords and clubs are making their way up the hill towards the king. The long procession of Judaeans who survived the battle of Lachish approach from the

left, escorted by warriors. They are on their way to captivity—men, women and children—with all that they have left partly carried on their backs, partly loaded on carts. All are barefoot. The first few are seen in the act of prostrating themselves. They wear their beards short and their hair curled. They are dressed in long coats and are bareheaded. Behind them comes a group with a two-wheeled cart full of children drawn by a pair of oxen. The women wear a short-sleeved garment with a full-length dress. Behind an Assyrian guard come some men with their hands raised in supplication. They wear short kilts and head-scarves knotted at the side. On the far left more warriors and chariots press on. Underneath, on the left, comes a pack-camel, and, centre, two naked men are being impaled by Assyrian soldiers.

249

"Behold, the days come, that all . . . shall be carried to Babylon . . ."
So said Isaiah to King Hezekiah (Isaiah 39: 6).
The conquest of Lachish likewise ended in deportation.
"Men and women, horses, mules, asses, camels, oxen and small
cattle did I lead forth out of it and counted as spoil"
says Sennacherib's campaign diary.
Above: Extract from the drawing of a relief on
p. 248—lower row left—in the original.

"As for Hezekiah of Judah, who did not submit to my yoke, forty-six of his strong walled cities, as well as innumerable small cities in their neighbourhood, I besieged with scaling ladders, siege engines, infantry, breaches, mines and tunnelling and I conquered them. Himself I shut up like a caged bird in his royal city of Jerusalem. I threw up earthworks against him, and whoever came out of the city gates was made to pay for his crimes. Those of his cities which I had plundered I cut off from his land . . . and diminished his land. I increased his former tribute and exacted a yearly tax in acknowledgment of my sovereignty. But as for Hezekiah, he was intimidated by the splendour of my power, and the Urbi and his best mercenary troops which he had brought in to strengthen his royal city of Jerusalem deserted him in terror . . ." So runs Sennacherib's lively and fascinating description of the stirring events during his Palestine campaign in 701 B. C. This account, which supplements the biblical record considerably, is to be found in cuneiform writing on a hexagonal prism extolling the campaigns of the Assyrian king.

"*And Hezekiah king of Judah sent to the king of Assyria to Lachish, saying . . . that which thou puttest on me will I bear. And the king of Assyria appointed unto Hezekiah king of Judah three hundred talents of silver and thirty talents of gold*"
(II Kings 18:14).

The official Assyrian record on Sennacherib's prism adds some interesting items to the list of the tribute that according to the Bible Hezekiah had to pay: "As well as thirty talents of gold he had to dispatch singers, both men and women, to my royal city of Nineveh." The Assyrian artist who made the above relief at Nineveh has depicted a procession of captive musicians, men and women, with harps, double flutes, kettledrums and zithers.

"And it came to pass that night, that the angel of the Lord went out, and smote in the camp of the Assyrians an hundred fourscore and five thousand" (II Kings 19:35).
Scene in an Assyrian camp. An officer, fully armed, is just entering a large tent. While one of his servants offers him a drink, another is busy making his camp-bed.
Camels, sheep and goats lie around the tents, and a man seems to be drawing water from a large cistern.

"And when they arose early in the morning, behold, they were all dead corpses. So Sennacherib king of Assyria departed, and went and returned, and dwelt at Nineveh" (II Kings 19:35-36).
This staggering discovery was made by the famous English archaeologist, James Lesley Starkey. In the light of this statement in II Kings it is of unusual interest. On the outskirts of the biblical site he discovered a mass-grave containing about 2000 human skeletons. The grave had been filled in with obvious signs of haste, suggesting, as some scholars now imagine, an outbreak of some epidemic in the Assyrian army.

"And it came to pass, as he (Sennacherib)
was worshipping in the house of Nisroch
his god, that Adrammelech and Sharezer his
sons smote him with the sword"
(II Kings 19:37).
Sennacherib was assassinated in 681 B.C.
These men formed part of the palace
guard and private bodyguard of the
great Assyrian monarch. They were
obviously not very efficient.

"And Esarhaddon his son reigned
in his stead" (II Kings 19:37).
This short matter of fact statement
in the Bible is amplified by Esarhaddon
himself, the son of Sennacherib,
who succeeded the murdered king.
He describes these turbulent days in
Nineveh: "Disloyal aspirations
overpowered my brothers . . . they
rebelled. To seize the kingdom they
killed Sennacherib. I became a raging
lion, I was consumed with fury . . ."
On this victory monument King
Esarhaddon stands over two of his
vanquished foes, Usanahuru, son of
Taharka of Egypt (kneeling) and King
Abdimilkutti of Sidon. He has these
dwarf-like princes roped through the
lips like wild beasts. "Because thy rage
against me, and thy tumult, is come up
into mine ears, therefore will I put my
hook in thy nose, and my bridle in thy
lips . . ." (Isaiah 37:29).

"The great and noble Asnapper" is how the Bible (Ezra 4: 10)
describes Ashurbanipal, the son of Esarhaddon, who succeeded his father
on the throne and reigned from 669–626 B. C. He was the last of the great
Assyrian despots. This scene on an alabaster relief takes place in the royal
park, which is planted with date palms, conifers and shrubs.
Vine tendrils, recognisable by the leaves and the grapes, provide
a shady bower in which the king reclines on a well-upholstered couch.
He is in a relaxed mood, and has laid aside his weapons—sword, bow
and arrows. For such an "off-duty" occasion he wears a head-band
with streamers and an embroidered coverlet with tassels at the corners is
spread over his legs. With his right hand he raises a goblet to his lips,
in his left hand he holds a flower. Beside the couch is a table laid with food.
Opposite him his wife Ashursharrat in a richly decorated robe sits on
an elegant throne with a footstool. She too is drinking. Menservants and
maidservants bring on food or wave fly-whisks. In the background a
musician plays a lyre with eleven strings. A peaceful scene indeed,
were it not for the human head hanging from a neighbouring tree (left).
It may have belonged to the King of Elam since Ashurbanipal is here seen
actually celebrating his victory over the Elamites at the decisive battle
of Susa in 655 B. C. "There is Elam and all her multitude round about her
grave; all of them slain, fallen by the sword . . ." (Ezekiel 32: 24).

"Asnapper brought over, and set in the cities of Samaria ... the Apharsites, the Archevites, the Babylonians, the Susanchites, the Dehavites, and the Elamites, and the rest of the nations ..." (Ezra 4:9–10).

Over and above this brief reference to Ashurbanipal's policy of resettlement, archaeology gives us a fascinating picture of his character. The great Assyrian king whose interests ranged through art, science and literature, and who founded a major library at Nineveh, was highly

talented in all directions, not least in his skill as a hunter, like so many of his predecessors. This relief shows his special delight in lion-hunting. Hunting from chariots in the ancient East was the sport of kings. In Israel, on the other hand, hunting was more a matter of necessity for protection from wild animals. Nimrod and Esau are pinpointed in the Bible as keen hunters (Genesis 10:8–9; 25:27). Neither of them was an ancestor of the Israelites. Assyria is specifically referred to as the "land of Nimrod" (Genesis 10:11).

"Art thou better than populous No, that was situate among the rivers . . . Ethiopia and Egypt were her strength, and it was infinite . . . Yet was she carried away, she went into captivity; her young children also were dashed in pieces at the top of all the streets . . ." (Nahum 3:8-10).

In 663 B. C. the Assyrians pulled off the greatest triumph in their whole history. King Ashurbanipal conquered Thebes, the capital of Upper Egypt, which is called No or No-Amon in the Bible. This event caused an enormous stir throughout the whole of the ancient East, for the "city of a hundred gates", as Homer styled it, had hitherto been regarded as impregnable. The Assyrians plundered the metropolis. The picture shows the great pillared hall at Karnak, whose temples contained untold treasure. "I conquered the whole city", exulted Ashurbanipal, ". . . silver, gold, jewels, the whole contents of the palace, coloured vestments, linen, splendid horses, slaves and slave-girls, two great obelisks of burnished bronze weighing 2500 talents, the gates of the temple I took from their place and brought them to Assyria. Colossal was the plunder of priceless worth that I took away from Thebes".

*"So shall the king of Assyria lead away the Egyptians prisoners and
the Ethiopians captives, young and old, naked and barefoot, even with
their buttocks uncovered, to the shame of Egypt"*
(Isaiah 20:4).
The scenes on this Assyrian relief look like an illustration
of Isaiah's forebodings. It shows Ashurbanipal attacking an
Egyptian city, which is fortified with high walls. While the battle
still rages above, the removal of the prisoners has begun below.
Some are chained at the wrist, others at the ankle.
Ashurbanipal's triumph over Egypt was, however, short-lived.
Psamtik, the regent he had appointed, seized the throne of
Egypt and drove out the Assyrians, whose power was by then
already on the wane.

"*For Gaza shall be forsaken, and Ashkelon a desolation: they shall
drive out Ashdod at the noonday, and Ekron shall be rooted up . . . In the
houses of Ashkelon shall they lie down in the evening . . .*"
(Zephaniah 2:4,7).
It was about this time that wild hordes of mounted nomads
from the Caucasus swept into Mesopotamia, looting and ravaging.
They forced their way through Palestine as far as the frontiers
of Egypt. These were the Scythians.
The Prophet Zephaniah foresaw with horror the havoc
they would wreak in Palestine.
Galloping Scythian horsemen, practising their characteristic
shooting over the shoulder, decorate the lid of this bronze
Etruscan urn.

"And he will stretch out his hand against the north, and destroy Assyria"
(Zephaniah 2:13).
This prophecy of Zephaniah was fulfilled only twelve years after the
death of Ashurbanipal. The Chaldeans, one of whom had been
Merodach-baladan, the ally of King Hezekiah of Judah, had succeeded
at last after a long and fruitless struggle against their mortal enemies
the Assyrians, in making themselves masters of Babylon, and had
allied themselves with a people from Iran, the Medes. The first city
to fall before their joint assault was Ashur, which was taken in 614 B. C.
This reconstruction shows the north-west side of this impressive
metropolis, the oldest of the great cities of the Assyrian empire,
lying on the west side of the Tigris, with its massive Temple of the god
Ashur, who was its patron deity.

"And (he) will make Nineveh a desolation, and dry like a wilderness. And flocks shall lie down in the midst of her . . . desolation shall be in the thresholds . . ." (Zephaniah 2:13-14). On the east bank of the Tigris massive mounds of ruins are now the sole indication of what was once the great capital city of the Assyrians. Here stood the splendid palaces of Sennacherib and Esarhaddon and the imposing library of Ashurbanipal, surrounded by spacious parklands and game preserves, with stables for the royal livery, with warehouses and government buildings. This mighty city of Nineveh met the fate that Zephaniah and Nahum had predicted when it was destroyed by the Chaldeans and the Medes in 612 B. C.

*"An oracle concerning Nineveh . . . The shatterer has come up
against you . . . The shield of his mighty men is red, his soldiers are
clothed in scarlet. The chariots flash like flame when mustered in
array . . ."*
(Nahum 1:1; 2:1–3–*R.S.V.*).

Red was the favourite colour of the Medes and Chaldeans,
whose combined forces attacked Nineveh, conquered it and
destroyed it. The head of a Mede wearing a round cap (left)
and of a Chaldean wearing a headband. "For, lo, I raise
up the Chaldeans, that bitter and hasty nation, which shall
march through the breadth of the land, to possess the
dwelling-places that are not theirs. They are terrible and
dreadful" (Habakkuk 1:6–7).

PLATE VII

"Is not this great Babylon, that I have built . . ." (Daniel 4:30).
The great Ishtar Gate, dedicated to the goddess of that name, and
one of the most impressive monuments rediscovered in the ancient
East, formed one of the principal entrances into Babylon. It was
one of the elaborate building projects of Nebuchadnezzar II
(605–562 B.C.) who was determined to beautify his capital, and
who also restored the temple of the chief god Marduk and built
himself a splendid new palace with the famous "Hanging Gardens".
We are told in the Bible that this was the king of Babylon who
brought the Kingdom of Judah to an end and carried off its people
into exile. King Jehoiachin, who spent many years in Babylon
as a prisoner, must have seen this massive gateway many times
like many other exiles. The Ishtar Gate was the starting point
for processions, which assembled in front of it, marched through
the triumphal arch and proceeded along the Sacred Way to the
seven-storied ziggurat which was crowned by the temple of
Marduk. The gateway, which is flanked by twin towers and
ornamented with pinnacles, is completely covered with coloured
enamelled bricks. Dragons and bulls are moulded in relief,
the animals symbolising the gods Marduk and Adad. The bright
yellow and brown beasts are surrounded by tiles of glorious blue,
tinted with lapis-lazuli dust. In front of the gateway outside the
city there was a road whose walls were decorated with lions,
in reliefs of glazed yellow tiles. The Ishtar Gate was reconstructed
in Berlin out of material excavated by Robert Koldewey
(see also p. 271).

"At that time the servants of Nebuchadnezzar king of Babylon came up against Jerusalem"
(II Kings 24:10).
Under this old masonry at the south-east corner of what used to be the temple
wall in Jerusalem, the foundations reach a depth of almost sixty feet and go back
to the early days of the monarchy. They were silent witnesses of the fearful
devastation which the Holy City suffered at the hands of the Chaldeans soon
after the final collapse of Assyria. King Nebuchadnezzar was the second ruler
of the Neo-babylonian Empire.

"*Jehoiachin was eighteen years old when he began to reign, and he reigned in Jerusalem three months ... At that time the servants of Nebuchadnezzar king of Babylon came up against Jerusalem, and the city was besieged. And Nebuchadnezzar king of Babylon came against the city, and his servants did besiege it. And Jehoiachin the king of Judah went out ... and the king of Babylon took him ... And he carried out thence all the treasures of the house of the Lord and the treasures of the king's house ... And he carried away Jehoiachin to Babylon ... And the king of Babylon made Mattaniah his father's brother king in his stead, and changed his name to Zedekiah*" (II Kings 24:8–17).

So far the only written evidence from Babylon dealing with these events described in the Bible is the cuneiform text above. It reads: "In the seventh year (i.e. of Nebuchadnezzar—599 B. C.) in the month Chislev (November/December) the King of Babylon assembled his army, and after he had invaded the land of Hatti (Syria-Palestine) he laid siege to the city of Judah. On the second day of the month Adara (16th March) he conquered the city and took the king (Jehoiachin) prisoner. He installed in his place a king (Zedekiah) of his own choice, and after he had received rich tribute, he sent (them) forth to Babylon".

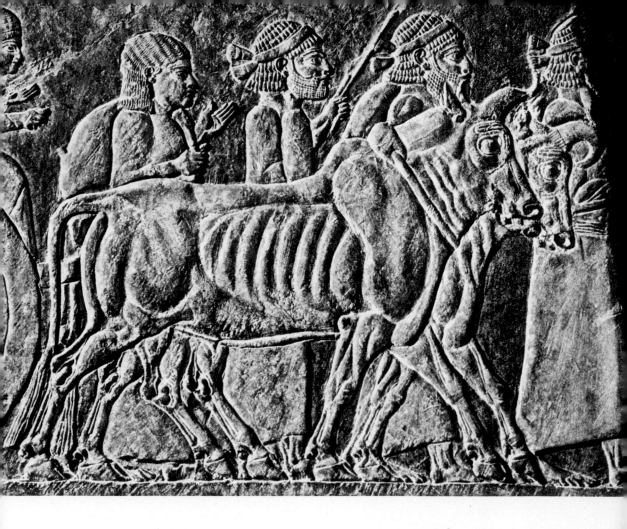

"*And he carried away all Jerusalem, and all the princes, and all the mighty men of valour, even ten thousand captives, and all the craftsmen and smiths: none remained, save the poorest sort of the people of the land*"
(II Kings 24:14).
After the capture of Jerusalem in 598 B. C. by King Nebuchadnezzar, the first deportation to exile in Babylon took place, which in this case affected only the moneyed and titled classes and specialised trades. A bas-relief from Nineveh shows this scene of a deportation such as the citizens of Jerusalem had to endure.

*"And for his (i.e. Jehoiachin's) diet,
there was a continual diet given him of the
king of Babylon, every day a portion,
until the day of his death, all the days of
his life"* (Jeremiah 52:34).
Two fragments of clay tablets which
were found in Babylon, and which
contain lists of rations delivered to
captives there. The cuneiform text
reads as follows:
"10 (sila of oil) for . . . Jaukin
(Jehoiachin), king of Judah,
2½ sila for . . . the sons of the king of
Judah, 4 sila for eight men from
Judah" . . . "1½ sila (of oil) for three
carpenters from Arvad, ½ sila each.
11½ for eight ditto from Babylon,
½ sila each, 3½ sila for seven ditto,
Greeks, ½ sila each . . . 10 (sila) for
Jakukinu (Jehoiachin), son of the
king of Judah, 2½ sila for the five
sons of the king of Judah by the hand
of Qanama . . ." The clay tablets
which date from 592 B. C. prove
that the king of Judah must have
lived in Babylon with his sons and
some retainers, since they are still on
the ration strength six years after the
fall of Jerusalem and the deportation.
They demonstrate the historical
accuracy of the biblical text.

"The property of Eliakim, steward of Jehoiachin".
So runs the inscription on these jar-seals which
have been unearthed at Debir and Beth-Shemesh in
Judah. They shed considerable light on the position of
Jehoiachin in Babylon, since they prove that between
598 and 587 B. C. a man by the name of Eliakim
must have been in charge of the crown lands of
Jehoiachin during his Babylonian captivity. Thus
it would appear that the estates of the King of Judah
were left unmolested by the Babylonians.

*"King Nebuchadnezzar . . . walked in the palace
of the kingdom of Babylon . . . and said, Is not this
great Babylon, that I have built for the house of the
kingdom, by the might of my power, and for the
honour of my majesty?"* (Daniel 4:28–30).
Reconstruction of the prospect of ancient
Babylon in the time of Nebuchadnezzar,
based on excavations. A solemn procession is
seen making its way through the great gateway
dedicated to the goddess Ishtar. As far as the
eye can travel, the broad processional way
bisects the vast metropolis. In the distance
(right) rises the massive ziggurat, the "Tower
of Babel" (Genesis 11:3–4), while more in the
foreground lie the famous "Hanging Gardens"
with their luxuriant palm-trees. Nearby stood
the royal palace, in which later on,
presumably after he had been pardoned,
King Jehoiachin with his sons and personal
attendants also lived. "And it came to pass,
in the seven and thirtieth year of the captivity
of Jehoiachin king of Judah . . . that Evil-
merodach king of Babylon, in the first year
of his reign, lifted up the head of Jehoiachin
king of Judah, and brought him forth out of
prison . . . and changed his prison garments;
and he did continually eat bread before him all
the days of his life" (Jeremiah 52:31–33).

"Into his right hand comes the lot for Jerusalem, to open the mouth with a cry, to lift up the voice with shouting, to set battering rams against the gates, to cast up mounds, to build siege towers" (Ezekiel 21:22–R.S.V.).

Nine years after the first deportation, "Nebuchadnezzar king of Babylon came, he, and all his host, against Jerusalem" (II Kings 25:1). In 587 B.C.—after a siege lasting eighteen months—the moment must have arrived which is pictured in this Assyrian relief, when under the impact of battering-rams "a breach was made in the city" (II Kings 25:4–R.S.V.). Jerusalem fell and was destroyed.

". . . when the king of Babylon's army fought against Jerusalem, and against all the cities of Judah that were left, against Lachish and against Azekah: for these defenced cities remained of the cities of Judah"
(Jeremiah 34:7).

Underneath the masses of rubble at Tell ed-Duweir in Judah, which covered the ancient city of Lachish (above), archaeologists found layers of ashes several feet thick, evidence of the destruction wrought by the Babylonians when they besieged and conquered the city. Nebuchadnezzar's technique was to seize a fortress by kindling huge fires against its walls. So between 589 and 587 B.C. Lachish was visited by the judgment pronounced by the Prophet Jeremiah when he said:
". . . his cities are burned without inhabitants" (Jeremiah 2:15).

Clay "message-pads", found in the rubble at
the gateway of Lachish, tell of the last days before
the fortress was captured by the Babylonians.
They contain hastily scribbled messages from
detached forts, observation posts and strongpoints
of Judaean troops who had not yet been overpowered. On this particular sherd is a message from
a certain Hoshaiah to Joash, commander of the
Lachish garrison: " . . .to let my lord know
that we are watching for the signals from Lachish
as we have been instructed, for we can no longer
see any signals from Azekah."

*"Now the rest of the people that were left in the city, and the fugitives
that fell away to the king of Babylon, with the remnant of the multitude,
did Nebuzaradan the captain of the guard carry away"* (II Kings 25:11).
Once more after the destruction of Jerusalem in 587 B. C. a large
number of the survivors were taken to Babylon. This time it was
deserters, middle class and working class people, and also many
poor folk. Assyrian reliefs have faithfully registered the miserable
plight of their vanquished enemies as they are marched off to exile.

"*So Judah was carried away out of their land*" (II Kings 25:21).
The road to exile. During a halt the captives are fed by their
guards.

"*And I looked, and behold . . . a fire . . . and out of the midst thereof
came the likeness of four living creatures. And this was their appearance;
they had the likeness of a man . . . As for the likeness of their faces,
they four had the face of a man, and the face of a lion on the right side;
and they four had the face of an ox on the left side; they four also had
the face of an eagle*" (Ezekiel 1:4, 5, 10).
The Prophet Ezekiel who came from an important priestly
family had already been banished to exile in 598 B. C.
together with King Jehoiachin and the aristocracy. The
Bible does not tell us which route the prisoners took to
Babylon, but somewhere on the journey Ezekiel must have
seen in one of the great cities the terrifying monsters—winged
oxen with human heads—which the Assyrian monarchs had set
up as guardians at their palace gates. As the Prophet's words
indicate, they combined in one figure the face of a man, the
head of a lion, the body of an ox and the wings of an eagle.
This winged ox accompanied by his tutelary spirit is from
the palace of Sargon II at Khorsabad.

"And as for the people that remained in the land of Judah, whom Nebuchadnezzar king of Babylon had left, even over them he made Gedaliah the son of Ahikam, the son of Shaphan, ruler" (II Kings 25:22).

A clay seal which was found in the ruins of Lachish may well serve as confirmation of what the Bible says, for the translation of the inscription runs: "Gedaliah, who is over the house." This is undoubtedly the same Gedaliah who was appointed regent by Nebuchadnezzar after the fall of Jerusalem and who was assassinated soon after: ". . . and (they) smote Gedaliah, that he died . . . at Mizpah" (II Kings 25:25; Jeremiah 41:2).

Seal of "Jaazaniah, servant of the king", which was found at Mizpah and which also takes us back to the time immediately after the fall of Jerusalem. Above a fighting cock is inscribed the name of the official of the royal household of Judah who is mentioned in II Kings 25:23: "And when all the captains of the armies, they and their men, heard that the king of Babylon had made Gedaliah governor, there came to Gedaliah to Mizpah . . . Jaazaniah the son of a Maachathite . . ." (also Jeremiah 40:8).

"*By the rivers of Babylon, there we sat down; yea, we wept, when we remembered Zion. We hanged our harps upon the willows in the midst thereof. For there they that carried us away captive required of us a song: and they that wasted us required of us mirth, saying, Sing us one of the songs of Zion*" (Psalm 137: 1–3).
There still exist a few narrow canals, overhung with trees, as a modest relic of what was once an elaborate system of irrigation, "the rivers of Babylon" (above).

Prisoners from Judah seen playing lyres and guarded by a soldier (right). Detail of an Assyrian relief.

IX Return and Renewal

". . . until the reign of the kingdom of Persia . . ." (II Chronicles 36:20)

From the Exile to the Maccabean Kingdom

(Ezra, Nehemiah, I and II Maccabees)

"And I will bring Israel again to his habitation" (Jeremiah 50:19)

IT WAS ONLY for a short while that the New Babylonian empire was able to maintain its predominance. No more than twenty-three years after the death of Nebuchadnezzar, who had sent the Jews into exile, Cyrus II of Persia seized Babylon in 539 B. C. as representative of the new world power that was for a time to decide the fate of the ancient East. With the coming of Cyrus the long yearned for moment of return to the homeland had arrived for the exiled Jews, impatiently waiting by the canals of Babylon. Before a year had passed Cyrus issued an edict permitting the Jews to return to their native land, with express instructions to rebuild the temple at the king's expense. Various groups of exiles began to make their way back from 538 B. C. onwards. The first group, under the leadership of Sheshbazzar, a prince of Judah whom Cyrus had appointed governor, began at once to clean up the ruins of the temple. Soon, however, work ceased on the site and it was not until 520 B. C. under Darius I (522–486 B. C.), who succeeded Cambyses, that building operations were resumed, and in 516 B. C. the temple was completed.

Two great figures emerge in this period of restoration. Ezra gave Judaism its distinctive character by his promulgation of the Law in 430 B. C. The achievements of Nehemiah lie more in the direction of material restoration, primarily the rebuilding of the walls of Jerusalem.

Thereafter the life of the Jewish people was relatively uneventful until the Maccabean rebellion broke out in 167 B. C. Judah was merely a district of the fifth satrapy within the Persian empire. The tiny area around Jerusalem was recognised by the imperial government as sacred territory, governed by its priests in accordance with the law of Moses.

When the Persian empire crumbled under the attack of Alexander the Great, the Jewish community accepted the new regime without protest. After Alexander's death in 323 B. C. Palestine became a buffer-state between the Seleucid dynasty in Syria and the Ptolemies in Egypt.

During the third century, until 198 B. C. it was under the suze-rainty of Egypt. Thereafter the Seleucids controlled the country. They attempted to Hellenize the natives by introducing Greek language and literature, Greek sports and Greek dress. When Antiochus IV (Epiphanes) who reigned from 175–163 B. C. finally set about exter-minating the Jewish faith and turning the temple at Jerusalem into a sanctuary of Zeus, the Jews revolted under the Maccabees. The second century B. C. was a time of bloodshed and strife throughout the land. Jewish independence came to an end when the Romans as-sumed control of the country in 63 B. C.

"Go up, O Elam, lay siege, O Media; all the sighing she has caused I bring to an end"
(Isaiah 21:2–R.S.V.).

In his oracle against Babylon, the prophet sees the Persians—"Elam"—and the
Medes—"Media"—sweeping over it victoriously like "whirlwinds in the Negeb",
to bring to an end the tyranny of the great city on the Euphrates over its
subject peoples.

This stone relief of two soldiers of the guard from the town hall in the royal
city of Persepolis show us what these warriors from "Elam" and "Media" looked
like. The Mede on the left wears the typical high round cap with a ribbon that
hangs down behind over a mass of ringlets coiled into a bun at the neck.

The short coat, trousers and boots indicate that this guardsman belongs to the
famous Persian cavalry. He is armed with a spear, which he holds with both hands.
The butt of the lance is decorated with a gold or silver pomegranate.

At his left side he carries a sheath that holds his bow and a quiverful of arrows.
Looped to his belt at his right side hangs the typical short sword of
the Indo-iranian cavalry.

The Persian on the right who belongs to the archers of the bodyguard,
wears the typical tall pleated hat on top of a fine head of curly hair.

A long carefully pleated robe reaches to his ankles, with a cape on top.
Apart from his lance this Persian guardsman carries a bow and quiver.

PLATE VIII

". . . when the king Ahasuerus sat on the throne of his kingdom, which was in Shushan the palace . . . he made a feast . . . when he showed the riches of his glorious kingdom . . ." (Esther 1:2–4). Persian troopers of the household guard from the royal palace at Susa. The discovery of these reliefs in highly coloured enamelled tiles, at one time covering whole walls, brought to life once more some of the pomp and ceremony that according to the book of Esther reigned in the royal palace of the kings of Persia. We see the archers in their brightly coloured attire—white or yellow garments with yellow or brown sleeves, yellowish-brown shoes and olive coloured hair and beard. Their clothes are decorated with little stars, and small squares enclosing little towers. Their weapons consisted of a long spear, with an ornamental gold or silver knob at the end of the shaft, as well as a bow and quiver.

"*. . . warriors from Persia . . .*" (Ezekiel 38:5–*Moffatt*).
The new masters of the ancient world belonged to a particularly handsome race.
Here are the heads of two gentlemen-in-waiting from the royal household at Persepolis.
Their beards are carefully arranged in little curls in Persian fashion.

*"Now in the first year of Cyrus king of Persia . . . the Lord stirred up
the spirit of Cyrus king of Persia"* (Ezra 1:1).
This damaged monument, decorated with a bas-relief of a four-winged
demon, recalls Cyrus the Great.
It formed part of the guardroom in a massive gateway
that once led into the monarch's vast game preserve at Pasargadae.
It was long thought to be a portrait of the king himself
because of the inscription "I am Cyrus, the Achaemenid".
It is now known, however, that these words
were commonly inscribed on a variety of buildings.

"When I entered Babylon in peace, and took up my royal
abode in the palace of the princes amid acclamation and
shouts of joy, the mighty lord Marduk inclined the great
hearts of the Babylonians towards me ... I liberated those
who dwelt in Babylon from the yoke that chafed them ...
I am Cyrus, king of all things, the great king ... king of all
the earth ..." So runs the inscription in Babylonian
characters on the clay cylinder of Cyrus. The last words
might almost suggest that the biblical Chronicler had them
in mind: "Thus saith Cyrus king of Persia, All the kingdoms
of the earth hath the Lord God of heaven given me ..."
(II Chronicles 36:23).
In 539 B. C.—a year after Cyrus had beaten the army
of Nabonidus, the Babylonian king—the occupation
of Babylon by the Persians settled the fate of the last
great empire of Mesopotamia. The time had come of which
it was said: "... after seventy years be accomplished
at Babylon I will visit you ... in causing you to return to
this place" (Jeremiah 29:10).

*"Come down, and sit in the dust, O virgin daughter of Babylon;
sit on the ground: there is no throne, O daughter of the
Chaldeans"* (Isaiah 47:1).
Among the innumerable envoys bearing tribute depicted
in relief in the Apadana, the great audience hall at
Persepolis, appears a group of the defeated Babylonians.
Three men in long robes and tasselled caps, bring a humped
bull as tribute.

"O man, whoever you are and wherever you come from, for I
know that you will come—I am Cyrus, and I won an empire for
the Persians. Do not grudge me this spot of earth which covers
my body." This inscription was carved on the tomb of Cyrus, the
liberator, who died in 530 B. C. while on a campaign in the
East. The small stone chamber on its ashlar platform, in which a
gold sarcophagus once enclosed the mortal remains of the great
Persian, is now an empty shell.

"*They sent a letter unto him, wherein was written thus:
Unto Darius the king, all peace*"
(Ezra 5:7).

These were the opening words of the letter in which the Persian
governor sought permission from his king to build the temple in
Jerusalem. We encounter this Darius I, son of Hystaspes,
who in 522 B. C. succeeded Cambyses, son of Cyrus,
on a relief from the treasury at Persepolis. He is in process
of giving an audience.

The monarch is seated on his carved throne with his feet resting on a
stool. In his right hand he holds the sceptre of his authority,
in his left hand, a symbolic lotus flower with two buds.
He wears a moustache and a very long beard, broken up into rows
of curls, and a tall hat. Two incense-burners have been placed before
the throne. The grand vizier makes his obeisance, one hand raised
to his lips as a mark of respect, the other holding his wand of office.
This high dignitary combined in his own person the offices
of chief of the general staff, commander of the guard and prime minister.
He wears the round cap and uniform of a Mede.
On the right two attendants in Persian dress complete the scene;
one carries a spear, the other, a bucket presumably containing incense.

"About that time . . . Antiochus . . . had entered the city called Persepolis,
and went about to rob the temple, and to hold the city; whereupon the multitude running to
defend themselves with their weapons put them to flight."

When the defeated Seleucid king referred to here in II Maccabees 9:1–2
"returned with shame", more than three hundred years had passed since
Darius I had begun to build his palatial city, the greatest of the monuments
he has left behind him.

Adjoining the rocky slopes of the "Mountain of Mercy",
Persepolis overlooked a wide plain. Here, surrounded by his closest
relatives and the imperial guards, Darius chose to live where the
countryside lent itself most to riding, hunting and jousting.

Even today the ruins are more than ordinarily impressive.
The magnificent lay-out is without parallel in the Near East both in design
and execution. From the massive stone terraces, past monumental gates
and huge portals with gigantic guards, long staircases covered with reliefs
lead up to the main buildings—the throne hall, the hall of a hundred
columns, the assembly hall of the nobles, and the palace area itself,
consisting of the royal residence, the harem and the palaces of members
of the royal family. Darius was unable to complete his imperial city.
Xerxes I and his successors built more palaces to add to his
architectural achievements.

A wide staircase leads up to the "Apadana" the elaborate
throne hall in the royal city of Persepolis.
This was the first of Darius's building projects.
All that now remains of the fabulous "hall of a hundred pillars"
are a few fragmented columns.
On the facade of the staircase are stone carvings of Persian
and Median guardsmen; above them is the emblem
of Ahuramazda, chief of the gods according to the new
teaching of Zoroaster, with sphinxes to right and left of it.
Behind the soldiers on each side, a lion is attacking an ox.
The main wall of the staircase on the right is adorned with
reliefs of Persian and Median nobles.

"Now it came to pass in the days of Ahasuerus, (this is Ahasuerus which reigned from India even unto Ethiopia, over an hundred and seven and twenty provinces) . . ." (Esther 1:1).

This was Xerxes I, son of Darius the Great, whose portrait in stone shows him while he was still crown prince. Acceding to the throne in 486 B. C. he reigned until 465 B. C. Here he is wearing a tall hat and a long curled beard. His right hand is outstretched and in his left hand he is holding some kind of lotus symbol. A long robe pleated at the side is worn under a wide-sleeved pleated cape, together with high-heeled shoes. Behind Xerxes I comes a magician with his head swathed in a cowl. He is followed by an esquire attached to the light cavalry of the imperial guard, armed with a battleaxe, a sheathed bow and short sword. Two guards with tall lances complete the scene (left).

*"When he shewed the riches of his glorious kingdom,
and the honour of his excellent majesty, many days . . ."*
(Esther 1:4).
This colossal bull adorned the capital of a pillar in a great
palace hall. The animal once supported the great wooden
rafters on his neck. This work of art in grey marble was found on
the site of ancient Susa. At one time the chief city of the kingdom
of Elam (Daniel 8:2), Susa under Persian rule became the
winter residence of the kings.
"As I was in Shushan (i. e. Susa) the palace" says Nehemiah
at the beginning of his book.
The story of Esther also had its setting in Susa.

"In the third year of his reign, he made a feast unto all his princes and his servants; the power of Persia and Media, the nobles and princes of the provinces, being before him . . ." (Esther 1:3).

On the facade of the throne-room, the famous Apadana at Persepolis, archaeologists discovered a unique relief that might almost be a contemporary illustration to accompany these words from the book of Esther.

Two long rows of Persian and Median dignitaries march in solemn procession at a New Year festival.

Some of the Medes—with their tall round bonnets—wear the uniform of the royal horse guards, knee-length tunics and tight-fitting trousers, while others have draped over their shoulders a long cloak with sleeves. Some of the Persians—with tall pleated hats—have the short sword stuck in their belts on top of their pleated coats, others, like some of the Medes, wear the bow-and-quiver-sheath at their side. Above, servants leading the king's horses and war-chariot.

The great feast that Xerxes I, the "Ahasuerus" of the Bible, made in the third year of his reign for his princes, his servants and his nobles, according to the biblical narrative, may have been the occasion for a secret conference of the general staff.

For at that time, 482 B. C., preparations were already being made in Persia for the famous campaign of Xerxes against Greece (480 B. C.).

This led to the conquest of Athens but ended with the destruction of the Persian fleet at the battle of Salamis.

"If it please the king, and if thy servant have found favour in thy sight, that thou wouldest send us unto Judah, unto the city of my fathers' sepulchres, that I may build it" (Nehemiah 2: 5). In 445 B. C. Nehemiah, a Jew who was cupbearer to King Artaxerxes I Longimanus (Nehemiah 2: 1), was sent to Jerusalem as Persian governor. There he succeeded in rebuilding the city walls in fifty-two days (Nehemiah 3–5). Dating from this time, in which the province of Judah had the status of a semi-autonomous religious community, several jar-seals have been found bearing the inscription "Jehud" in old Hebrew characters—the official Aramaic style for "Judah" (above)—and the letters for "Jerusalem" (below).

Coins of the province of Judah from the time of the Persian sovereignty. Above, an imitation of the Greek tetradrachma with the owl of Athens and the letters JHD (Jehuda). Below, a Hebrew coin, also bearing the letters JHD above a god sitting in a chariot with a falcon on his hand. Both coins are from the first half of the fourth century B. C., about the time when Ezra gave the Law a new status in Jerusalem.

*"Alexander, son of Philip the Macedonian, who came out of the land
of Chettim . . . reigned in his stead, the first over Greece and made many
wars, and won many strongholds . . ."*
(I Maccabees 1 : 1–2).
The first book of the Maccabees, going far back into history,
begins with this reference to the victorious campaigns
of Alexander the Great. This is a portrait of Alexander on a
gold coin, showing him with a horn as a sign of his divinity.
"An he goat came from the west", says Daniel 8 : 5, 21,
"And the rough goat is the king of Grecia: and the great horn
that is between his eyes is the first king."

"Alexander . . . had smitten Darius king of the Persians and Medes"
(I Maccabees 1:1).
In 336 B. C. Darius III Codomanus became king of Persia.
He was twice defeated by Alexander the Great, at Issus in 333
and at Gaugamela in 331 B. C. Alexander thus brought to an
end the power of the Achaemenids and the empire of Persia.
The famous mosaic that was preserved under the volcanic ash
of Vesuvius at Pompeii gives an impression of the battle of Issus
dating from about 100 B. C. Left, the head of Alexander;
right, Darius III in battle.

*"So Alexander . . . died . . . and his servants bare rule
every one in his place. And after his death they all put crowns
upon themselves; so did their sons after them many years:
and evils were multiplied in the earth"*
(I Maccabees 1:7-9).
With the partition of the empire after Alexander's
death in 323 B. C., the little theocracy of Judah
was first of all incorporated into the third of the
succession states, the kingdom of the Ptolemies
of Egypt. Its founder and first ruler, Ptolemy I,
whose head is shown in the sculpture above, brought
the tiny state into the Hellenistic sphere of influence.
This meant more than a change of overlords.
It was rather the first step on the road to the fulfilment
of the pregnant words of Genesis:
"God shall enlarge Japheth, and he shall dwell
in the tents of Shem" (Genesis 9:27).
Among the progeny of Japheth—
the third son of Noah after Shem and Ham—
the Greeks are expressly referred to under
the name of Kittim.

299

*"Antiochus surnamed Epiphanes, son of Antiochus the king, . . . reigned
in the hundred and thirty and seventh year of the kingdom of the Greeks.
In those days went there out of Israel wicked men, who persuaded
many, saying, Let us go and make a covenant with the heathen that
are round about us . . ."* (I Maccabees 1:10–11).

Antiochus III, called the Great—above—was the sixth of the
Seleucid rulers, masters of the greatest of the succession kingdoms,
with Antioch in Syria as its capital. After his victory over
Ptolemy V the Seleucids took possession of Palestine in 198 B. C.
With this further change of overlords Greek culture became
a real threat to the Jewish faith. When "he (i. e. Jason, the high
priest) had gotten into his hand the rule, he forthwith brought
his own nation to the Greekish fashion" (II Maccabees 4:10).

"For he built gladly a place of exercise under the tower itself, and brought the chief young men under his subjection . . . Now such was the height of Greek fashions, and increase of heathenish manners, through the exceeding profaneness of Jason, that ungodly wretch, and no high priest; that the priests had no courage to serve any more at the altar . . . but hastened to be partakers . . . in the place of exercise, after the game of Discus called them forth" (II Maccabees 4:12–14).

The "place of exercise" was a stadium. If nakedness appeared provocative to the orthodox Jews—compare the kilted Semitic boxers (above) with the contestants on the Greek vase (centre) —Jewish gymnasts were soon guilty of a more serious offence against the Law—they "made themselves uncircumcised" (I Maccabees 1:15).

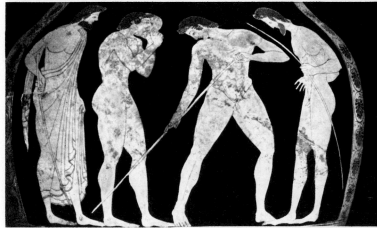

"For the king had sent letters by messengers unto Jerusalem and the cities of Juda, that they should follow the strange laws of the land, . . . and pollute the sanctuary and holy people: set up altars, and groves, and chapels of idols, and sacrifice swine's flesh, and unclean beasts: that they should also leave their children uncircumcised . . ." (I Maccabees 1:44–48).

These crimes, which Antiochus IV Epiphanes—pictured on the coin—added to his looting and desecration of the temple in 168 B. C., sparked off rebellion and war, under the leadership of the Maccabeans, three brothers—Judas, Simon and Jonathan, with the nickname "Maccabaeus" meaning "the hammer."
The first book of the Maccabees tells the story of what followed up to the death of Simon, the great champion of freedom, in 134 B. C.

301

X When the Fulness of the Time was Come

"... *God sent forth his Son* ..." (Galatians 4:4).

In the Time of Jesus and the Apostles

(The historical books of the New Testament)

"Now when Jesus was born in Bethlehem of Judaea, in the
days of Herod the king . . ." (Matthew 2:1).

IN ST LUKE'S gospel the story of Jesus is put in its historical setting.
Jesus was born under Octavian, who was given the title Augustus,
and who reigned as Roman emperor from 31 B.C. to A.D. 14. At
that time Herod, who had been placed on the throne by the Roman
senate at the request of Mark Antony and Octavian, was king of
Judaea. The account of the "Massacre of the Innocents" at Bethlehem
is, however, the only information that the Bible gives us about this
bloodstained tyrant. When Herod "the Great" died in 4 B.C., three
of his sons were appointed to rule in his place. Archelaus became
ethnarch of Judaea (4 B.C.–A.D. 6) during which time Joseph
returned to Nazareth from Egypt with the infant Jesus. Herod Antipas
became tetrarch of Galilee and Peraea (4 B.C.–A.D. 39). He is referred to simply as "Herod" in the gospels. Jesus was one of his
subjects (Luke 23:7) and compared him on one occasion to a fox
(Luke 13:32). The tetrarch of the northern territories was a third son
of Herod, Philip (4 B.C.–A.D. 34), who is mentioned in Luke 3:1.
Caesar Augustus was further responsible for deposing Archelaus in
A.D. 6. His territory was handed over to a Roman procurator who
lived in Caesarea, and came to Jerusalem only at festivals or other
special occasions.

It was under the Emperor Tiberius (A.D. 14–37), the son of
Augustus' third wife, Livia, by a former marriage, that John the
Baptist made his appearance, Jesus began his public ministry and was
also crucified. Pontius Pilate was appointed procurator (A.D. 26–36)
by this emperor.

Apart from Claudius, none of the Roman emperors who followed
Tiberius within the first century A.D. is mentioned in the New
Testament. Their history is nevertheless important, especially in the
time of the apostles. Caius Caligula (A.D. 37–41), who followed
Tiberius, was the friend and patron of Herod Agrippa I, King of

Judaea (A. D. 37–44), who is mentioned in Acts 12. He had made him king of Judaea after he had deposed and banished Herod Antipas, whose wife Herodias was responsible for the death of John the Baptist. It was Herod Agrippa I who had St Peter thrown into prison, from which—and indeed from execution—he escaped only by a miracle (Acts 12:1–10).

After the death of Herod Agrippa in A. D. 44 the greatest part of his territory was again put under Roman procurators by the Emperor Claudius (A. D. 41–54). Among them was the Antonius Felix mentioned in Acts 23:33, who governed from A. D. 52–60, and to whom St Paul was taken at Caesarea after his arrest in Jerusalem. We are further told in Acts 18:2 that the Emperor Claudius, in whose lifetime the first two missionary journeys of St Paul took place, expelled the Jews from Rome.

Claudius was succeeded as emperor by Nero (A. D. 54–68). It was in his reign that St Paul in his famous letter counselled the church in Rome to be obedient to the state (Romans 13:1 ff). Nero appointed Porcius Festus procurator (A. D. 60–62) and it was during his trial before this man that St Paul appealed to Caesar (Acts 25:11–12) and was subsequently sent to Rome. Before that, Porcius Festus had given the apostle an opportunity to state his case before Herod Agrippa II—son of Herod Agrippa I (Acts 26). We are told nothing in the Bible about the great fire of Rome and the persecution of the Christians under Nero in A. D. 64, nor are we told that it was under this emperor that the Jewish rebellion broke out in A. D. 66. The upheaval that followed the death of Nero and the end of the first imperial dynasty was stabilised only when Flavius Vespasianus, an army commander, became the Emperor Vespasian (A. D. 69–79). The name of his son, later the emperor, Titus, will always be associated with the destruction of Jerusalem in A. D. 70 which Jesus had foreseen.

*"And it came to pass in those days, that there went
out a decree from Caesar Augustus, that all the world should
be taxed . . . And all went to be taxed, every one
into his own city"* (Luke 2:1,3).
The likeness of the monarch expressly mentioned in
St Luke's gospel, in whose reign Jesus was born at
Bethlehem, has been preserved by this statue in the
Vatican. He was Octavianus the first Roman emperor—a
grand-nephew of Julius Caesar—who ruled from 31 B.C. to
A.D. 14, and on whom the Roman senate in 27 B.C.
conferred the title of "Augustus"—"reverend".

"And Joseph also went up from Galilee, out of the city of Nazareth, into Judaea, unto the city of David, which is called Bethlehem ... To be taxed with Mary his espoused wife, being great with child. And so it was, that, while they were there, the days were accomplished that she should be delivered. And she brought forth her firstborn son, and wrapped him in swaddling clothes, and laid him in a manger; because there was no room for them in the inn" (Luke 2:4–7).

Southward of Jerusalem in the heart of the desolate wilderness of Judah, whose rocky knolls can be seen stretching down to the shores of the Dead Sea, lies Bethlehem. Its name, which means "house of bread", is mentioned first in patriarchal times as the burial place of Rachel (Genesis 35:19), and, later, as the home of David (I Samuel 16:1 ff.). Above the supposed birthplace of Jesus—a limestone cave—the Emperor Constantine built the Church of the Nativity in A. D. 330. It is the prominent building in the centre of the picture.

"Now in the fifteenth year of the reign of Tiberius Caesar, Pontius Pilate being governor of Judaea . . ."
(Luke 3:1).

Once again, as at the birth of Jesus, St Luke gives us further details of the historical background at the beginning of his third chapter, which sets the stage for Jesus' public ministry. After dealing with John the Baptist's revival campaign, he comments: "And Jesus himself began to be about thirty years of age" (v.23).— This portrait in marble of an elderly man with a veil over his head is that of the Emperor Tiberius, in whose reign Jesus began his ministry and was also crucified. Tiberius, who succeeded Augustus in A.D. 14 and died in A.D. 37, appointed Pontius Pilate procurator of Judaea in A.D. 26.

As governor of the province Pilate minted the bronze coin seen on the left. It has on one side three ears of corn (above) and on the other a Roman ladle used in religious ceremonies.

And Joseph *"came and dwelt in a city called Nazareth"*
(Matthew 2:23).
On a cypress-clad hill, near the great trade-route from Damascus
to Egypt and on the edge of the Plain of Jezreel, lies the home
of Jesus and his family (Luke 1:26; Mark 6:3). It was here
that he lived from the time his parents brought him back from
Egypt until the beginning of his public ministry. In this lovely
countryside he learned the parables of nature, the time of sowing
and harvest, growth and decay.
Yet it was in Nazareth that Jesus was later to find no faith
in himself: "A prophet is not without honour, but in his own
country, and among his own kin, and in his own house"
(Mark 6:4).

"And he came to Nazareth, where he had been brought up: and, as his custom was, he went into the synagogue on the sabbath day, and stood up for to read. And there was delivered unto him the book of the prophet Esaias" (Luke 4:16–17).

This was the kind of "book" that Jesus held in his hands. This scroll of Isaiah was recently found in a cave by the Dead Sea—a copy in the original language dating from at least a century before Christ. The rolls at each side show clear signs of constant use. The manuscript consists of pieces of parchment sewn together into a roll of just over 24 feet long. In the second line of the column which is completely visible are the words: "A voice cries: In the wilderness prepare the way of the Lord" (Isaiah 40:3)— words which are specifically quoted with reference to John the Baptist's mission in relation to the impending commencement of Jesus' public ministry (Luke 3:4).

"Now when Jesus had heard that John was cast into prison, he departed into Galilee: and leaving Nazareth, he came and dwelt in Capernaum, which is upon the sea coast . . ." (Matthew 4:12–13). At the north end of the Lake of Galilee, beside a bay, lie the remains of what was once a handsome synagogue. They have something to tell us of old Capernaum, for they formed part of a building erected about A. D. 200 on the ruins of the place of worship in which Jesus often stood and taught (Mark 1:21). Capernaum is called "his own city" in Matthew 9:1 for it was the main centre of his activity. It was from Capernaum that Jesus set out with his twelve disciples to go to Jerusalem, where death on a cross was to bring to an end his earthly ministry.

"Now as he walked by the sea of Galilee, he saw Simon, and Andrew his brother, casting a net into the sea: for they were fishers. And Jesus said unto them, Come ye after me, and I will make you to become fishers of men"
(Mark 1:16–17).
It was from these shores, fringed by Capernaum and Chorazin (Matthew 11:21), the scene of recent excavations, that Jesus launched his ministry. The sea of Galilee, overlooked on the west by a ridge of bare hills and in the north by the snowy slopes of Hermon, is still well stocked with fish. Fishing boats with sails and oars (Mark 6:48) are there in plenty today, as they were in the time of Jesus.
So also are the sudden squalls (Mark 4:37) which can be quite dangerous.

"And Jesus went out, and departed from the temple: and his disciples came to him for to shew him the buildings of the temple"
(Matthew 24:1; Luke 21:5).

Model of the temple at Jerusalem, which Herod the Great began to rebuild, enlarge and embellish, to curry favour with the Jews. Bit by bit the sacred edifice was taken to pieces and built afresh, without any interruption of the religious services. The interior was reconstructed with the old dimensions but at a greater height. In the new temple the courts were built in terrace fashion on ascending levels leading up to the sanctuary. A massive wall, the foundations of which can still be seen at the Wailing Wall, surrounded the whole precinct. To the west (left) was the main entrance. Through these gates one came first into the outer court, or Court of the Gentiles. In the middle of this great square, with colonnades on all sides, lay the temple area proper, built on a higher level and surrounded by a low wall. Notices were inscribed here forbidding non-Jews to pass beyond this point on pain of death (Acts 21:28) (see illustration on p. 315). To the east of the outer court was "Solomon's portico" (John 10:23; Acts 3:11; 5:12), on the south side was the "Royal Portico". In one of these porches Jesus as a twelve year old boy sat at the feet of the rabbis (Luke 2:46). At the north-west corner the temple area was dominated by a massive fort— the old Baris of Maccabean times, rebuilt and enlarged by King Herod and renamed "Antonia" after his friend, Mark Antony. Steps led up to this castle from the temple area (Acts 21:35, 40). From the Court of the Gentiles, nine gates led into the inner temple, four to the north and four to the south. The east gate was the most splendid—the "Beautiful Gate" (Acts 3:2, 10)—giving entrance to the Women's Court. From here a staircase led up to the Court of Israel. This was separated by a parapet from the Court of the Priests,

in which stood the altar of burnt offerings and the "brazen sea". Only a few years after the reconstruction was complete, the temple was destroyed by the Romans in A. D. 70. They forced their way into the temple area from the tower of Antonia, after the Jews themselves had set fire to the outbuildings. A Roman soldier threw a firebrand through a window adjacent to the Holy of Holies. There was enough wood in the construction to start a blaze, the fire spread, and the temple crashed in flames.

"And as he went out of the temple, one of his disciples saith unto him, Master, see what manner of stones and what buildings are here"
(Mark 13:1).
On the outer west boundary of the old temple area lies the "Wailing Wall" of Jerusalem, a relic of Herod's bastion. The size of these huge stone blocks gives us some idea of the grandeur and beauty of this holy place which Jesus frequented. It was here that the Jews mourned the destruction of their temple until, by the division of the city, this too became part of Jordan and access was made impossible for them.

"... and further, (he, i.e.Paul) brought Greeks also into the temple, and hath polluted this holy place ... And they took Paul, and drew him out of the temple: and forthwith the doors were shut"

(Acts 21:28–30).

Paul was accused of having brought Greeks into the temple, thus disregarding this notice which has since been rediscovered in Jerusalem. It was inscribed on the Court of the Gentiles in the temple and forbade any non-Jew on pain of death to pass beyond that point into the inner courts. "Whoever is caught doing so will have himself to blame that his death ensues" – thus the inscription in red letters on a block of white limestone which dates from the time of Jesus and his disciples.

"Then Solomon began to build house of the Lord at Jerusalem in mount Moriah, where the Lord appeared unto David his father, in the place that David had prepared in the threshing floor of Ornan the Jebusite"

(II Chronicles 3:1).

On the "rock of the plain" (Jeremiah 21:13) – now called el-Haram es-Sharif—stands the Mohammedan Dome of the Rock built in the seventh century. It encloses the "holy rock", a solid mass of stone measuring about 60 × 40 feet, hollow in the centre (right foreground). Solomon built his temple here, and probably the altar of burnt offerings stood on this spot (I Kings 9:25). After the return from exile in Babylon, the new temple was built on the same site, later to be renovated by Herod.

315

*"Shew me the tribute money. And they brought unto him a penny.
And he saith unto them, Whose is this image and superscription? They say
unto him, Caesar's. Then saith he unto them, Render therefore unto
Caesar the things which are Caesar's, and unto God the things
that are God's"* (Matthew 22:19–21).

This was what the silver coin looked like, which was brought
to Jesus, and which sponsored the famous parable
of the tribute money. It was the Roman denarius,
the commonest silver coin, translated in English as "penny"
(Matthew 18:28; Mark 6:37; Luke 7:41).
It was also called tribute or tax money,
because the annual Roman poll-tax amounted to a denarius.
In Jesus' day the face of the coin bore the portrait
of the Emperor Tiberius (left).

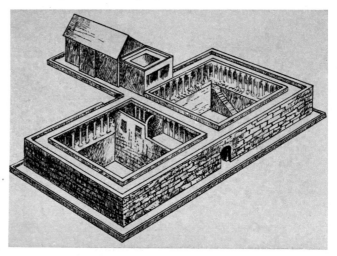

*"Now there is at Jerusalem by the sheep market, a pool, which is called
in the Hebrew tongue Bethesda, having five porches.
In these lay a great multitude of impotent folk, of blind, halt,
withered, waiting for the moving of the water"* (John 5:2–3).

North of the temple area remains of a double pool
were discovered. It lay in the midst of five
porticos, two along the length of the pool and one
at each end. A portico divided the whole building in two.
The reconstruction (above) based on the excavations shows
what the pool probably looked like.
It was here that Jesus healed the man who had
been ill for thirty-eight years:
"Rise, take up thy bed, and walk" (John 5:8).

"*And he came out, and went, as he was wont, to the
mount of Olives; and his disciples also followed him . . .
And he that was called Judas, one of the twelve, went before them,
and drew near unto Jesus to kiss him*" (Luke 22:39,47).
The Mount of Olives, to the east of Jerusalem, forms part
of a chain of hills about two thousand five hundred feet high.
On his way from Jericho, Jesus had looked down from the top
of the hill upon Jerusalem, and it was "as he sat upon the Mount
of Olives, over against the temple" that he spoke of the
last things (Mark 13:3 ff.). In the Garden of Gethsemane at the
foot of the Mount of Olives, Jesus was arrested. Some ancient
gnarled olive trees are still standing there today.

*"And when Joseph had taken the body, he wrapped it in a clean
linen cloth, and laid it in his own new tomb, which he had hewn
out in the rock: and he rolled a great stone to the door
of the sepulchre and departed"* (Matthew 27:59–60).
This tomb, hewn out of the rock face, dates back
to New Testament times. It gives us some idea of the tomb
of Joseph of Arimathaea in which Jesus was laid.
There is a low doorway (John 20:5) which could be closed by
rolling a stone over it (seen to the right
of the entrance) "And when they looked,
they saw that the stone was rolled away:
for it was very great" (Mark 16:4).

*"And there was a certain disciple at Damascus, named Ananias; and to him said
the Lord in a vision . . . Arise, and go into the street which is called
Straight, and enquire in the house of Judas for one called Saul,
of Tarsus"* (Acts 9: 10–11).

Today, after almost two thousand years, "Straight Street",
where St Paul lodged after the shattering experience of his conversion,
still runs from east to west across the centre of Damascus.
The ancient capital of Syria, lying east of Mt Hermon on
the edge of the desert, has been bound up with biblical history
since the time of Abraham (Genesis 15: 2).

"*And it came to pass ... that Paul ... came to Ephesus*"
(Acts 19:1).
Ephesus was the capital of the Roman province of Asia on
the west coast of Asia Minor. Shown above are the ruins of the
theatre, where games were held in honour of the Roman emperor.
It was in this semi-circular building, capable of holding
more than 24,000 spectators, that the scene took place
which is described in Acts 19:24–29: "And the whole city was
filled with confusion: and having caught ... Paul's
companions in travel, they rushed with one accord into the
theatre". The remains of the temple of Artemis were also
discovered under many feet of rubble. This was once one of the
seven wonders of the world.
The Ephesian coin (left) gives a picture of the temple
with a statue of the goddess.
Her many breasts mark her out as a deity of a fertility cult.
It was about her that the mob in the story cried:
"Great is Diana of the Ephesians" (Acts 19:28,34).

"After these things, Paul departed from Athens, and came to Corinth ..." (Acts 18:1).

There are still some columns standing which formed part of the temple of Apollo on the hill at Corinth, the busy commercial and industrial centre on the isthmus where the apostle on two occasions stayed for some time (Acts 18:1-18; 20:2).

Excavations have also revealed the site of the law-court with the governor's "judgment seat" (Acts 18:12) and the meat-market (I Corinthians 10:25), which lay near the main square or Agora. On his second visit here St Paul wrote his famous epistle to the Romans (Romans 16:23).

*"Paul, a servant of Jesus Christ, called to be an apostle . . . to all
that be in Rome, beloved of God . . ."* (Romans 1:1, 7).
So begins St Paul's letter to the Romans.
This is the first page of that great letter,
which the apostle wrote in Corinth, from the Codex
Sinaiticus. This manuscript of the Bible in Greek,
dating from the fourth century A. D., was found in
the monastery of St Catherine on the Sinai peninsula.

"And . . . he . . . landed at Caesarea" (Acts 18:22).
Thirty miles north-north-east of Tel Aviv, a few fragmented pillars,
washed by the Mediterranean waves, are all that now remains of the
once proud Palestinian city of Caesarea. King Herod, whose
improvements made it into a superb seat of government for the Roman
procurators of Judaea, equipped it with its own harbour and called it
"Caesarea" in honour of Caesar Augustus. Within its walls
—where Pontius Pilate also lived (Matthew 27:11 ff.)—
St Paul lodged on various occasions while on his missionary journeys
(Acts 9:30; 18:22; 21:8). After an imprisonment in Caesarea
lasting two years St Paul set out from there on his last journey to Rome.
"And when it was determined that we should sail into Italy,
they delivered Paul and certain other prisoners unto one named Julius,
a centurion of Augustus' band" (Acts 27:1).

*"And so we went toward Rome. And from thence,
when the brethren heard of us, they came to meet us as
far as Appii forum . . ."* (Acts 28: 14–15).
It was along this famous Appian Way that St Paul
entered Rome as a prisoner. He had come by
sea as far as Puteoli, a port on the bay of Naples,
where he had spent a week (Acts 28: 13).
A day's journey from Rome—about forty miles—
along this imperial highway which stretched south
from the capital, lay the Forum of Appius.
Here in this place which had an unsavoury
reputation on account of its light-fingered inhabitants
and its malarial sickness, St Paul met the first
Roman Christians, who had hastened to greet him.

"And when we came to Rome ... Paul was suffered to dwell by himself with a soldier that kept him ... And Paul dwelt two whole years ... preaching the kingdom of God, and teaching those things which concern the Lord Jesus Christ, with all confidence, no man forbidding him" (Acts 28:16, 30–31).

St Paul saw also the Forum Romanum, right in the heart of the old city on the Tiber, which in the time of the apostles was also the centre of the world. On the left, the Temple of Saturn, which still has eight of its tall pillars remaining, had been standing there for many centuries when St Paul came as a prisoner to Rome. It was consecrated in 497 B.C. and restored about 44 B.C. In front of the trees on the right rise three pillars of a temple which had been dedicated in 484 B.C. to the twin gods Castor and Pollux. To the left of it can be seen the triumphal Arch of Titus, built in A.D. 94 to commemorate the conquest of Jerusalem. The Colosseum and the other buildings are also of later date. On the other hand when St Paul was here there stood in front of the Temple of Saturn the "Miliarium Aureum", a gilt column erected by the Emperor Augustus giving the names of the most important cities of the Empire and their distance from Rome, including Londinium (London) in the west, and Jerusalem in the east. When St Paul began to preach the gospel in Rome, the first stage of Christianity's world-mission was completed. It was here that the apostle wrote his letters to the Ephesians and to the Colossians, perhaps also the letter to the Philippians, the second letter to Timothy and the letter to Philemon. St Peter, like St Paul, also lived in Rome, as did St Mark and St Luke.

"I appeal unto Caesar", said St Paul emphatically when on trial
at Caesarea before the procurator, Porcius Festus (Acts 25:11).
The emperor whom the apostle invoked as the highest
court of appeal was none other than Nero (above).
For two years after his transfer from Caesarea,
St Paul lived in Rome as a prisoner under surveillance.
Clearly his confinement was not strict (Acts 28:16, 30)
and he was released, as we learn from his letters to Timothy
and Titus. Then, of course, his destiny caught up with
St Paul as with St Peter in Rome under the Emperor Nero.

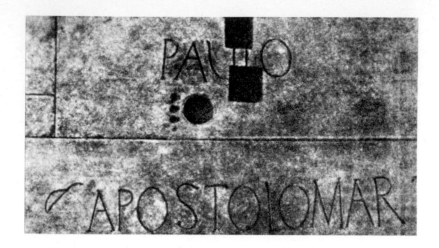

"Paulo, Apostolo Martyri". The inscription on this marble slab is written in lettering typical of the period of the Emperor Constantine. It was found under the high altar in the church of St Paul-outside-the-Walls in Rome during its reconstruction after a fire which almost completely destroyed it in 1823. The Emperor Constantine is said to have built the first church on this site above the grave of the apostle Paul.

"... when thou shalt be old, thou shalt stretch forth thy hands, and another shall gird thee, and carry thee whither thou wouldest not. This spake he, signifying by what death he should glorify God" (John 21:18–19).
According to tradition, the martyrdom of St Peter by crucifixion, as foretold by Jesus in John 21:19, took place in the reign of Nero and at the same time as St Paul was beheaded. Far below the crypt and the high altar in St Peter's in Rome, amid pagan tombs, lie these remains of a memorial which was probably erected about A. D. 160 over the reputed grave of St Peter.

"Verily I say unto you, There shall not be left here one stone upon another, that shall not be thrown down"
(Matthew 24:2).
The destruction of Jerusalem in A. D. 70, which Jesus had predicted (Luke 19:41–44), was the work of Titus, who had been made commander-in-chief of the Roman army in Judaea by his father Vespasian when he became emperor in A. D. 69. Titus himself became Roman emperor from A. D. 79–81. This is his head on a coin. He wears the victor's laurels.

"... *it shall strip his treasury of every precious thing*"(Hosea 13:15—*R.S.V.*).
A last testimony, carved in stone, to the costly vessels
of the temple at Jerusalem stands in the heart
of the ancient Roman Forum. It is a relief on the inside of the
triumphal arch which was erected in honour of Titus,
the conqueror of Jerusalem. The Arch of Titus itself, through
which the procession is passing, can be seen on the right
of the picture. After the general—the victorious Titus—has passed
through, Roman soldiers follow on, wearing laurel wreaths
and dressed in light tunics. Among them march manacled Jewish
captives. The Romans are carrying on their shoulders the spoils they
have acquired in Jerusalem. Each group has a placard bearing
the name of the particular item of plunder: (from the right) first,
the Table of the Bread of the Presence—"And you shall make
a table of acacia wood" (Exodus 25:23—*R.S.V.*).
On top of it sits a cup—the "cup of Yahweh"—and two silver
trumpets rest crosswise on the stays: "Make two silver
trumpets ... and you shall use them for summoning the
congregation, and for breaking camp" (Numbers 10:2—*R.S.V.*).
A second placard indicates the seven-branched Candlestick—
"And thou shalt make a candlestick of pure gold ... And thou
shalt make the seven lamps thereof ..." (Exodus 25:31,37).

"... and Jerusalem shall be trodden down of the Gentiles,
until the times of the Gentiles be fulfilled" (Luke 21:24).
"Judaea capta"—"Judaea conquered"—is written on this
Roman coin minted to commemorate the fall of
Jerusalem in A. D. 70. A Roman warrior stands under
a palm tree (left), while, on the right, a crouching woman
in tears symbolises the humiliation of Judaea.

Synoptic Chronological Table of Biblical History

THE AGE OF THE PATRIARCHS (c. 2000–1700 B. C.)

Period	Biblical Events	Bible Reference	Ancient East	
c.2000–1700	Journeys of the Patriarchs	Genesis 11:31ff.	Mesopotamia: c. 2000 B. C. End of the 3rd dynasty of Ur 2000–1700 B. C.: Invasion of the Amorites and founding of Amorite dynasties. Age of Mari. First Babylonian dynasty c. 1850–1550	Egypt: Middle Kingdom. 12th dynasty: c. 2000–1780. Palestine under Egyptian control
c. 1700	Jacob's family moves to Egypt	Genesis 42ff.	Invasion of Indo-Aryans and Hurrians into Northern Mesopotamia: 18th and 17th centuries	Egypt: Age of the Hyksos c. 1720–1550 Palestine: Prosperity under Hyksos rulers

THE SOJOURN IN EGYPT (c. 1700–1300 B.C)

Period	Biblical Events	Bible Reference	Ancient East	
	The Children of Israel in Egypt	Exodus 1:6–7 Exodus 12:40	Asia Minor: Great Hittite Empire (1600–1200) Northern Mesopotamia: Mitanni (Hurrian) kingdom 1500–1370	Egypt: New Kingdom: 18th dynasty: c.1546–1319. Expansion across Syria to the Euphrates (boundary at Mitanni kingdom)
				Palestine: Egyptian province 1400–1360: Letters from Canaanite city governors to the Egyptian court (Amarna letters): Amenophis III (c. 1413–1377), Amenophis IV (Akhnaten, c. 1377–1360)

FROM EGYPT TO CANAAN (c.1300–1225 B. C.)

Period	Biblical Events	Bible Reference	Ancient East	
	Bondage in Egypt	Exodus 1:11ff.		Egypt: 19th dynasty: c. 1319–1200. Conflict with the Hittites attempting to recover power in Asia
Shortly after c. 1300	Exodus of the Israelites Sojourn in the desert	Exodus 12:37ff. to Deuteronomy		Pharaoh Seti I: c. 1319–1301 Pharaoh Ramesses II: c. 1301–1234 Battle of Kadesh against the Hittites: 1297. Treaty with Hittites 1280
c. 1250–1225	Occupation of the Promised Land	Joshua		Pharaoh Merneptah, c. 1235–1227, mentions "Israel" on a victory stela dated around 1230

THE AGE OF THE JUDGES (c. 1225–1020 B. C.)

Period	Biblical Events	Bible Reference	Ancient East	
c. 1100	Battle against the Canaanites in the Plain of Jezreel (Song of Deborah)	Judges 4–5	Asia Minor: c. 1200: End of the Hittite empire Palestine: Philistines settle in the southern coastal plain: early 12th century	Egypt: 20th dynasty: 1200–1085. Attack by the 'Sea Peoples', among them the Philistines of the Bible. Successful repulsion by Pharaoh Ramesses III in a great sea and land battle, c. 1190. After c. 1150: Decline of Pharaoh's power, rule of priests. Loss of Asiatic possessions.
	Gideon defeats the Midianites	Judges 6:1–8,21		
	First battles against the Philistines	Judges 15–16		
c. 1050	Fall of Shiloh	I Samuel 4		

THE AGE OF THE KINGS (c. 1000–587 B.C.)

List of Kings		Period	Biblical Events
1 The united kingdom (c. 1000–926 B.C.)			
Saul c. 1020–1004			Battles with Philistines
David c. 1004– 998 (King of Judah)			Capture of Jerusalem
c. 998– 965 (King of all Israel)			
Solomon c. 965– 926			Construction of temple. Building "store-cities" and "chariot-cities" Ship-building at Ezion-Geber

List of Kings				Period	Biblical Events
2 The divided kingdom. 926–721 B.C.					
Israel		Judah			
Jeroboam I	926–907	Rehoboam	926–910	c. 926	Division of the kingdom
				c. 922	Sheshonk raids Israel and Judah
Nadab	907–906	Abijam	910–908		
Baasha	906–883	Asa	908–872		
Elah	883–882				
Zimri	882				
Omri	882–871			c. 880	Omri founds Samaria
Ahab	871–852	Jehoshaphat	872–852		Ahab's battles against Damascus
Ahaziah	852–851	Jehoram	852–845		
Jehoram	851–845	Ahaziah	845–844		Moabites revolt against Israel
Jehu	845–818	Athaliah	845–839		Jehu destroys the House of Ahab
Jehoahaz	818–802	Jehoash	839–800		
Jehoash	802–787	Amaziah	800–785		
Jeroboam II	787–747	Uzziah (Azariah)	785–747		
Zachariah	747	Jotham			
Shallum	746	(Regent and King)	758–743		
Menahem	746–737	Ahaz	742–725	734	Tiglath-pileser (Pul) conquers Isr
Pekahiah	736–735				
Pekah	734–733			733–732	Tiglath-pileser captures Damascus Northern Israel, Transjordan
Hoshea	732–724	Hezekiah	725–697	732	Tiglath-pileser sets Hoshea on the t Shalmaneser defeats Hoshea
				724–Feb. 721	Assyrians besiege Samaria
				721	Fall of Samaria; 27,290 deported

List of Kings		Period	Biblical Events
3 THE SOUTHERN KINGDOM OF JUDAH: 725–587 B.C.			
Hezekiah	725–697	711	Sargon's Tartan conquers Ashdod
		701	Sennacherib besieges Hezekiah Tribute from Jerusalem Tirhakah advances
Manasseh	696–642		Manasseh captured by Assyrians
Amon	641–640	663	Ashurbanipal captures Thebes
Josiah	639–609	612	Fall of Nineveh
		609	Josiah killed in battle against Pharaoh Necho
Jehoahaz	609		
Jehoiakim	608–598	605	Battle of Carchemish
		605	Nebuchadnezzar before Jerusalem
		598	King Jehoiakim rebels against Ba
Jehoiachin	598	598	Nebuchadnezzar conquers Jerusale for the first time First deportation to Babylon
Zedekiah	598–587	589–587	Nebuchadnezzar conquers Jerusale for the second time
		587	Fall and destruction of Jerusalem Second deportation to Babylon

Bible Reference	Ancient East
Samuel 13:1–14, 46; 17; 31 I Samuel 5:7 Kings 6:1 ff. Kings 9:26	Assyrian kingdom: *c.* 1000–612 King Hiram of Tyre
Kings 12 Kings 14:25	Egypt: Pharaoh Sheshonk I (Shishak) founder of the 22nd dynasty: from *c.* 935
Kings 16:24 Kings 20 II Kings 1:1; 3:4 ff. II Kings 9:10	Mesopotamia: King Shalmaneser III of Assyria: 859–824 853: Invasion of Syria. Battle of Karkar (Ahab takes part) Memorial stela of King Mesha of Moab 841: Jehu pays tribute to Shalmaneser III
II Kings 15–16 II Kings 15:29 II Kings 15:30 II Kings 17:3 II Kings 17:5–18, 9–12	Tiglath-pileser III of Assyria 745–727; Founder of the world-wide Assyrian Empire Tiglath-pileser invades 733–32: Israel and Judah become tributary states King Shalmaneser V of Assyria, 727–722: reduces Israel in size after rebellion King Sargon II of Assyria, 722–705
Isaiah 20:1 II Kings 18:13–19, 36 Isaiah 37:9 II Chronicles 33:11 Nahum 3:8–10 Nahum 2:2 ff. II Kings 23:29 Jeremiah 46:1–12 Daniel 1:1–2 II Kings 24:1 II Kings 24:10–13 II Kings 24:14–16 II Kings 25:1–10 Jeremiah 39:1–14; 52 II Kings 25:11	Mesopotamia: Sargon II of Assyria: 722–705; Merodachbaladan of Babylon: 721–709 Sennacherib of Assyria: 705–681 Egypt: Pharaoh Taharka: *c.* 689–663 (Ethiopian dynasty) Esarhaddon of Assyria: 681–669: conquers Lower Egypt *c.* 670 Ashurbanipal of Assyria: 669–626: conquers Thebes 663 Medes and Neo-Babylonians conquer Ashur: 614 End of the Assyrian Empire: 612; Medes and Neo-Babylonians conquer Nineveh Neo-Babylonian Empire: 612–539 Egypt: Pharaoh Necho II: 609–597 King Nebuchadnezzar II of Babylon: 605–562. Victory over Necho at Carchemish Nebuchadnezzar occupies Syria, Palestine: Judah becomes a tributary state 604: Nebuchadnezzar conquers Askelon Exile in Babylon: 587–538

FROM THE EXILE TO THE KINGDOM OF THE MACCABEES (587–163 B. C.)

Period	Biblical Events	Bible Reference	Ancient East
from 587 538	Exile in Babylon Edict of Cyrus Return of the Jews to Jerusalem	Psalm 137 Ezra Nehemiah	Persian Empire: Cyrus unites the Medes and Persians: 549, conquers Lydia: 546 and Babylon: 539 (ruled by Nabonidus and the crown prince Belshazzar)
520–516	Reconstruction of the temple under Zerubbabel		Cambyses: 530–522, conquers Egypt: 525. Darius I: 522–486, campaign against Greece, defeat at Marathon: 490. Xerxes I: 486–465, campaign against Greece, battle at Thermopylae, defeat at Salamis: 480
458	Return of Ezra		
445	Return of Nehemiah		Artaxerxes I: 465–424
			Hellenistic period: Alexander the Great: 336–323, conquers the Persian Empire 332: Palestine becomes a Greek province
			Kingdoms of the Diadochi: Palestine under Egyptian rule (Ptolemies)
168	Antiochus suppresses the Jewish faith	I and II Maccabees	198: Palestine transferred to Syria (Seleucids) Antiochus III, the Great; 223–187 Antiochus IV, Epiphanes: 175–163
167	Revolt of the Maccabees		
166–160	Judas Maccabaeus		
160–142	Jonathan		
142–134	Simon		140: Beginning of the Hasmonean dynasty with Simon
			63: Pompey conquers Jerusalem, start of Roman rule over Palestine
			48–47: Julius Caesar in Egypt
			47: Julius Caesar appoints Antipater, the Edomite, as procurator of Judaea.

JESUS AND THE AGE OF THE APOSTLES

Period	Biblical Events	Bible Reference	Palestine	Roman Empire
7 B. C.	Birth of Jesus	The books of the New Testament	Herod the Great, King of Judaea: 40–4 B. C. 4 B. C.–A. D. 6: Archelaus (Tetrarch of Judaea, Samaria) 4 B. C.–A. D. 39: Herod Antipas (Tetrarch of Galilee, Peraea) From A. D. 6: Roman governors in Judaea.	Augustus 31 B. C.–A. D. 14 Tiberius 14–37
A. D. 28	John the Baptist The works of Jesus Crucifixion of Jesus		26–36: Pontius Pilate, Governor of Judaea	
32/33	Paul's conversion on the road to Damascus			37–41: Caligula
44	Peter's imprisonment			41–54: Claudius
50–52	Paul visits Greece			
52–55	Paul visits Ephesus			
56	Paul taken prisoner in Jerusalem			54–68: Nero 64: Great fire of Rome, first
58–59	Paul journeys to Rome; Paul is imprisoned in Rome		66–70: first Jewish revolt against Rome 70: Titus destroys Jerusalem and the temple 132–135: second Jewish revolt against Rome	persecution of Christians 69–79 Vespasian 79–81: Titus 117–138: Hadrian

Bibliography

Adams, J. M. K., *Ancient Records and the Bible* (1946)
Albright, W. F., *From the Stone Age to Christianity* (1946)
—, *Archaeology and the Religion of Israel* (1953)
—, *Archaeology of Palestine* (1954)
Andrae, W., *Das wiedererstandene Assur* (1938)
Avi Yonah, M. and Kraeling, E. G. *Our Living Bible* (1962)

Barrois, A. G., *Manuel d'archéologie biblique I/II* (1939/53)
Benzinger, I., *Hebräische Archäologie* (1927)
Bittel, K., *Die Ruinen von Bogazköy* (1937)
Breasted, J. H., *Ancient Records of Egypt* (1907)
—, *The Dawn of Conscience* (1934)
—, *History of Egypt* (1950)
Bruin, P., Giegel, P., *Welteroberer Paulus* (1959)

Cermont-Ganneau C. S., *La Stèle de Mésa* (1887)
Childe, V. G., *New Light on the most Ancient East* (1952)
Contenau, G., *L'Antiquité orientale* in *Histoire Générale de l'Art I*, S. 35–65 (1950)
—, *Manuel d'Archéologie orientale* (1927–47)
Crowfoot, J. W., *The Buildings at Samaria* (1942)

Davis, J. D., *Dictionary of the Bible* (1953)

Finegan, J., *Light from the Ancient Past* (1954)

Glueck, N., *The other Side of the Jordan* (1940)
—, *The River Jordan* (1946)
Götze, A., *Hethiter, Churritter und Assyrer* (1936)
Gressmann, H., *Altorientalische Bilder zum Alten Testament* (1927)
Grollenberg, L. H., *Atlas of the Bible* (1957)

Huyghe, R., (ed.) *L'art et l'homme I* (1959)

Jacob, E., *Ras Shamra-Ugarit et l'Ancient Testament* (in *Cahiers d'Archéologie Biblique* No. 12) (1960)
Jeremias, J., *Die Wiederentdeckung von Bethesda*
Jirku, A., *Die Welt der Bibel* (1960)

Koldewey, R., *Das wiedererstehende Babylon* (1925)
—, *Das Ischtar-Tor in Babylon* (1918)
—, Wetzel, Fr., *Die Königsburg von Babylon* (1931)
Kramer, S. N., *From the Tablets of Sumer* (1956)

Layard, A. H., *Discoveries in the Ruins of Nineveh and Babylon* (1853)
—, *Nineveh and its Remains* (1849)
Lenzen, H. *Die Sumerer* (1948)
Lepsius, C. R., *Denkmäler aus Ägypten und Äthiopien* (1849/56)
Lexikon zur Bibel, (ed.) F. Rienecker (1960)
Loud, G., *Megiddo Ivories* (1939)
—, *Megiddo II* (1948)
Lüpsen, F., *Palästina* (1961)

Macalister, R. A. S., *A Century of Excavations in Palestine* (1925)
Mader, E., *Mambre* (1957)
Mallowan, M. E. L., *Twenty-five Years of Mesopotamian Discovery* (1958)
Malraux, A., *Le musée imaginaire de la sculpture mondiale* (1953)
Mati, F., *Kreta, Mykene, Troja* (1956)

Metzger, H., *Les routes de Saint Paul* (in *Cahiers d'Archéologie Biblique*) (1956)
Meyer, G. R., *Staatl. Museen zu Berlin. Durch vier Jahrtausende altvorderasiatische Kultur* (1956)
Miller, M. S. and J. L., *Plants of Bible Life* (1944)
—, *Harpers Bible Dictionary* (1952)
Montet, P., *L'Egypte et la Bible* (in *Cahiers d'Archéologie Biblique*) (1960)
Moortgat, A., *Altvorderasiatische Malerei* (1959)

Olmstead, A. T., *A History of Assyria* (1923)
Osten, H. H. v. d., *Die Welt der Perser* (1956)
Otto, E., *Ägypten, Der Weg des Pharaonenreiches* (1953)
Otto, W., (ed.) *Handbuch der Archäologie I* (1939)

Parrot, A., *Sumer* (1960)
—, *Assur* (1961)
—, *Cahiers d'Archéologie Biblique*, Neuchâtel (1955–62): *Déluge et Arche de Noé / La Tour de Babel / Ninive et l'Ancient Testament / Le Temple de Jérusalem / Abraham et son temps / Samarie, capitale du Royaume d'Israel / Babylone et l'Ancient Testament / Le musée de Louvre et la Bible*
—, *Mission Archéologique de Mari I-III*, (1956, 58, 59)
Pillis, S. A., *The Antiquity of Iraq* (1956)
Posner, G., *Dictionary of Egyptian Civilization* (1963)
Pritchard, J. B., *The Ancient Near East in Pictures* (1954)

Ricciotti, G., *Storia d'Israele* (1949)
Riemenschneider, M., *Die Welt der Hethiter* (1961)
Rothenberg, B., *God's Wilderness* (1961)
—, *Ancient Copper Industries in the Western Arabah, Palestine Exploration Quarterly*, London (1962)
Rowe, A., *The Topography and the History of Beth-Shan* (1930)
—, *The Four Canaanite Temples of Beth-Shan I* (1940)
Rowley, H. H., *The Old Testament and Modern Study* (1952)

Schaeffer, C. F. A., *Ugaritica I-II* (1939/1949)
Schmöckel, H., *Ur, Assur und Babylon* (1957)
Schöne, G., *Jerusalem* (1961)
Schubert, K., *Israel, Staat der Hoffnung* (1960)
Stéve, M.-J., *Sur les chemins de la Bible* (1961)

Unger E., *Die Reliefs Tiglatpilesers III. aus Nimrud* (1917)
—, *Assyrische und babylonische Kunst* (1927)

Vaux, R. de, *Ancient Israel* (1961)

Watzinger, C., *Denkmäler Palästinas I-II* (1933/35)
The Westminster Historical Atlas to the Bible (1953)
Wetzel, Fr., *Assur und Babylon* (1949)
Wiseman, D. J., *Illustrations from Biblical Archaeology* (1958)
Wolf, W., *Die Welt der Ägypter* (1954)
Woolley, L., *Ur of the Chaldees* (1929)
—, *Excavations at Ur* (1954)
—, *History unearthed* (1958)
Wreszinski, *Atlas zur ägyptischen Kulturgeschichte I-II* (1923/40)
Wright, G. E., *Biblical Archaeology* (1959)
—, (ed.) *The Bible and the Ancient Near East* (Essays in Honor of W. F. Albright) (1961)
For further references see Keller, W., *The Bible as History*. (1962)

337

Index of Bible References _(Numbers in heavy print refer to the acknowledgements of illustrations)_

OLD TESTAMENT

NEW TESTAMENT

Acknowledgements of Illustrations with Commentary

13 Tell Nimrud (biblical Calah, Assyrian Kalchu), a capital of Assyria and one of the four cities built by Nimrod (Genesis 10:10), 18 miles south-east of Nineveh. British excavation: Austin Henry Layard, 1845–51; M. E. L. Mallowan, 1949. *(Drawing by A. H. Layard in 'Monuments of Nineveh', fig. 98)*

16 The Tigris at Jebel Khanuke below Ashur *(After Groeber, Palestine, Arabia and Syria, 1925)*

16 Impression of a cylinder-seal: called "The Temptation". Mesopotamian mid-third millennium B. C. British Museum. *(Photo: Courtesy of the Trustees of the British Museum)*

17 Flood layer at Ur. Part of Sir Leonard Woolley's excavations, 1929. *(Photo: Arthaud-Mikaël Audrain)*

18 Ruins of the ziggurat at Aqar-Quf (Dur Kurigalzu) west of Baghdad. Kassite period: 14th/13th centuries B. C. *(Photo: Arthaud-Mikaël Audrain)*

19 Impression of a cylinder-seal: priest in front of a ziggurat. Assyrian. From Babylon (Babel). End of 2nd millennium B. C. *(Photo: Courtesy of the Staatliche Museen, Berlin)*

19 Stela depicting a lion hunt. Mesopotamian. Warka (ancient Uruk). Beginning of 3rd millennium. Black basalt. Height 32 inches. Iraq Museum, Baghdad. *(Photo: Courtesy of the Directorate General of Antiquities, Iraq)*

20 Discovery of a winged bull with human head in Tell Nimrud. *(Drawing by A. H. Layard in "Nineveh and its Remains", pl. 2, London, 1849)*

21 The "White Temple" with staircase at Warka (ancient Uruk, Sumerian name for Erech) (Genesis 10:10; Ezra 4:9), 125 miles southeast of Babylon on the left bank of the Euphrates, one of the four cities of Nimrod. Sumerian metropolis, one of the oldest cities in Mesopotamia, city of Gilgamesh. Mesopotamian, latter half of the 4th millennium. German excavation: Jordan 1912–13, 1928–31; Nöldeke, Heinrich 1931–39, Lenzen from 1954. *(Photo by Heinrich Lenzen's expedition)*

22 Vase from Warka (ancient Uruk) with cultic designs (religious procession). Mesopotamian. 4th/3rd millennium B C. Alabaster, height 3¼ ft. Iraq Museum, Baghdad. *(Photo: Courtesy of the Directorate General of Antiquities, Iraq)*

23 Bronze head of a king, probably Sargon I of Accad [Accad: name of (a) town in northern Babylonia —one of the four cities of Nimrod in the Land of Shinar (Genesis 10:10), exact position not yet discovered, possibly ruins at Tell ed-Der near Sippar, (b) a dynasty with Sargon (probable reign 2467–2412 B. C.) as its first king]. From Nineveh. Latter half of the 3rd millennium B. C. Height 12 inches. Iraq Museum, Baghdad. *(Photo; Courtesy of the Directorate General of Antiquities, Iraq)*

24 Stela of Naram-Sin, a king of the Accad dynasty, grandson of Sargon (c. 2300 B.C.). The king rests his foot on his dead opponent. Accadian. From Susa, second half of the 3rd millennium B. C. Rose-coloured sandstone, height 6¼ ft. Discovered by Jacques de Morgan, who started the excavations at Susa in 1897. Louvre. *(Photo: Archives Photographiques)*

25 Ur-Nammu stela, detail. Neo-Sumerian. From Ur. 22nd century B. C. Total height of the stela: 10 ft. Philadelphia University Museum. *(Photo: Courtesy of the Philadelphia University Museum)*

27 Statuette of a man carrying a sacrificial lamb. Babylonian. From Mari (Tell Hariri) on the right bank of the middle Euphrates. Beginning of the second millenium B. C., gypsum, height 9 inches. French excavation under André Parrot, Paris, since 1933. Aleppo Museum. *(Photo: Courtesy of the Directorate General of Antiquities, North Syria.)*

29 Lower Euphrates. *(Photo: Arthaud-Mikaël Audrain)*

30 Statuettes from the cache found in the temple of Abu. Mesopotamian. From Tell Asmar (ancient Eshnunua), ruins in the region of the river Dyala, an eastern tributary of the Tigris. This region contains many ruins. First half of 3rd millennium. American excavation under H. Frankfort, 1930–36. Iraq Museum, Baghdad; Oriental Institute of the University of Chicago. *(Photo: Courtesy of the Oriental Institute, Chicago)*

31 The ziggurat of Ur with the ruins of the town (foreground). Built by Ur-Nammu, founder of the 3rd dynasty of Ur, 22nd century B. C. Ur: Tel al Muqayyar (arab.: "Mound of Bitumen"), today lies app. 9½ miles west of the Euphrates near the Persian Gulf (see Map I). Anglo-American excavation under Sir Leonard Woolley 1922 to 1934. *(Photo: Courtesy of the Trustees of the British Museum)*

32 Nomads with their herds at the old fountain at Haran on the River Balikh (an eastern tributary of the middle Euphrates), c. 280 NNE of Damascus. Mentioned in letters to the palace at Mari and in the Bible (II Kings 19:12; Ezekiel 23:23). In the background ruins of the medieval castle of Qal'at (the Temple of the Moon is said to be situated under its foundations). *(Photo: Courtesy of Seton Lloyd)*

33 Statuette bearing the inscription: "Ishtup-Ilum, shakkanaku (governor) of Mari". Babylonian. From the palace of Mari, hall 65. Beginning of the 2nd millennium B.C. Black stone, height 4¾ ft. Aleppo Museum. *(Photo: Courtesy of the Dir. Gen. of Antiquities, North Syria)*

34 Aerial photograph of the palace of Mari. Excavation by A. Parrot at Tell Hariri on the middle Euphrates (so far the largest royal residence of the 2nd millennium found in the East, more than 6 acres). *(Photo: Aviation Française du Levant)*

36 Nomads with their herds at a new water-hole in the Syrian-Arabian desert. *(Photo: Courtesy L. Grollenberg O.P., Nijmegen)*

37 Scene on the upper reaches of the Jordan. Source on Mt Hermon, "Mountain of Snow" (7400 ft. in the SE corner of Anti-Lebanon). *(Photo:Israel Government Tourist Office, London)*

38 Shechem (Tell Balata) 31 miles north of Jerusalem in the heart of Samaria. The massive ruins of the rectangular temple of Baal-Berith at the highest point of the hill. The ramparts in the foreground formed part of the defences which at one time surrounded the whole town. German excavation: E. Sellin, 1913/14. *(Photo: Lee C. Ellenberger, courtesy of the Drew-McCormick Archaeological Expedition)*

343

39 Painted potsherd bearing the profile of a Canaanite. From Beth-Shan (Tell el-Husn near Beisan, *c.* 16 miles south of the sea of Galilee). 16th/15th centuries B.C. Aleppo Museum. *(Photo: Arthaud-Mikaël Audrain)*

40 Landscape in the Negeb (in southern Palestine). *(Photo: Hed Wimmer, Karlsruhe)*

42 Starving bedouin leads three oxen in a procession bringing gifts for Ukh-hotep. Meir (*c.* 31 miles south of Tell el-Amarna), south wall, time of Sesostris I (1971–1928 B.C.), Middle Kingdom. *(Photo: Courtesy of the Metropolitan Museum of Art, New York)*

42/43 "Step-pyramid" of Djoser at Saqqara. View from the Nile delta. Egypt's earliest stone monument built by the first pharaoh of the 3rd dynasty (beginning of the Old Kingdom) *c.* 2700 B.C. Saqqara: the burial ground of Memphis, one of the main cities of Lower Egypt, 13 miles south of Cairo on the left bank of the Nile, has now disappeared. *(Photo: Courtesy L. Grollenberg O.P.)*

45 Semite caravan. Painting on stucco (reproduction), from the tomb of Khnumhotep in Beni Hasan, situated on the Nile north of Tell el-Amarna. Dates back to the time of Sesostris II (*c.* 1897–1879 B.C.), 12th dynasty. *(After C.R.Lepsius, Denkmäler aus Aegypten und Aethiopien, 1849–59. Volume 2, pl.133)*

46 Pharaoh Sesostris III (*c.* 1878–43 B.C.), 12th dynasty. Red granite. Cairo Museum. *(Museum photograph)*

47 Aerial photograph of the Jordan valley. *(Photo: Thames and Hudson Archives)*

48 Nomads at a well near Beersheba (located in the deep south of Judah in the desert) (Genesis 21:22 ff.), 25 miles SW of Hebron. *(Photo: Hed Wimmer, Karlsruhe)*

49 Tamarisk in full bloom. *(Photo: Paul Popper, London)*

50 Fragment of a stela of Untash-Huban, King of Elam (the highlands east of Babylon with Susa as capital). Detail. From Susa, *c.* 1250 B.C. Louvre. *(Photo: Archives Photographiques)*

50 Bronze lion with stone commemoration tablet. Dedicated by the early Hurrian ruler Tishari of Urkish. [Hurrians: probably the Horites of the Bible, migrants into northern Mesopotamia; later Mitanni kingdom (*c.* 1500–1370 B.C.) bears strong resemblance to

Hurrians]. Accadian art, second half of the 3rd millennium B.C. Height 5 inches, length of the sides of the small stone tablet 4^1/$_2$ inches. Louvre. *(Photo: Museum)*

51 The Dead Sea with the peninsula of el-Lisan. *(Photo: Government Press Office, Jerusalem, Israel)*

52 Remarkable salt formation on the high sloping banks of the Dead Sea, called "Lot's Wife". *(Photo: Ecole Biblique et Archéologique Française, Jerusalem)*

53 Extracting salt from the Dead Sea near Sodom. *(After K.Schubert, Israel, Staat der Hoffnung, 1957)*

53 Ancient terebinth near Hebron. *(Photo: Palestine Exploration Fund)*

54 Site of ancient Mamre. Abraham's well in the south-west corner, pre-Herodian pavement in the foreground. On the left, a hole in the pavement, where presumably a terebinth once stood, bears witness to a date as late as the time of the Emperor Constantine and his successors. Excavation by Fr.E.Mader, 1927. *(After E. Mader, Mambre, 1957, illustration 101)*

54 Country woman drawing water at an ancient well with a covering stone. *(Photo: Willem van der Poll, Amsterdam)*

55 Household gods (teraphim) from Nuzu (present-day Yorgan-Tepe near Kirkuk). Excavation: American School of Oriental Research and Harvard University, under E. Chiera 1925/28. *(Photo: Courtesy of Prof. G. E. Wright)*

55 Quffa on the Euphrates. Quffa: vessel made from plaited reeds and caulked with pitch still used for crossing rivers. *(Photo: Ewing Galloway, New York)*

56 Assyrian coracle covered with animal hides. Detail from a relief in the palace of Sennacherib at Nineveh, dating from around 700 B.C. British Museum. *(Photo: Courtesy of the Trustees of the British Museum)*

57 Egyptian high official. Time of Amenophis III (*c.* 1413–1377 B.C.), 18th dyn. Limestone. Birmingham Museum.*(Photo:Courtesy ofBirmingham Museum and Art Gallery)*

59 Hyksos: Name of a group of peoples meaning "rulers of foreign lands" which ruled Egypt about 1700–1580. Their capital was Avaris in the NE of the Nile delta. Under Ramesses II this moved to Pi-Ramesses-Meri-Amon, the biblical "treasure city Raamses" (Exodus 1:11).

60 Syrians offering tribute to Pharaoh

Thutmose IV (predecessor of Amenophis III). Among the gifts: leather quivers, an oil horn, goblets in the form of griffins' heads, gold vases and a naked child. Fragment of a wall-painting from Thebes [No-Amon of the Bible, Homer's "city of a hundred gates", capital of Upper Egypt and after the expulsion of the Hyksos capital of the whole kingdom. Ruins on the eastern bank of the Nile near the villages of Karnak and Luxor. Burial city on the west bank (among others the Valley of Kings, the burial temple of Deir el-Bahri and the temple palace of Medinet Habu)]. Tomb of Sibek-hotep. *(Photo: Courtesy of the Trustees o the British Museum)*

61 Sphinx and pyramids at Giza. The large pyramids were built during the Old Kingdom of the 3rd and 6th dynasties (*c.* 2700–2200 B.C.). Right: pyramid of Khafre (height 472 ft., length of the sides 710 ft.). The largest of the surviving pyramids is that of Cheops, 485 ft. high. It lies to the right just outside the picture. (Khafre: 4th pharaoh of the 4th dynasty, about 2620 B.C., son and second successor of Cheops). *(Photo: Ewing Galloway, New York)*

62 A Shardana in the role of bodyguard to pharaoh. In the Battle of Kadesh against the Hittites (*c.* 1297 B.C.) the Shardana—probably of Sardinian origin—fought as mercenaries on the side of Egypt. Their helmet with two horns and a ball on a stem is typical. The Shardana later joined the coalition of Sea Peoples against the Egyptians. They were defeated around 1190 B.C. by Ramesses III in a sea and land campaign. Detail from a relief on the SW wall of the temple-tomb of Ramesses II (1301–1234 B.C.) at Thebes. *(Photo: Courtesy of the Staatliche Museen, Berlin)*

62 Reconstruction of an Egyptian house at Tell el-Amarna, a village near the ruins of Akhetaton on the Nile. The latter was for a short time the capital of Amenophis IV (Akhnaten) (*c.* 1377–1360 B.C.), 18th dynasty. *(After Seton Lloyd, Art of the Ancient Near East, illustration 240)*

63 Wall-painting depicting a garden with a pond. Tomb of Neb-Amon at Thebes, *c.* 1400 B.C., 18th dynasty. *(Photo: Eileen Tweedy)*

64 Side view of the sarcophagus of Princess Kawit: Milk is being poured from a bottle into a bowl

and offered to the princess. From a limestone relief at Deir el-Bahri. 11th dynasty (*c.* 2135–2000 B.C.). Cairo Museum. *(Photo: Marburg)*

64 Royal bakehouse. Wall-painting on stucco. From the tomb of Ramesses III in the Valley of Kings at Thebes. 20th dynasty. *(After H. Gressmann, Altorientalische Bilder zum Alten Testament, illustration 184)*

65 Pharaoh Seti I (*c.* 1319–1301 B.C.) invests an official with his gold chain of office. Stela of Marmin, guard of the royal harem. From his tomb at Saqqara. 19th dynasty. Louvre. *(Photo: Archives Photographiques)*

66 Amenophis IV (Akhnaten) drives his chariot to the temple. Detail from a relief in the tomb of Merya, Tell el-Amarna. 14th century B.C., 18th dynasty. *(After Davies, Rock Tombs of El-Amarna I, 10)*

67 Ruler sitting at a sacrificial table and servants with sacrificial gifts. Wall-painting on stucco. From a tomb in Saqqara. Old Kingdom. 5th dynasty (*c.* 2500 B.C.). *(After C. R. Lepsius, Denkmäler, Volume II, p. 67)*

68 Servants with flocks of geese. Wall-painting from a tomb at Thebes. 18th dynasty, *c.* 1400 B.C. British Museum. *(Photo: Courtesy of the Trustees of the British Museum)*

68 Geese are prepared for pickling in clay jars. Wall-painting from tomb of Nakht, Thebes, 18th dynasty. *(After Wreszinski, Atlas zur altägyptischen Kulturgeschichte, I, 178)*

69 Scribes record the harvest. Wall-painting from the tomb of Menna, No. 69, at Thebes, *c.* 1420 B.C., 18th dynasty. Reproduction by N. de G. Davies. *(Photo: Courtesy of the Trustees of the British Museum)*

69 Winnowing and measuring of the corn in the presence of the lord of the manor, Nakht. Wall-painting from the tomb of Nakht at Thebes, 18th dynasty. N. de G. Davies, Tomb of Nakht, pl. 20. *(Photo: Courtesy of the Oriental Institute, Chicago)*

70 Painted wooden model of a granary. Tomb of Meket-ra, Middle Kingdom (*c.* 2000–1780 B.C.). *(Photo: Courtesy of the Trustees of the British Museum)*

71 Collecting taxes from defaulters. Limestone relief from the tomb of the vizier Mereruka, chamber A 4, Saqqara, 6th dynasty (*c.* 2400–2200 B.C.). *(Photo: Courtesy of the Oriental Institute, Chicago)*

71 Starving people. Limestone relief from the inner wall of the Temple Way of King Una at Saqqara. 5th dynasty (*c.* 2400 B.C.). *(Photo: Courtesy Service des Antiquités, Cairo)*

72 Harvest scene. Centre: granaries. Above, men carry away fruit, below, baskets full of grapes for the wine-press. Painted limestone relief from the tomb of the vizier Mereruka, Saqqara, 6th dynasty. *(Photo: Courtesy of the Oriental Institute, Chicago)*

73 Syrians and Libyans as petitioners before a royal official. Relief from the tomb of Pharaoh Haremheb (*c.* 1349–1319 B.C.) at Memphis. 18th dynasty. *(Photo: Rijksmuseum van Oudheden, Leiden)*

74 Captives are transported to Egypt, probably Semites. Painted limestone relief from the tomb of Haremheb (see above). Memphis. 18th dynasty. Rijksmuseum van Oudheden, Leiden. *(Photo: Max Hirmer)*

74 Ass laden with a basket of corn. Wall-painting (reproduction) from a tomb at Thebes. Time of Ramesses II (*c.* 1301–1234 B.C.), 19th dynasty. *(H. Gressmann, Altorientalische Bilder zum Alten Testament, illustration 166)*

75 Banquet with dancing-girls and musicians. Wall-painting from the tomb of Neb-Amon, Thebes, 18th dynasty. *(Photo: Courtesy of the Trustees of the British Museum)*

76 Cows and calves with herdsmen in the shallow waters of the Nile delta. [Goshen: part of Egypt, present-day Kesem with the town of Saft el-Henna, to the west of Wadi el-Tumilat, was leased to the Israelites as grazing land (Genesis 45:10; 46:28 ff.)]. Limestone relief in the tomb of Ti at Saqqara, 5th dynasty, mid-3rd millennium B.C. *(Photo: Max Hirmer)*

77/78 "Foreign prince", leader of a Semitic caravan. Detail from the illustration on page 45. Painting on stucco, from the tomb of Prince Khnumhotep at Beni Hasan, age of Sesostris II (*c.* 1897–1879 B.C.), 12th dynasty. *(After C. R. Lepsius, Denkmäler, Volume II, pl. 133)*

79 Driving home herds of oxen. Wall-painting from a tomb at Thebes. 18th dynasty. British Museum. *(Photo: Courtesy of the Trustees of the British Museum)*

80 Measuring a piece of land. Wall-painting from the tomb of Menna, Thebes. 18th dynasty. *(After Wreszinski, Atlas zur ägyptischen Kulturgeschichte I, 232)*

80 Embalming. Above: Corpse on the embalming table, in front of it stands Anubis, below: preparation of the body. From the sarcophagus of Dje-bastit-ef-onkh. Late period (*c.* 1000 B.C.). Pelizaeus Museum, Hildesheim. *(Museum photo)*

81 Group of professional mourning-women and girls. Wall-painting from the tomb of Ramose, a high official of Amenophis IV (Akhnaten) (*c.* 1377–1360 B.C.), Thebes. From a copy by N. de G. Davies. *(Photo: Courtesy of the Trustees of the British Museum)*

82 Egyptian burial procession. Wall-painting from the tomb of the vizier Roi. Beginning of the 19th dynasty (*c.* 1300 B.C.). *(After Wilkinson-Birch, Manners and Customs of the Ancient Egyptians, III, 68)*

83 Gigantic head of Ramesses II (*c.* 1301–1234 B.C.). Memphis. *(Photo: Dr Paul Wolff and Tritschler)*

85 Seti I (*c.* 1319–1301 B.C.). From a relief in the temple of Seti I, NW wall, Abydos, north of Thebes. *(Photo: Max Hirmer)*

86 Relief showing heads of Hittites. [Hittites: Indo-European people from Anatolia, played a significant part in the history of the ancient East, repeatedly named in the Old Testament. Between *c.* 1800 and 1200 B.C. great Hittite empire with capital city Hattusas (Bogazköy, 94 miles east of Ankara). After the collapse of the empire, several late-Hittite city states survived, among others Zinjirli, Carchemish.] Relief, probably a scene from the battle of Kadesh on the Orontes (*c.* 1297 B.C.). Pharaoh Ramesses II against the Hittites, ended with a peace treaty. 19th dynasty. *(Photo: Courtesy of the Staatliche Museen in Berlin)*

87 Hittite war-chariots in battle with Egyptians. Detail from a relief in the temple-tomb of Ramesses II at Thebes. *(Photo: Marburg)*

88 Bronze statuette of a vassal king of the Mitanni kingdom (*c.* 1500–1370 B.C., at times stretching from Nuzu to the Mediterranean, people of Indo-European origin; settlements between the Tigris and Khabur). He wears an Egyptian crown and the Mitannian robe with padded edge. Cairo Museum. *(Photo: Courtesy of the Service des Antiquités, Cairo)*

88 Footstool belonging to Tutankhamen. Wood inlaid with gold, silver and blue faience. Seen from above, it shows Egypt's traditional enemies. From Thebes, *c.* 1350

B. C., 18th dynasty, Cairo Museum. *(Photo: Harry Burton, The Metropolitan Museum of Art, New York)*

89 Slaves working in the fields. Relief from the tomb of Khaemhat at Thebes, 18th dynasty. *(Photo: Audrain—Mission Samivel)*

90 Slaves making bricks. Wall-painting from the tomb of Rekhmire at Thebes. Age of Thutmose III *(c. 1490–1436 B.C.). (Copy after C. R. Lepsius, Denkmäler aus Aegypten und Aethiopien III, 40)*

91 Peasant being beaten for non-payment of taxes. Wall-painting from the tomb of Menena, Thebes, 18th dynasty. *(Photo: Arpag Mekhitarian, Brussels)*

91 In the land of Midian, east of the gulf of Aqabah. *(Photo: Department of Antiquities, Amman)*

92 Massive rock temple of Ramesses II at Abu Simbel. The four figures of the pharaoh are each 66 ft. high. The temple, hewn 208 ft. into the rock is sacred to Amon, Re and Ptah and to the deified Ramesses II. 19th dynasty. *(Photo: Marburg)*

93 Bricks made from Nile clay and pieces of straw, stamped with the name and title of Ramesses II. Unfired clay, 15 inches in length. British Museum. *(Photo: Courtesy of the Trustees of the British Museum)*

94 Lake Maruit. *(Photo: Audrain—Mission Samivel)*

95/96 Pharaoh Tutankhamen in his war-chariot leads his troops against the Asians. On the right of the picture lie broken chariots and dying soldiers; Egyptian troops collect heads and hands. Front of chest No. 21 from the tomb of Tutankhamen at Thebes. Wood covered with plaster, height 18 inches. 18th dynasty, c. 1350 B.C. Cairo Museum. *(Photo: F.L.Kenett: copyright George Rainbird Ltd.)*

97 Chest from the tomb of Tutankhamen. Detail from the side depicting chariots, each manned by two soldiers. Thebes *(c. 1350 B.C.).* Wood covered with plaster and painted. *(Photo: Cairo Museum)*

97 Egyptian infantry. Two wooden models depict Nubian archers (right) and Egyptians with spears and shields. 40 soldiers to each board. From the tomb of the provincial governor Mesehti at Asjut. First intermediate period *(c. 2260–2040 B.C.). (Photo: Archives Photographiques)*

98 Women and girls with timbrels and castanets. Limestone relief from the tomb of Khai. 18th or 19th dyn. Height 16 inches. *(Photo: Courtesy*

of the Oriental Institute, Chicago)*

99 Ain Hawara, biblical Marah: the first encampment after the passage though the Red Sea. Ancient water-hole, today covered with sand and surrounded by a few date palms. *(Photo: Dr B. Rothenberg, God's Wilderness, London 1961)*

100 Oasis in Wadi Garandel, probably the biblical Elim, the second resting-place on the Exodus. *(Photo: Archives, Tel Aviv)*

101 Wooden model of an Egyptian slaughterhouse. In the upper storeys meat is hung out to dry. From the tomb of chancellor Mekti-re, at Qurneh near Thebes. 11th dynasty *(c. 2000 B.C.). (Photo: Courtesy of the Metropolitan Museum of Art, New York)*

101 Women baking bread. Wooden model from a tomb of the 11th/12th dynasties. Royal Scottish Museum, Edinburgh. *(Photo: Courtesy of the Scottish Museum)*

102 Catching quails. Wall-painting on stucco from a tomb at Thebes, 18th dynasty *(c. 1546–1319 B.C.).* Egyptian Museum, Berlin. *(Photo: Courtesy of the Staatliche Museen, Berlin)*

103 View of the chain of mountains which includes Jebel Musa, 7293 ft. high, according to Christian tradition the mountain (Sinai) of the commandments. *(Photo: Radio Times Hulton Picture Library)*

104/105 View from the peak of Jebel Musa. *(Photo: Dr Beno Rothenberg, God's Wilderness London 1961)*

106 Bronze statuette of Apis, the bull-god of Memphis. 4th millennium B.C. *(Photo: Courtesy of the Trustees of the British Museum)*

107 Fishing in Egypt. Painted limestone relief from the tomb of Mereruka at Saqqara, 6th dynasty *(c. 2400–2200 B.C.). (Photo: Courtesy of the Oriental Institute, Chicago)*

107 Women returning from market. Painted limestone relief from the tomb of Ti at Saqqara, middle of 5th dynasty *(c. 2500 B.C.). (Photo: Courtesy of the Oriental Institute, Chicago)*

108 Egyptian attack on a fortified Syrian town. Limestone relief from Medinet Habu (near Thebes). Age of Ramesses III, 20th dynasty. Height 14 ft. *(Photo: Courtesy of the Oriental Institute, Chicago)*

110 Oasis at Ain Qudeirat (with Ain Qedeis, 5 miles away, the Kadesh-barnea of the Bible), the largest spring in the fertile area of southern Palestine. Most important resting-place on the journey through the

desert. *(Photo: Middle East Archives, Tel Aviv)*

111 Roman road east of Wadi La'aban, built over the biblical "kings high way". *(Photo: The Royal Air Force, 1938. Courtesy of Dr Nelson Glueck)*

112 The River Arnon close to its entry into the Dead Sea. Its deep canyon cuts far into the highlands east of the Dead Sea, as does that of the "stream Zared". *(Photo: Courtesy P. J. Cools O.P.)*

113/114 Harvest scenes and field work in Egypt. Painted limestone relief from the tomb of the vizier and town governor of Memphis, Mereruka, at Saqqara. Chamber A13, east wall. 6th dynasty, c.2360 B.C. *(From a painting by Vcerold Strekalowsky. Courtesy of the Oriental Institute, Chicago)*

115 Two statues from Amman (Transjordan), probably depicting kings. Both made of soft limestone. Found in the citadel at Amman. Age of the Israelite kings. *(Photo: Department of Antiquities, Amman)*

116 Aerial photograph of the Jordan valley and the mountainous district of Judah, taken in 1930. *(Photo: The Times)*

119 Bas-relief of a Semite with arms tied behind his back, over a list of conquered countries. Luxor, temple of Ramesses II. *(Photo: K. Lange)*

122 View across the plain of Jericho from Transjordan towards the west. *(Photo: Radio Times Hulton Picture Library)*

123 Lower reaches of the River Jordan near its entry into the Dead Sea. View from the Allenby Bridge, near Jericho. *(Photo: Ewing Galloway, New York)*

124 Egyptian circumcision ceremony. In ancient Egypt every male was circumcised. The operation was performed on young boys, probably with a flint knife – compare Exodus 4:25 –, by a "servant of Ka" (otherwise a burial priest), who seems to take the place of a doctor. Here the young men are depicted without the usual forelock worn by boys. Relief from the tomb of Ankh-mar-Hor near Saqqara, 6th dynasty, Old Kingdom. *(Photo: Courtesy of the Oriental Institute, Chicago)*

125 View towards the "Mountain of Temptation" through the deep shaft dug into Tell es-Sultan during the excavation of Jericho. German excavation: E. Sellin, C. Watzinger 1907/09; British excavation: J. Garstang 1930, Kathleen M. Kenyon

since 1953. *(Photo: V. Böckstiegel, F. Lüpsen)*

126 Ain es-Sultan, a spring near Jericho with date-palms which were already a characteristic of the "city of palm trees" in biblical times. *(Photo: Willem van der Poll, Amsterdam)*

127 An Assyrian king places his foot on the back of a vanquished foe. Louvre, Paris. *(After A. Parrot, Le Musée du Louvre et la Bible, fig. 7)*

127 The young Amenophis II on the lap of his nurse, his feet resting on the heads of captured enemies. *(c. 1430 B.C.)*, 18th dynasty. *(After J. Wilkinson, op. cit.)*

128 Squatting stone figure, probably a god (Baal?), with sacrificial libation bowl and stelae. From a small Canaanite sanctuary at Hazor (Tell el-Qeda, north of the sea of Galilee). 13th century B.C. *(Photo: Richard Lannoy)*

129 Statue of Pharaoh Merneptah with "nemes", the royal headdress *(c. 1235–1227 B.C.)*, 19th dynasty. Granite. From Qurneh near Thebes. Cairo Museum. *(Photo: Courtesy of the Metropolitan Museum of Art, New York)*

130 The name "Israel" written in ancient Egyptian script. Excerpt from column 27 on the Merneptah stela (see following). Cairo Museum. *(Photo: Archives Photographiques)*

131 Granite stela of Pharaoh Merneptah *(c. 1235–1227 B.C.)*, relating his victories over the Libyans. In column 27 the word Israel is mentioned for the only time in Egyptian documents. From the temple-tomb of Merneptah at Thebes. Gezer (Geser) in Tell ed-Djezer (6 miles east of Ekron), royal Canaanite city (Joshua 12:12). Solomon received Gezer from the pharaoh as part of a dowry (I Kings 9:16). Excavation by Macalister 1902/05; 1907/09. Cairo Museum. *(Photo: Archives Photographiques)*

132 The god Ningirsu, a club in his hand, imprisons enemy captives in a net. Detail from the "Stela of the Vultures". Sumerian. Memorial to Eannatum, King of Lagash, in honour of the victory over Umma, a rival Sumerian city. Ningirsu, god of fertility, was worshipped in Lagash. His emblem: lion-headed eagle. First half of the 3rd millennium B.C. From Tello (ancient Lagash), a Sumerian city *c.* 43 miles NNE of Ur. Interrupted French excavations 1877–1933: Sarzec, Cros, Genouillac, Parrot. *(Photo: Archives Photographiques)*

133 Terracotta figures of Canaanite fertility goddesses. Found in Israelite and Canaanite layers throughout Palestine. Hair styles and lotus flowers illustrate Egyptian influence. *(Photo: Palestine Exploration Fund)*

133 Statuette of a Canaanite god, probably Baal, wearing a high crown (similar to that of Upper Egypt). Bronze. Head and crown are gilded, body silver-plated, gold ring on right arm. From Minet el-Beida, near Ras Shamra (ancient Ugarit). 15th/14th century B.C. Louvre. *(Photo: Maurice Chuzeville)*

135 Ramesses II conquers Askelon (massive ruins on the Mediterranean 31 miles SSW of Tel Aviv; one of the five cities of the Philistines, site of Samson's feat of strength (Judges 14:19), birthplace of Herod). Relief in the temple of Amon at Karnak. 19th dynasty, Ramesses II. *(c. 1301–1234 B.C.)*. *(Photo: Courtesy of the Oriental Institute, Chicago)*

136 Ruins of a large villa dating from the time of the judges at Bethel, about 11 miles north of Jerusalem. Site of Jacob's dream (Genesis 28:12). *(Photo: Courtesy of Prof. G. E. Wright)*

137 Gold salver showing a hunting scene: Canaanite prince hunting wild bulls from his chariot. From Ras Shamra (ancient Ugarit) on the coast of North Syria, one of the largest Mediterranean metropoli during the 2nd millennium B.C. French excavation under C. F. A. Schaeffer since 1929. 8 inches diameter. Louvre, Paris. *(Photo: Archives Photographiques)*

138 Mount Tabor (Jebel et-Tor), 5½ miles ESE of Nazareth in the NE corner of the Plain of Jezreel. *(Photo: Middle East Archives, Tel Aviv)*

139 Scene at the court of a king (or prince). Carved ivory tablet, 8 inches in length. From Megiddo, layer VII A. Between 1350–1150 (estimation of the excavator G. Loud). Palestine Archaeological Museum, Jordan. *(Museum photo)*

140 A battle by Ashurbanipal against the Arabs, who are fleeing on camels. Alabaster limestone. 7th century B.C. Assyrian. From Nineveh, north palace (discovered by Hormuzd Rassam, 1854, who on behalf of Britain dug at most of the Assyrian and Babylonian sites). British Museum. *(Photo: Courtesy of the Trustees of the British Museum)*

141 Measuring the dew. Gideon's experience repeated in a scientific experiment by Dr Duvdevani in Israel. On the right his daughter Jael. *(Photo: Courtesy of Dr S. Duvdevani)*

142 An Egyptian leads two chained captives (Philistines) to Ramesses III, pharaoh of the 20th dynasty *(c. 1195–1164)*. Detail from a relief at Medinet Habu (temple-palace in west Thebes. The lay-out planned by Ramesses III included temple-tomb, palace and fort. The walls were decorated with reliefs showing the pharaoh's deeds in battle, including the victorious wars waged on land and sea against the Sea Peoples. From the outer north wall, height *c.* 4 ft. *(Photo: Courtesy of the Oriental Institute, Chicago)*

143 Sea battle between the Egyptians and the allied Sea Peoples, including the Philistines. Drawn from a relief in the temple of Ramesses III at Medinet Habu. 20th dynasty. Nekbet: vulture-goddess of Upper Egypt, later tutelary goddess of the whole south. *(After Champollion, Monuments de l'Egypte et la Nubie)*

144 Detail from the above sea battle in the original. An Egyptian ship engages one of the Philistine vessels. The latter are recognised by their feathered helmets. *(Photo: Courtesy of the Oriental Institute, Chicago)*

145 Ox-drawn carts of the Philistines. Relief from the temple of Ramesses III at Medinet Habu. Detail from the land battle between the Egyptians and the combined Sea Peoples. *(Photo: Courtesy o the Oriental Institute, Chicago)*

145 Philistine clay jar with characteristic spiral and bird designs. Redbrown on a rose background. From Beth-Shemesh (Tell Rumeilah), 16 miles west of Jerusalem. (The Philistines sent the captured Ark of the Covenant back to Beth-Shemesh from Ekron (I Samuel 6:9 ff.). *c.* 1150–1000 B.C. *(Photo: Palestine Archaeological Museum, Jordan)*

147 Painted potsherd depicting a king. Black and red colouring on a rose background. From Ramat Rahel, layer V. (Ramat Rahel: 2½ miles south of Jerusalem on the road to Bethlehem). Ramat Rahel expedition under Y. Aharoni, first excavation 1959. *(Photo: Courtesy of Y. Aharoni, Ramet Rahel expedition, Hebrew University of Jerusalem and University of Rome)*

149 The ruins of Gibeah. Remains of Saul's residence on the hill of Tell el-Ful, about 3 miles north of Jerusalem, excavated by W. F. Albright. *(Photo: Courtesy of Prof. G. E. Wright)*

150 View of the site of the battle of

347

Michmash, also called "Allenby's battlefield". (Photo: Radio Times Hulton Picture Library)

151 Captured Philistines being ed off. Detail from a relief in the temple of Ramesses III at Medinet Habu. (Photo: Hassia, Paris)

152 Harpist. Terracotta relief. Babylonian. From the region of Dyala. Beginning of 2nd mill. Height 5 inches. Oriental Institute of the University, Chicago. (Photo: Courtesy of the Oriental Institute, Chicago)

153 Ashurbanipal in single combat with a lion. Assyrian. Relief from the palace of Nineveh. 7th century B.C. (Photo: Courtesy of the Trustees of the British Museum)

154 Site of biblical Azekah (Tell Zakarije), 17 miles NW of Hebron, with the "valley of the terebinth" (Wadi es-Sunt) in the foreground. Scene of David's triumph over Goliath. (Photo: Middle East Archives, Tel Aviv)

155 A sling-stone dating back to Israelite times. (Photo: Courtesy of Prof. G. E. Wright)

155 Basalt relief of a slinger. Orthostat from Tell Halaf (ancient Guzan), ruins near the source of the River Khabour (eastern tributary of the upper Euphrates); excavation: Max Frhr. v. Oppenheim, 1911/13, 1929. (Photo: Courtesy of the Trustees of the British Museum)

156 Dead Philistine. Detail from a relief in the temple of Ramesses III at Medinet Habu. (Photo: Courtesy of the Oriental Institute, Chicago)

157 Foundations of the temple of the god Mikal at Beth-Shan. 13th century B.C. Excavation in Tell el-Husn near Beisan, Jordan Valley. (After A. Rowe, The Topography and History of Beth-shan, pl. 17)

157 Temple of Pharaoh Ramesses III in biblical Beth-Shan. Still in use until app. 1000 B.C. Reconstruction. Possibly the "House of Dagon". Dagon: god worshipped by the Philistines (Judges 16:23; I Samuel 5:2–7), god of fertility, originating in Mesopotamia; depicted with the head and shoulders of a man, and lower body of a fish. (After A. Rowe, The Four Canaanite Temples of Beth-shan, fig. 5)

158 Land battle between the Egyptians and the combined Sea Peoples including the Philistines. Detail from a relief in the temple of Ramesses III at Medinet Habu. Copy from The Epigraphic Survey, Earlier Historical Records of Ramesses III, Medinet Habu, 1938, Chicago.

(Photo: Courtesy of the Oriental Institute, Chicago)

159 Meagre ruins in Jerusalem of the Jebusite wall and a tower of Solomon's time. Jebusites: People who inhabited Canaan before the Israelites (Genesis 10:16) and who still dwelt in Jerusalem during David's reign (II Samuel 5:6). (Photo: Arthaud-Mikaël Audrain)

160 Four Egyptian scribes. Limestone relief, c. 1350 B.C. 18th dynasty. Museo Archeologico, Florence. Scribes were employed in temple administration (I Chronicles 24:6), in the civil service and the armed forces (Isaiah 33:18; II Chronicles 26:11). (Museum photo)

161 Scribes seated with quills and palettes. Relief from the tomb of Kani-nesut, son of Pharaoh Snefru, 4th dynasty, at Giza. (H. Junker, Giza, Volume II, Leipzig, 1934)

162 The equipment of an Egyptian scribe. Length of the palette 3 inches. (Photo: Courtesy of the Oriental Institute, Chicago)

163 Egyptian princess. Probably from Amarna. Painted limestone, 6 inches high. Late 18th dynasty. Louvre, Paris. (After Archives Photographiques)

164 Group of Egyptian ladies. Painting in the tomb of Nakht at Thebes. 18th dynasty. Detail from a picture of a banquet. (Photo: Marburg)

165 A glimpse into an Egyptian harem. Copy of a relief in Tell el-Amarna, 18th dynasty, time of Amenophis IV (c. 1377–1360). (Photo: N. de G. Davies, El-Amarna VI 28)

166 Bronze model of an adoration ceremony from the time of King Shilchak-Inshushinak, called "Sit Shamsi", "This sacrificial plaque is a model of an Elamite sanctuary with all the marks of a Semitic cult." (A. Parrot). Elamite. From Susa, 12th century B.C., length 24 inches, width 16 inches. Louvre, Paris. (Photo: Archives Photographiques)

167 Excavation at Megiddo (Tell el-Mutesellim in the Plain of Jezreel). Eastern side of layer III, town gateway after the earth has been removed and layer IV revealed. First excavation by the Deutsche Orientgesellschaft under J. Schumacher 1903/05; demonstration excavation by the Oriental Institute of the University of Chicago under G. Loud, P. L. O. Guy since 1925. (Photo: Courtesy of the Oriental Institute, Chicago)

167 Reconstruction of the triple gateway at Megiddo dating back to Solomon's day. (Photo: as above)

168 Excavation of the stables at Megiddo. According to layer IV the buildings must have been erected c. 975–925 B.C. King Solomon's reign: c. 965–925 B.C. (Photo: as above)

169 Reconstruction of the southern part of the stables at Megiddo. Solomon's period. (Eglon: town in the Plain of Shephelah [Joshua 10:3,5]. According to Prof. W. F. Albright Eglon is to be found in Tell el-Hesi, east of Gaza, on the borders of Philistia with its five cities.). (Photo: as above)

170 Reconstruction of the palace at Megiddo dating back to Solomon's time. Seat of the district governor Baana. (Photo: as above)

171 Egyptian horse's head. Sculpture. Limestone, c. 1350 B.C., 18th dynasty. Egyptian Museum, Berlin. (Photo: Courtesy Staatliche Museen in Berlin)

172 Chariot from the tomb of the parents-in-law of Amenophis III in the Valley of Kings. Wood and gilded leather. Length 8 ft., 18th dynasty. Cairo Museum. (Photo: Archives Photographiques)

172 Hittite, probably a war-god with lance, shield and sword fixed in his waistband. Dolerite relief from Zinjirli (ancient Sam'al), ruins in Turkey. Capital of a kingdom during the latter days of the Hittites (c. 1200–700 B.C.). Height 4½ ft. Near East Museum, Berlin. (Photo: Marburg)

173 Hittite chariot with archer and driver runs over the naked corpse of a speared enemy soldier. Zinjirli (Sam'al). Late Hittite. (Photo: Archaeological Museum, Istanbul)

174 Ships' carpenters at work. From a picture of an Egyptian shipyard. Relief in the tomb of Ti at Saqqara, 5th dynasty. (Photo: Courtesy of the Oriental Institute, Chicago)

175 Two Syrian ships at anchor in an Egyptian harbour. Traders and shop-owners exchange goods on the quay. Copy of an almost completely destroyed wall-painting at Thebes. Time of Amenophis III (c. 1413–1377 B.C.). (Photo: John Freeman, courtesy of the Egyptian Exploration Fund)

176 Above: The present-day township of Aqabah (Eloth of the Bible) on the gulf of Aqabah. Photograph 1939. (Photo: Courtesy of Dr Nelson Glueck)

176 Below: View of the excavations in Tell el-Kheleifeh, biblical Ezion-Geber. Discovered and excavated by Nelson Glueck, 1937–40. (Photo: Courtesy of Dr Nelson Glueck)

177 Potsherd bearing the inscription "Gold from Ophir for Beth-horon, thirty shekels". Tell Qasile near Tel Aviv, excavation by B. Maisler, 1949. *(Photo: Department of Antiquities, Jerusalem, Israel)*

177 Queen Hatshepsut's ship returning Punt. Copy of a picture from in the temple of Deir el-Bahri, opposite Karnak on the westbank of the Nile. Around 1500 B. C., 18th dynasty. *(Photo: Marburg)*

178 Sarcophagus of King Ahiram of Byblos. Detail of a sculptured relief showing King Ahiram on his throne. Phoenician. W. F. Albright places the inscription on the sarcophagus in the 10th century B. .C, the time of Solomon. Byblos: Phoenician coastal town north of Beirut. Probably the "Gebal" of the Bible (Ezekiel 27:9 etc.). Byblos is the origin of the word 'Bible'; for the Greek word 'biblion' meaning book owes its origin to this town, through which Egyptian papyrus was exported to Greece. *(Photo: Courtesy of the National Museum, Beirut)*

179/180 Horses and mules with a warchariot in a cornfield. (The warchariot was introduced into Egypt by the Hyksos (see note to 59). Colourful painting on the wall of an unnamed tomb dating back to the 18th dynasty. British Museum. *(Photo: Eileen Tweedy)*

181 Aerial photograph of Tyre. *(Photo: Courtesy of the Uitgeversmaatschappij Elsevier, Amsterdam)*

182 Campaign against Phoenicia by Shalmaneser III of Assyria. Above: Picture of the fortified city of Tyre, surrounded by the sea.
Below: Assyrian charioteers and infantry on the way to battle. Detail from a bronze relief on the doors of the summer palace belonging to Shalmaneser III at Tell Balawat east of Mosul. British excavation by H. Rassam (1882) and M. E. L. Mallowan (1956). Main finds: Bronze door mountings with reliefs showing the achievements of Ashurnasirpal II and Shalmaneser III (c. 859–824 B. C.). Height 11 inches. *(Photo: Courtesy of the Trustees of the British Museum)*

183 Cedars of Lebanon. *(Photo: Middle East Archives, London)*

184 Felling cedars in the Lebanon for a flag-pole for the temple of Amon. (Amon: god worshipped at Thebes, capital of Upper Egypt, to whom the ram was sacred.) Detail from a limestone relief from the temple of Amon at Karnak. Time of Seti I

(c. 1319–1301 B. C.). (Photo: Courtesy of the Staatliche Museen, Berlin)

185 Shipping cedar wood. Six boats with shipping heads on the bows and high sterns; fish and other marine creatures swim in the water. Assyrian. Alabaster relief from Khorsabad, time of Sargon II (722–705 B. C.). *(Photo: Marburg)*

186 The "Quarries of Solomon" in Jerusalem. *(Photo: Radio Times Hulton Picture Library)*

187 Reconstruction of Solomon's temple, drawn by Stevens based on details from W. F. Albright and G. E. Wright. *(After The Biblical Archaeologist, XVIII 2, illustration 9)*

188 Metallists at work. Below: casting a bronze door. Wall-painting from the tomb of the vizier Rekhmire at Thebes, 18th dynasty. *(Photo: Arpag Mekhitarian, Brussels)*

189 Reconstruction of the Bronze Sea by William Morden. *(Photo: Courtesy of the Oriental Institute, Chicago)*

190 Mobile laver made of bronze. From a tomb at Larnaka, Cyprus. Late Mycenean, c. 1400–1200 B. C. Antiquarium, Berlin. *(After L. H. Grollenberg, Atlas of the Bible, 194)*

191 King Solomon's copper mines in Wadi Timna (in the Arabah, the region of the large depression between the Dead Sea and the gulf of Aqabah). Discovered by Dr Beno Rothenberg 1959. *(Photo: Dr Beno Rothenberg)*

193 Assyrian soldiers wearing knee-length garments and carrying lances, swords and rounded shields running into a point. Relief from the palace of the Assyrian king, Sennacherib (705–681 B. C.) in Nineveh. *(Photo: Courtesy of the Staatliche Museen, Berlin)*

196 Record of the towns in Palestine and Syria conquered by Pharaoh Sheshonk I, Shisak of the Bible. According to I Kings 14:25 Shisak's invasion took place c. 922 B. C. Limestone relief from the temple of Amon at Karnak. *(Photo: A. Gaddis, Luxor)*
Right: Copy of the relief. *(After C. R. Lepsius, Denkmäler III, 252)*

197/198 Two Assyrian court officials. Detail from an Assyrian wall-painting showing Tiglath-pileser III holding an audience (see p. 215/216). From a palace in Tell Ahmar (ancient Til Barsip), NE Syria on the east bank of the Euphrates. Main city of the Aramaic state of Bit-Adini conquered by Shalmaneser III. Excavated by Expedition Thureau-Dangin (France) 1929/31. *(Photo: Schneider-Lengyel)*

199 Reconstruction of the fortress of Mizpah, present-day Tell en-Nasbeh, 7 1/2 miles north of Jerusalem. The outer wall was 1980 ft. long, 13–20 ft. thick and covered with plaster. At its N E corner stood a strongly fortified gateway c. 900 B. c. Excavation by the Pacific School of Religion, 1927–35 under W. F. Bade. *(After C. C. McCown, Tell en-Nasbeh I pl. II, 5)*

200 View towards the hill of Samaria, c. 7 1/2 miles N W of Shechem. Once the capital of the northern kingdom of Israel; present-day Sebaste. *(Photo: Palestine Archaeological Museum)*

201 Walls of the palace of King Omri at Samaria. (Omri c. 882–871 B.C.) Excavation by G. A. Reisner, C. S. Fisher, D. G. Lyon, Harvard University, USA, 1908/10; Anglo-American excavation under J. W. Crowfoot 1931/35. *(Photo: Bavaria Verlag, Heinrich Frese)*

202 Basalt statue of the Assyrian king, Shalmaneser III (859–824 B. C.). *(Photo: Courtesy of the Archaeological Museum, Istanbul)*

203 Shalmaneser III's campaign against North Syria. Above: Capture of the town of Dabiju near Aleppo, 858 B. C. Detail from a bronze relief mounting, on the doors of the summer palace of Shalmaneser III in Tell Balawat. Height 11 inches. British Museum. *(Photo: Courtesy of the Trustees of the British Museum)*

203 Remains of the pillared hall built by King Ahab (c. 871–852 B. C.) at Hazor. *(Photo: Middle East Archives, London)*

204 Carefully built stonework; remains of the walls of King Ahab's palace at Samaria. *(Photo: Palestine Archaeological Museum)*

204 Fragment of ivory beading with stylised plant motif, found at Samaria. Israelite period. *(Photo: Palestine Exploration Fund)*

205 Head of a Phoenician woman. Ivory relief, probably part of the decoration on a sumptuous bed. Eyebrows, pupils and hair black, lips lightly reddened. Archaic smile. Phoenician workmanship, 9th–8th century B. C. Found at Nimrud. National Museum, Baghdad. *(Photo: Courtesy of the Directorate General of Antiquities, Baghdad)*

206 "Baal with thunderbolt". From Ras Shamra (Ugarit), a sanctuary west of the Great Temple. Excavation by C. F. A. Schaeffer, discovered 1932. Dated: 1900–1750 B. C. (Schaeffer); 1650–1500 B. C. (Albright). Limestone, height 4 3/4 ft.

Louvre, Paris. (*Syria*, Volume 16, 1935, pages 410–411)

207 Woman applying cosmetics. Egyptian. Detail from Turin papyrus No. 145. New Kingdom. (*Photo: Courtesy of the Museo Egizio, Turin*)

207 "Woman at a window". Syrophoenician work. Assyrian loot. From Nimrud. 9th century B. C. Ivory carving, height 4 inches. (*Photo: Courtesy of the Trustees of the British Museum*)

208 The Moabite stone. Dating from time of King Mesha of Moab (*c.* mid-9th century B. C.). Found at Diban, Transjordan, in 1868 by the German missionary F. Klein. Black basalt, height 3¹/₄ ft. Louvre, Paris. (*Photo: Archives Photographiques*)

209 Relief in black-green basalt, probably depicting a Moabite. Discovered at Diban, Transjordan, in 1851 by de Saulcy. 3¹/₄ ft. high. Louvre, Paris. (*Photo: Service de documentation photographique*)

210 King Jehu of Israel (*c.* 845–818 B. C.) bringing tribute. Detail from the obelisk of Shalmaneser III, King of the Assyrians. Monument in black basalt, Nimrud. British Museum. (*Photo: Courtesy of the Trustees of the British Museum*)

210 Scribes count the severed heads of a defeated tribe of Chaldeans. Assyrian. Relief from hall XVIII in the palace of Sennacherib, Nineveh. 7th century B.C. (*Photo: Courtesy of the Trustees of the British Museum*)

211 Ivory carving showing a bearded figure, probably that of the biblical King Hazael of Damascus. Found at Arslan Tash [ruins in North Syria (ancient Hadatu); French excavation by the expedition of Thureau-Dangin, 1928; discovered primarily reliefs, statuettes and a marvellous collection of ivory carvings]. 9th century B.C. Height 6¹/₂ inches. (*Photo: Archives Photographiques*)

212 Ivory carving used as decoration of wooden objects. The tablet showing two winged beings (above) came from the palace of Hazael at Damascus, as did the fragment showing fantastic winged animals with rams' heads and lions' feet (below). Found at Arslan Tash, Syria. Period of the Israelite kings. Aleppo Museum North Syria. (*Photo: Courtesy of the General Director of Antiquities, North Syria*)

213 The obelisk of Shalmaneser III of Assyria. This monument made of black basalt is shaped like a temple tower at the top, ending in three

steps. Assyrian. 9th century B. C. Height 6¹/₂ ft. Found in 1845 at Nimrud by A. H. Layard. British Museum. (*Photo: Courtesy of the Trustees of the British Museum*)

214 Detail from the obelisk of Shalmaneser III. Second row showing Israelites bringing tribute, led by King Jehu—prostrate in the dust before Shalmaneser.(*Photo:Courtesy of the Trustees of the British Museum*)

215/216 Tiglath-pileser III of Assyria holds audience. Behind the throne stand two beardless youths with red headbands. (In the Bible Tiglath-pileser is also referred to as Tiglath-Pilneser and by his nickname of Pul—Assyrian Pulu.) Assyrian wall-painting from the palace at Til Barsip (Tell Ahmar) in North Syria. 8th century B. C. (*Copy by L. Cavro, Paris*)

217 Part of the tribute paid by King Benhadad III of Damascus, son of Hazael, to Adadnirari III, King of Assyria. Syro-phoenician. 8th century B. C. From Arslan Tash. Louvre, Paris. (*Photo: Archives Photographiques*)

218 Winged "Cherub" sphinx. Ivory carving from Samaria. 8th century B. C. (*Photo: Palestine Archaeological Museum*)
Note: the picture has been reversed.

219 Hebrew seal engraved with a roaring lion, inscribed: "Shema servant of Jeroboam". Time of King Jeroboam II of Israel (787–747 B. C.). Found at Megiddo. Archaeological Museum, Istanbul. (*J. B. Pritchard, The Ancient Near East in Pictures, illustration 276*)

220 Outer wall of the palace of King Uzziah of Judah (785–747 B. C.). The fortress-like building was 264 ft. by 165 ft. with a casemate wall three storeys high, rising in steps. Gateway. Excavation in 1959 by Y. Aharoni (Hebrew University, Jerusalem) at Ramat Rahel, two and a half miles south of Jerusalem. (*Photo: Courtesy of Y. Aharoni, Ramat Rahel Expedition*)

221 Tombstone of King Uzziah of Judah. This is the longest inscription in Aramaic from the time of Christ, when the bones were reinterred. Because he was a leper, Uzziah was not buried in the royal tombs. The inscription on the ossuary (a limestone casket into which the bones of the dead were placed) reads: "The bones of Uzziah, King of Judah, rest here— do not open!" Discovered by Prof. Sukenik, 1931, Jerusalem. (*Photo: Courtesy of A. H. Philpot*)

221 Seal of Jotham, Regent and King of Judah (758–743 B. C.), son of King Uzziah. Found at Ezion-Geber, 8th century B. C. (*Photo: Courtesy of Dr Nelson Glueck*)

222 Portrait of Tiglath-pileser III, King of Assyria (745–727 B. C.). Fragment of the upper part of a plaster tablet. Height 3¹/₂ ft. From Nimrud, central palace. British Museum. (*Photo: Courtesy of the Trustees of the British Museum*)

223 Assyrian cavalry engaged in battle with Syrian rebels. The leg-muscles of the horsemen are particularly emphasised and their beards and hair are waved according to regulations. Their armour: pointed helmet, chain-mail shirt, lance and sword. Relief. Time of Tiglath-pileser III. 8th century B. C. Height about 3¹/₂ ft. British Museum. (*Photo: Courtesy of the Trustees of the British Museum*)

224 Hebrew seal bearing the inscription "Ushna, servant of Ahaz". 8th century B. C. (*Photo: Courtesy of Prof. G. E. Wright*)

224/225 Assyrian attack on the town of Gazru (Geser?). The inhabitants stand on the towers and walls and signal their capitulation. Gypsum relief from Nimrud. Time of Tiglath-pileser III. 8th century B. C. British Museum. (*Photo: Courtesy of the Trustees of the British Museum*)

226 Aerial photograph of the excavations in Zone A at Hazor. (Tell el-Queda, in Upper Galilee, about 9 miles north of the sea of Galilee.) Excavation by Y. Yadin. (*Photo: Courtesy of Prof. Y. Yadin, Hebrew University—J. A. de Rothschild's expedition to Hazor*)

227 Sargon II of Assyria (722–705 B. C.). The ruler wears the fez-like crown of Neo-Assyria, which is topped by a squat ball and has ribbons flowing onto the king's back. The king's hair and beard are carefully waved and he wears ear-rings. During the first year of his rule, Sargon II conquered Samaria after it had been besieged by his predecessor Shalmaneser V (727–722 B. C.) since 724 B. C. Limestone relief, 36 inches high. From Khorsabad. Museo Egizio, Turin. (*Museum photo*)

227 Captives being led away by Tiglath-pileser III. Plaster relief from Nimrud. 8th century B. C. Length 9³/₄ ft. British Museum. (*Photo: Courtesy of the Trustees of the British Museum*)

228 Reconstruction of the buildings of Khorsabad (Dur Sharrukin) in-

cluding the palace of Sargon II, temples and the staged tower. Sargon II built this residence shortly before his death (705 B.C.). 9½ miles NNE of Nineveh, 10 miles NNE of Mosul. After that it was deserted. Discovered by Paul-Emile Botta, French excavation 1843/44. Reconstruction by Charles Altmann, excavated by Gordon Loud at Khorsabad from 1933. *(After G. Loud, Khorsabad II,1)*

229 Cuneiform tablet describing Sargon II's 8th campaign in Syria. The report is addressed to the god Ashur. 8th century B.C. Louvre, Paris. *(Photo: Archives Photographiques)*

230 Assyrians storming a city. Drawing by A. H. Layard from a relief at Nineveh. *(After A.H.Layard, Ruins of Nineveh and Babylon, 1853)*

231 Inhabitants and their sheep being driven out of a captured city by Assyrian warriors. The city: Astartu (?), possibly Ashtaroth of the Bible, is situated like Samaria on top of a hill and is surrounded by a double wall with prominent towers. Both the walls and the towers are crenellated. Gypsum relief from Nimrud, the time of Tiglath-pileser III, 8th century B.C. Height app. 3½ ft. British Museum. *(Photo: Courtesy of the Trustees of the British Museum)*

233 Snake-griffin from the Ishtar Gate at Babylon. The snake-griffin (Griffin = a combination of lion and bird), also called a "dragon", was the fabulous animal ascribed to the god Marduk. It is depicted with a snake's head (with horns), a lion's body (with scales); the forefeet are lions paws, the hind-feet bird's claws, the tail is like a snake. Enamelled bricks with a blue and green glaze, height 3¾ ft., length 5 ft.Neo-Babylonian, time of Nebuchadnezzar II (605–562 B.C.). *(Photo: Arthaud-Mikaël Audrain)*

236 Sargon II and his Tartan (Assyrian *tartanu*), the title given to the commander-in-chief of the Assyrian army (II Kings 18:17). Detail from a relief in the palace of Sargon II at Khorsabad. 8th century B.C. *(Photo: Courtesy of the Trustees of the British Museum)*

237 View of the Siloam tunnel, dug by King Hezekiah of Judah (725–697 B.C.) through the rock of Jerusalem. The underground tunnel is 23–26 in. wide and a maximum of 4¾ ft. high. It runs westwards straight through the hill, has a drop of 7¼ ft. and starts on the east side

of the "city of David" at Jerusalem's main spring in the bottom of the valley. This spring, called "Gihon" in the Bible (I Kings 1:33), is today known as "The Virgin's spring". *(Photo: Courtesy of the Palestine Archaeological Museum)*

238 The Siloam inscription from Jerusalem. 15 inches high, 29 inches wide (c. 700 B.C.). This inscription, carefully chiselled into a flattened rock at the southern entrance to the underground canal, is now in the Istanbul Museum. The inscription in ancient Hebrew places the date in the reign of Hezekiah. *(Photo: Palestine Archaeological Museum)*

239 Drawing of the course of the Siloam tunnel through the rock of Jerusalem. *(Drawn by S. Molnar from a sketch by Dr W. Keller)*

239 The pool of Siloam at Jerusalem. The water is brought to this pool by way of Hezekiah's canal from the spring of Gihon, Jerusalem's main well outside the city. *(Photo: F.A.Brockhaus)*

240 King Merodachbaladan II of Babylon (Marduk-apal-iddin = "Marduk has given a son") bestows estates on a noble. Inscribed boundary stone (Babylonian kudurru). Black basalt, height 18½ inches. 8th century B.C. Origin unknown. Staatliche Museen, Berlin. *(Photo: Courtesy of the Staatliche Museen)*

241 Two soldiers from Elam with bows and quivers, marching to the left, one looking backwards. Both have beards and their bushy hair arranged in straight curls, is held together with a headband. Their short-sleeved robes reach to their knees, the second soldier carries on his back a quiver with an Elamite covering. Elam [first-born son of Shem (Genesis 10:22)]: ancient name for the region of Persia southeast of Babylon. Exiled Israelites were brought as far as Elam (Isaiah 11:11; Esther 2:5,6). Asnapper (Ashurbanipal) later transported Elamites to Samaria (Ezra 4:9,10). Limestone relief from Nineveh, 8 inches high, probably 7th century B.C. Museo Barracco, Rome. *(Photo: Oscar Savio, Rome)*

242 King Sennacherib of Assyria (705–681 B.C.) seated on his throne in front of Lachish. Detail from a relief in Nineveh. 690 B.C. British Museum. *(Photo: Courtesy of the Trustees of the British Museum)*

243 Reconstruction of the fortified Judaean city of Lachish (Tell ed-Duweir), 43 miles south-east of

Jerusalem. The walls, the gateway and the palace of the local governor which were discovered during the excavations, were probably built during the reign of King Rehoboam (926–910 B.C.) *(Photo: Copyright by courtesy of the Trustees of the late Sir Henry S. Wellcome)*

244 The capture of Lachish by Sennacherib, King of Assyria, in the year 701 B.C. Relief from Nineveh. 690 B.C. Gypsum, height 5¾ ft. British Museum. *(Photo: Courtesy of the Trustees of the British Museum)*

246 Breaches in the walls of Lachish, made by Assyrian siege-engines. Discovered during the excavations at Tell ed-Duweir. *(Photo: Copyright by courtesy of the Trustees of the late Sir Henry S. Wellcome)*

246 Four-wheeled siege-engine used by the Assyrians. Detail of a gypsum relief from Nineveh, time of Tiglath-pileser III. 8th century B.C. British Museum. *(Photo: Courtesy of the Trustees of the British Museum)* Note: the picture has been reversed.

247 Pharaoh Taharka, Ethiopian king of Egypt and Nubia (c. 689–663 B.C.), called Tirhakah in the Bible. Was defeated by Esarhaddon, King of Assyria, in 670 B.C. The latter invaded Lower Egypt and captured Memphis (see victory stela of Esarhaddon, p. 254). Taharka is mentioned by Esarhaddon and Ashurbanipal in inscriptions. 25th dynasty (Ethiopian). Bronze statuette. Hermitage, Leningrad. *(Photo: Society for Cultural Relations with the USSR, London)*

248/249 Seated on his throne Sennacherib receives loot and captives from defeated Lachish. Drawing by A.H. Layard from a relief in the palace of Sennacherib at Nineveh. 690 B.C. *(After A.H.Layard, Monuments of Ninevis, plates 21–22)*

250 Captives from Lachish are led away. Detail in the original from the relief in the palace of Sennacherib at Nineveh. British Museum. *(Photo: Courtesy of the Trustees of the British Museum)*

251 Hexagonal prism of Sennacherib. It lists the details of his 8th campaign, including the besieging of "Hezekiah the Judahite" in Jerusalem in the year 701 B.C. From Nineveh, Taylor-Prism, British Museum. *(Photo: Courtesy of the Trustees of the British Museum)*

252 Captive musicians pay homage to the king. After a successful battle against the Elamites, musicians, men and women, from the defeated

town perform: in front are five men, three with harps, one with double-flute and one with a zither which was played horizontally in front of the body. Six women follow behind, four with harps, one with double-flute and one with kettledrum. Alabaster relief from Nineveh, time of Ashurbanipal (669–626 B.C.). (Photo: Courtesy of the Trustees of the British Museum)

253 Scene in the tent of an Assyrian officer. The camp-bed and a meal are being prepared. Alabaster relief from Nineveh. Height 15 inches. Time of Ashurbanipal, 7th century B.C. Berlin Museum. (Photo: Courtesy of the Staatliche Museen, Berlin)

253 Human skulls in Tomb 120 at Lachish. (Photo: copyright by courtesy of the Trustees of the late Sir Henry S. Wellcome)

254 Sennacherib's bodyguard. Drawing from relief in the palace of Sennacherib at Nineveh. 690 B.C. Louvre, Paris, Salle XXIV. (After A. Parrot, Le musée de Louvre et la Bible, fig. 59)

254 Victory stela of Esarhaddon, King of Assyria (681–669 B.C.). The monument lists Esarhaddon's victories over Pharaoh Taharka of Egypt and Ethiopia (see p. 247) and King Abdimilkutti of Sidon (port on the Mediterranean, modern Saida; see Joshua 19:18; Isaiah 23:2). The king is wearing royal regalia and holds in his right hand a beaker, in his left the club-sceptre and ropes tied to two captives. The one on the left (kneeling) bound and with a ring through his lips, wears the viper insignia on his head, the pharaohs' mark of royalty, which suggests he is probably Usanahuru, Taharka's son (or the pharaoh himself, as both are mentioned in the text). The one on the right (standing) with beard, pointed cap and long robes: King Abdimilkutti of Sidon. Above right: gods with their symbols, some riding on the animals sacred to them, as well as a crescent moon, winged sun and eight-pointed star. Dolerite, height 10¹/₂ ft. 7th century B.C. From Zinjirli [ruins in Turkey, capital of a kingdom in late Hittite times (1200–700 B.C.)]. Excavation: F. v. Luschan 1888–1902. Staatliche Museen, Berlin. (Photo: Courtesy of the Staatliche Museen, Berlin)

255 Ashurbanipal and his wife in a vine bower. Assyrian king (669–626

B.C.) famous for his palace with reliefs showing hunting and war scenes and for his library at Nineveh (Tell Kuyunjik). British excavation: including A. H. Layard (discoverer of Nineveh, 1845), H. Rassam, under the leadership of H. C. Rawlinson. Alabaster relief from Nineveh (discovered by W. K. Loftus). 7th century B.C. (Photo: Courtesy of the Trustees of the British Museum)

256/257 Ashurbanipal hunting lions. Alabaster relief, Nineveh. 7th century B.C. Length 21¹/₄ ft., height 5³/₄ ft. British Museum. (Photo: Courtesy of the Trustees of the British Museum)

258 The great pillared hall in the temple at Karnak. Started by Ramesses I, completed by Ramesses II. Each of the 61 pillars is decorated with reliefs and rises to a height of about 50 ft. in the two aisles of the temple which covers an area of 6000 sq. yds. 19th dynasty. (Photo A. Jänicke)

260 Ashurbanipal attacking an Egyptian city. Limestone relief from Nineveh. 7th century B.C. Width 6 ft. British Museum. (Photo: Courtesy of the Trustees of the British Museum)

261 Bronze urn showing four horsemen, presumably Scythians [people from the steppes of southern Russia who, after crossing the Caucasus invaded Uratu (Armenia) and Assyria in droves from the 8th century B.C. onwards (see also II Maccabees 4:47)]. Two of the horsemen wearing swan-shaped helmets are shooting arrows over their shoulders. The horses' manes are cropped short to avoid hindering the archers. Campanian, around 500 B.C. British Museum. (Photo: Courtesy of the Trustees of the British Museum)

262 Reconstruction of Ashur (Qalat Shergat), one of the main cities of the Assyrian kingdom situated on the west bank of the Tigris. (German excavation: Walter Andrae 1913/14.) (After W. Andrae, Das wiedererstandene Assur, p. 29)

263 Mound of Nineveh (Tell Kuyunjik) on the east bank of the Tigris, north of Mosul in Iraq. Nineveh was one of the main cities of the Assyrian kingdom. A second mound, Nebi Junus (after the Prophet Jonah), concealed the palace of Esarhaddon. (Photo: Arthaud-Mikaël Audrain)

264 Head of a Mede. He wears a round cap with a ribbon at the back, and

ear-rings. (Medes: a confederation of Persian tribes famous for their horsemanship). Detail of a relief from a staircase at Persepolis. Beginning of the 5th century B.C. (Photo: Courtesy of the Oriental Institute, Chicago)

264 Head of a Neo-Babylonian (Chaldean). He wears a full beard and long hair held by a headband in Semitic-Babylonian style. The long square beard is artistically curled. Detail from the black basalt boundary stone of Merodach-baladan. Staatliche Museen, Berlin. (Photo: Courtesy of the Staatliche Museen, Berlin)

265/266 The Ishtar Gate at Babylon. Reconstruction. Glazed brick. Total height 47 ft. Neo-Babylonian. 7th–6th centuries B.C. Staatliche Museen, Berlin, Department of the Near East. (Photo: Courtesy of the Staatliche Museen, Berlin)

267 A corner of the wall of Jerusalem built in the Middle Ages. (Photo: Arthaud-Mikaël Audrain)

268 Babylonian chronicle for 605–594 B.C. The cuneiform text on this clay tablet tells, amongst other things, of the Battle of Carchemish [Nebuchadnezzar defeated Pharaoh Necho, 605 B.C., who himself had killed Josiah, King of Judah, four years previously (II Kings 23:29)], the accession to the throne of Nebuchadnezzar II, the Chaldean (605 B.C.), and the capture of Jerusalem on the 16th March, 598 B.C. The same paragraph mentions the nomination of Zedekiah as king and the exile in Babylon of Jehoiachin. British Museum. (Photo: Courtesy of the Trustees of the British Museum)

269 Deportation of civilians. Men and a woman carrying a bundle on her back march beside the oxen. A child looks down from the cart. Detail from a relief at Nineveh, 7th century B.C. Alabaster, total height 39 inches. Louvre, Paris. (Photo: Marburg). Note: In contrast to the Assyrians the Chaldeans left no pictorial record of their history and only very few written texts of historical substance. As their manner of fighting and handling of prisoners lacked none of the severity and cruelty shown by their Assyrian predecessors, Assyrian pictures can also illustrate what happened under the rule of Babylon.

270 Clay tablet from Babylon listing the rations allowed to captives in Babylon. Mentioned among them

are: "Jehoiachin, king of Judah" and his family. *(Photo: Courtesy of the Staatliche Museen, Berlin)*

271 Seal inscribed "The property of Eliakim, steward of Jehoiachin". From Debir (Tell Beit Mirsim, 13 miles WSW of Hebron, USA excavation: W.F. Albright, M. G.Kyle 1926). 6th century B.C. *(Photo: Courtesy of Prof. W.F. Albright)*

271 View of the Ishtar Gate, decorated with 575 dragons and bulls, and of the processional way at Babylon (metropolis on the Euphrates, 50 miles south of Baghdad, revival under the Neo-Babylonian kings, the Chaldees of the Bible). (German excavation: Robert J. Koldewey 1899–1917.) Reconstruction by Prof. E. Unger, drawn by H. Unger. *(After E. Unger, Babylon, die heilige Stadt, 1931)*

272 Assyrian battering-ram destroying a city wall. Detail from the bronze gates at the summer palace of Shalmaneser III at Tell Balawat. 9th century B.C. British Museum. *(Photo: Courtesy of the Trustees of the British Museum)*

272 The mound of Lachish (Tell ed-Duweir) in SW Palestine. First excavated in 1932–38 by the Wellcome-Marston expedition under J. L. Starkey. In 1935 and 1938 clay tablets (ostraka) bearing Hebrew script were found here and have become famous as the "Lachish letters". *(Photo: Copyright by courtesy of the Trustees of the late Sir Henry S. Wellcome)*

273 Lachish letter No. IV. Short message from Hoshaiah, commander of an outpost north of Lachish. Ostrakon (clay tablet with writing in ink) from Lachish. *(Photo: Copyright by courtesy of the Trustees of the late Sir Henry S. Wellcome)*

273 Deportation of civilians. Detail from a relief at Nineveh. Assyrian. 7th century B.C. Alabaster. Total height 5¹/₄ ft. *(Photo: Archives Photographiques)*

274 Scene of an encampment during a deportation with soldiers and their captives. Relief from Nineveh. 7th century B.C. Staatliche Museen, Berlin. *(Photo: Marburg)*

275 Winged bull with human head, from Khorsabad. Once stood guard against evil spirits at the gateway to the palace of Sargon II at Dur Sharrukin. It wears a crown with horns. The sculptors gave these animals five legs so that they were in proper perspective both from the front and from the side. The monster bull, which stands

14¹/₂ ft. high, is accompanied by his winged tutelary spirit. British Museum. *(Photo: Courtesy of the Trustees of the British Museum)*

276 Seal inscription "Gedaliah, who is over the house", probably the name of the governor of Judah, appointed by the Babylonians. From Lachish, 6th century B.C. *(Photo: Copyright by courtesy of the Trustees of the late Sir Henry S. Wellcome)*

276 Seal showing a fighting cock and with the inscription "The property of Jaazaniah, servant of the king". From Mizpah (Tell en-Nasbeh), 6th century B.C. *(Photo: Palestine Archaeological Museum)*

277 Canal off the Euphrates (near the ruins of Babylon). *(Photo: Radio Times Hulton Picture Library)*

277 Captive musicians, from Lachish, wander through a mountain forest, accompanied by an Assyrian warrior carrying a club and a quiver. They are wearing shirts and are barefoot; one has no hat, the others wear caps with headbands. Detail of an alabaster relief from the palace of Sennacherib at Nineveh. 7th century B.C. British Museum. *(Photo: Courtesy of the Trustees of the British Museum)*

279 Bearded sphinx seated. Fragment of a relief from the façade of an outside staircase in a palace at Persepolis, the Achaemenid royal city, famous for its palaces. Situated about 31 miles NE of Shiraz (excavated by E. F. Schmidt, USA). The relief shows the various influences on Achaemenid art: the Egyptian sphinx with wings, which probably originated in Phoenicia or the Aegean, and a horned crown, the Mesopotamian symbol of a deity. 5th century B.C. *(Photo: Courtesy of the Trustees of the British Museum)*

282 Mede and Persian guards. The Mede on the left. Detail from a relief in the council chamber at Persepolis, c. 500 B.C. *(Photo: Courtesy of the Oriental Institute, Chicago)*

283/284 Archer of the Persian royal guard. Achaemenid. From Susa. height of the archer app. 5 ft. Louvre, Paris. *(Photo: Maurice Chuzeville)*

285 Heads of two royal servants. Detail from a frieze in the harem of Xerxes at Persepolis. 5th century B.C. *(Photo: Courtesy of the Oriental Institute, Chicago)*

286 Four-winged demon from the

guardroom of the gateway at Pasargadae. Known as the Cyrus relief. Built by Cyrus the Great (c. 559–529 B.C.). *(Photo: Courtesy of the National Museum, Teheran)*

287 Cylinder of Cyrus, which tells of the bloodless occupation of Babylon. The king declares that he made good the wrong done by his predecessors by sending captives home. He helped in the rebuilding of their temples and the return of their gods. This edict included the Jews. From Babylon, fired clay. *(Photo: Courtesy of the Trustees of the British Museum)*

288 A group of Babylonians bearing tribute. They wear long robes reaching to their ankles and, on their carefully curled hair, caps with long tassels. From Persepolis, eastern staircase in the Apadana, time of Xerxes I (486–465 B.C.). *(Photo: Courtesy of the Oriental Institute, Chicago)*

289 Tomb of Cyrus. Six steps of irregular height lead up to a simple chamber with a gabled roof. A double door leads into a room with no windows. Pasargadae. *(Photo: A. Costa)*

290 King Darius I holds audience. Behind stands the crown-prince, Xerxes. Dark grey limestone relief from Persepolis, reception chamber of the treasury. Height 8¹/₄ ft. Time of Darius I (522–486 B.C.). *(Photo: Courtesy of the Oriental Institute, Chicago)*

291 Aerial photograph of the palace terrace at Persepolis. *(Photo: as above)*

292 Outside staircase of the Apadana. Persepolis. *(Photo: as above)*

293 Xerxes I, while still crown-prince, accompanied by court officials. Detail from a relief at Persepolis. *(Photo: as above)*

294 Double-headed bull capital. Grey stone, total length 19 ft. 5th/4th century B.C. Achaemenid. From Susa, now Shush, in modern Iran. Excavations since 1897. Louvre, Paris. *(Photo: Maurice Chuzeville)*

295 New Year's procession of Medes and Persians. Relief from the Apadana, Persepolis. Time of Xerxes I (486–465 B.C.). *(Photo: Courtesy of the Oriental Institute, Chicago)*

296 Official seals of the province of Judah from the 5th–4th centuries B.C. *(After G. E. Wright, Biblical Archaeology, fig. 145)*

296 Judaean coins from the 4th century B.C. *(Photo: Courtesy of the Trustees of the British Museum)*

297 Head of Alexander the Great. Gold coin of Lysimachus, King of Thrace. Cabinet des Médailles, Paris. *(Photo: Courtesy of the Bibliothèque Nationale, Paris)*

298/299 Alexander the Great fighting against Darius III in the battle of Issus (333 B.C.). Mosaic from the house of the Faun, Pompeii, 1st century B.C. Naples Museum. *(Photo: Alinari)*

299 Bust of Ptolemy I (323–283 B.C.), a general under Alexander the Great and founder of the Ptolemy dynasty in Egypt. *(Photo: Courtesy of the Trustees of the British Museum)*

300 King Antiochus III (c. 223–187 B.C.). Ruler of the Seleucid kingdom (part of Alexander's empire, embracing Persia and the Near East, 4th–1st centuries B.C.). Marble bust. *(Photo: Giraudon)*

301 Scene showing boxers dressed in knee-length, fringed garments. Babylonian—Larsa period, beginning of 2nd millenium B.C. Terracotta relief from Eshnunna (Tell Asmar, ruins in the region of Dyala, excavated by H. Frankfort 1930–36). Height 4¼ inches. Louvre, Paris. *(Photo: Archives Photographiques)*

301 Greek athletes: on the left a bearded man leaning on a staff, probably a spectator. One naked youth holds a discus in his raised hand, another tries a spear before throwing it, on the right an older athlete holds a javelin. Design on an amphora by Phintias (525–510 B.C.). Louvre, Paris. *(Photo: Max Hirmer)*

301 Coin picturing the head of Antiochus IV Epiphanes (175–163 B.C.), Seleucid ruler. British Museum. *(Photo: John Freeman)*

303 The Good Shepherd. Marble statue from Rome, Museo Cristiano Lateranense. 3rd–4th centuries. *(Photo: Alinari)*

306 The Emperor Augustus (31 B.C.–14 A.D.). Statue in the Vatican at Rome. *(Photo: Vatican)*

307 Aerial photograph of Bethlehem. *(Photo: The Times)*

308 The Emperor Tiberius (14–37) as an old man, wearing a veil. Marble bust. British Museum. *(Photo: Alinari)*

308 Bronze coin of Pontius Pilate, Roman procurator of Judaea at the time of the Crucifixion (in office A.D. 26–36). It pictures a Roman simpulum (ladle for religious ceremonies) and three ears of corn. British Museum. *(Photo: John Freeman)*

309 View of Nazareth. *(Photo: Radio Times Hulton Picture Library)*

310 Scroll of Isaiah. Found in Cave I near Qumran on the Dead Sea 1947. c. 100 B.C. Leather. Jerusalem. *(Photo: A.S.O.R.)*

311 Capernaum. Remains of the synagogue probably rebuilt in 200 A.D. on the foundations of the synagogue in which Jesus preached. *(Photo: Hed Wimmer, Karlsruhe)*

312 Fishermen on the Sea of Galilee. *(Photo: Radio Times Hulton Picture Library)*

313 Reconstruction of the temple of Herod (40–4 B.C.) at Jerusalem. *(Photo: Courtesy of the Palestine Exploration Fund)*

314 The "wailing wall" of Jerusalem, a remnant of the wall built by Herod to surround the temple area. The stone blocks show signs of workmanship typical of the stone-masons of King Herod. *(Photo: Radio Times Hulton Picture Library)*

315 Notice forbidding entry to any non-Jew into the temple at Jerusalem. White limestone slab, 34¹/₁ inches wide. From Jerusalem, c. 30 A.D. Istanbul Museum. *(Photo: Courtesy of the Palestine Exploration Fund)*

315 The "holy rock" in the Mohammedan Dome of the Rock in Jerusalem. The rock is still sacred to the Muslims. Above it rises the Dome of the Rock (wrongly-called Mosque of Omar). Built by 'Abd el-Malik ibn Merwan (A.D. 688–691), who was not recognised as ruler by the citizens of Mecca and Medina and who therefore tried to supersede the Kaaba with this new Dome. On a mountain in the "land of Moriah" Abraham was supposed to sacrifice his son Isaac (Genesis 22:2). According to II Chronicles 3:1 the temple hill in Jerusalem is called "Mount Moriah" and David was instructed to build his temple there (I Chronicles 21:18–26). *(Photo: Arthaud-Mikaël Audrain)*

316 Silver denarius ("penny") with head of the Emperor Tiberius, the tax money mentioned in Matthew 22:19. *(Photo: John Freeman)*

316 Reconstruction of the porticoes around the pool of Bethesda. *(After J. Jeremias, Die Wiederentdeckung von Bethesda, p. 26)*

317 Excavations by the pool of Bethesda. Prof. J. Jeremias discovered a part of Jerusalem dating back to the time of Jesus, when he unearthed, under several feet of rubble, this bathing pool in the vicinity of the sheep gate on the eastern side of the north wall (John 5:2). *(Photo: Bavaria Verlag, Heinrich Frese)*

318 On the Mount of Olives at Jerusalem. *(Photo: Rapho, Paris)*

319 View from inside a rock tomb with its stone cover near Jerusalem. 1st century A.D. *(Photo: Arthaud-Mikaël Audrain)*

320 "Straight Street" in Damascus. On the left Roman arcades. *(Photo: Courtauld Institute of Art, London)*

321 The great theatre at Ephesus where St Paul probably preached. Built under the Emperor Claudius (41–54), completed under the Emperor Trajan (98–117). It could hold 24,500 spectators arranged in 66 rows. *(Photo: Paul Popper)*

321 Ephesian coin with a picture of the statue of Diana in the temple. *(After Brockhaus Lexikon zur Bibel, p. 293)*

322 The temple of Apollo at Corinth. *(Photo: Courtesy of L. Grollenberg O.P.)*

323 A page from the Codex Sinaiticus: beginning of St Paul's Epistle to the Romans. The "Codex Sinaiticus" is a valuable parchment manuscript in Greek, covering the Old Testament and parts of the New Testament, dating back to the 4th century. Discovered in 1859 in the monastery of St Catherine on the Sinai peninsula by v. Tischendorf. Since 1933 in the British Museum. *(Photo: Courtesy of the Trustees of the British Museum)*

324 Ruins of the ancient port of Caesarea, 24 miles SSW of Haifa, the place where St Paul was imprisoned for two years (Acts 24–26). *(Photo: Arthaud-Mikaël Audrain)*

325 The Via Appia. *(Photo: Alinari)*

326 The Forum Romanum at Rome. *(Photo: Alinari)*

327 Marble bust of Nero, Roman emperor (54–68). British Museum. *(Photo: Courtesy of the Trustees of the British Museum)*

328 Marble slab over the supposed grave of St Paul. Basilica S. Paolo fuori le mura, Rome. *(After Finegan, Light from the Ancient Past, illustration 186)*

329 Memorial under the high altar of St Peter's in Rome. *(Photo: Thames and Hudson Archives)*

330 Head of the Emperor Titus (79–81). Cabinet des Médailles, Paris. *(Photo: Bibliothèque Nationale, Paris)*

331 Relief from the inside of the arch of Titus in Rome. *(Photo: Alinari)*

332 Bronze coin of Vespasian (69–79) inscribed "judaea capta". Struck in honour of the capture of Jerusalem and Judah 67–70. *(Photo: John Freeman)*

General Index

(Key: a) normal figure [I] = reference to text, b) heavy figure [I] = reference to corresponding number in the Acknowledgements of Illustrations, c) figure with asterisk [1*] = reference to Illustration.)

Raamses (Avaris)

LAND OF GOSHEN

Pithom

Succoth

Saqqara

Giza

Memphis

Nile

M E

Beni Hasan

Tell el-Amarna

Marah

Elim

GULF OF SUEZ

Dophkah

S I N A I

Rephidim

Mountain of Moses

GULF OF AQABAH

Abydos

(Thebes)

Medinet Habu

Deir el-Bari

Luxor

Karnak

E G Y P T

R E D   S E A